The Politics of Intervention

The MR/Censa Series on the Americas is dedicated to publishing new work on the critical issues affecting the nations of the Americas, whose destinies are becoming increasingly interlinked in the late twentieth century.

*T*he Politics of Intervention
*T*he United States in Central America

Edited by Roger Burbach and Patricia Flynn

Monthly Review Press
Center for the Study of the Americas

Photo credits:

Introduction: United Fruit Company workers, 1920s—collection of Philippe Bourgois. *Chapter 1:* San Salvador: demonstration, 1980—Harry Mattison/ NACLA. *Chapter 2:* Honduras: U.S. Ambassador John Negroponte and President Suazo Cordoba—Patricia Flynn. *Chapter 3:* Honduras: U.S. Green Berets—Patricia Flynn. *Chapter 4:* El Salvador: U.S. food shipment unpacked at orphanage—Anne Nelson/Visions. *Chapter 5:* Nicaragua: Coyolito farm cooperative—Jamey Stillings. *Chapter 6:* Guatemala—Jean Marie Simons/ Visions. *Chapter 7:* Guatemala—Pat Goudvis.

Copyright © 1984 Roger Burbach and Patricia Flynn
All rights reserved

Library of Congress Cataloging in Publication Data
Main entry under title:
The Politics of intervention.
    Includes Index.
    1. United States—Foreign economic relations—Central America—Addresses, essays, lectures. 2. Central America—Foreign economic relations—United States—Addresses, essays, lectures. 3. United States—Foreign Relations—Central America—Addresses, essays, lectures. 4. Central America—Foreign relations—United States—Addresses, essays, lectures. I. Burbach, Roger, II. Flynn, Patricia.
HF1456.5.C4P65   1984   337.730728   83-42526
ISBN 0-85345-634-8
ISBN 0-85345-635-6 (pbk.)

Monthly Review Press
155 West 23rd Street, New York, N.Y. 10011

Center for the Study of the Americas
2288 Fulton Street, #103, Berkeley, Cal. 94704

Manufactured in the United States of America

10 9 8 7 6 5 4 3 2 1

Contents

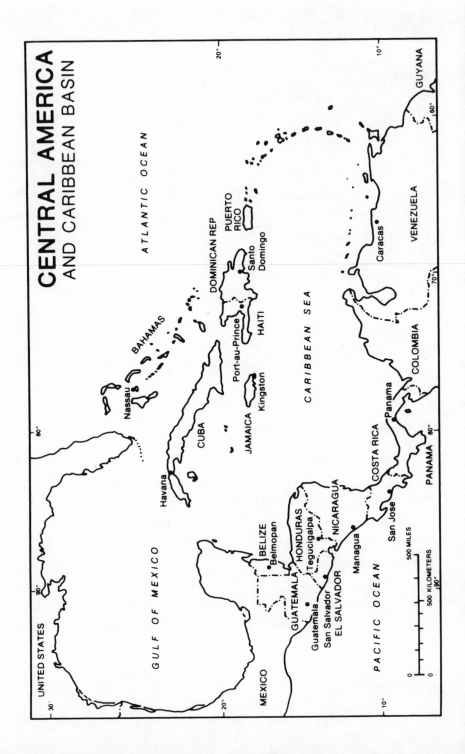

CENTRAL AMERICA
AND CARIBBEAN BASIN

Preface and Acknowledgments

The idea for this book grew out of a study and discussion group sponsored by the Center for the Study of the Americas (CENSA) in 1981 to monitor unfolding events in Central America. Though Washington was still playing a relatively low-profile role in the regional crisis, it was already clear that the United States was once again headed down the road to intervention. We felt it was important not only to document the course of that intervention, but also to probe and analyze the many facets of U.S. involvement in the crisis—historic, political, economic, and military. Our hope is that the articles in this book will help to counter some of the false arguments being used by U.S. officials to justify leading our country into an indefensible and tragic war against the people of Central America.

We would like to express our appreciation to the many people who made this book possible. Particular thanks go to Norma Chinchilla, Carmen Diana Deere, Nora Hamilton, Marc Herold, and David Landes for contributing articles and providing invaluable input and criticisms; to CENSA staff members and volunteers, especially Kay Baxter, Stephen Matchett, and Anna Marie Taylor, for helping with the equally important tasks of production and editing; Dorothy Marschak also provided last-minute copyediting assistance; to Bill Gasperini, Mark Hansen, David Kinley, Jim Morrell, Sarah Stewart, and Daniel Volman for providing research assistance; to our loyal friend and supporter Glenn Borchardt, whose skill with microcomputers liberated us from our typewriters; and to our editor at Monthly Review Press, Karen Judd, who held it all together with unflagging patience, calm, and hard work.

Thanks also to Marvin Collins for assistance with photographic printing, and to other members of the CENSA discussion group for their valuable input during the early stages of the project: Don Davis, Ilana Debare, Philippe Bourgois, Robert Girling, Luin Goldring, Peggy Handler, and Sherry Keith.

We also owe a debt of gratitude to many others whose work on Central America and U.S. foreign policy has been a source of inspiration and who have shared their invaluable insights with us: Robert

Armstrong, Tim Draimin, Richard Fagen, Elizabeth Farnsworth, Hank Frundt, Xabier Gorostiaga, Michael Klare, William LeoGrande, Harry Magdoff, Peter Marchetti, Orlando Nuñez, and Paul Sweezy.

Joel Burbach and Hans Langenberg provided support so this book could make it into print. We also want to thank those who have generously supported CENSA's work out of a sense of commitment to the overriding importance of preventing a full-scale war in Central America.

April 1984

*I*ntroduction
Revolution and Reaction

Roger Burbach

The only way to help protect the democracies [in Central America] might be for the United States to place forward deployed forces in these countries, as in Korea or West Germany.

—Fred C. Iklé, Assistant Secretary of Defense,
September 12, 1983

The national security of the United States is not threatened by the FMLN aspiring to be a sovereign government, independent and nonaligned. What is threatened are the unjust terms under which the United States has managed its economic and political relations with Latin America.

—Joaquín Villalobos, Salvadoran guerrilla leader,
September 1983

The United States today is locked into a war in Central America. It is a war between the forces of reaction and revolution, between a modern empire determined to defend the status quo and the social and political forces struggling to build a new society.

This conflict will not be over quickly. It will last certainly for the remainder of this decade, and perhaps even into the next century. It is, of course, impossible to predict the exact trajectory of the war. A year from now, U.S. troops may be fighting in Central America. Or the United States could still be clinging to its strategy of war overlord, in which it trains, arms, and directs the established armies of the region, while employing a private army to wage war on the Sandinista government in Nicaragua.

There will be ebbs and flows in the war. Temporary truces may occur, the revolutionary forces may suffer momentary setbacks, or the opposition of the North American people may compel the U.S. government to back off at times. But the underlying dynamic will be one of conflict and confrontation. Even if the guerrillas in El Salvador were to be victorious in six months, or if the anti-Sandinista forces collapsed, Central America would not find peace. The struggle between the forces of reaction and revolution would simply assume new forms or shift elsewhere to Guatemala or Honduras or, perhaps, even to Costa Rica.

Why is this so? The fundamental reason is that Central America and parts of the Caribbean are involved in a process of intense class conflict which will be prolonged. This has profound implications for U.S. imperialism. As the leading capitalist nation in the world and the hegemonic power in the Caribbean Basin, the United States is committed to sustaining governments and political systems that maintain capitalist relations in the economic, political, and social spheres. The primary thrust of the revolutionary movements, on the other hand, is aimed at overturning the established systems of class rule and setting up governments that bring new social and political forces into power. This battle over alternative political and economic projects is the fundamental reason why the United States and the revolutionary movements are locked into prolonged conflict.

This reality can be more fully understood by looking at the concrete forces that have shaped U.S. relations with Central America and the Caribbean. They are (1) the particular role that the region has played in the evolution of the U.S. imperial system, (2) the extensive U.S. economic interests in the Caribbean Basin, and (3) the role of the region in the U.S. National Security State. These factors have created a tightly knit web of historic and contemporary interests that the United States can only maintain by opposing the revolutionary forces and by maintaining its strategic alliance with the local ruling classes.

The Historic Role of Central America in the U.S. Empire

To understand why Central America and the Caribbean are so important to the U.S. empire, it is first necessary to understand what distinguishes the U.S. imperial system from previous empires. Beginning in the latter part of the nineteenth century, the United States broke with previous imperial systems in that it established an "informal empire," one in which it did not exercise direct territorial or colonial control.* Rather than joining in the rush for colonies in Africa and Asia as the European powers did at that time, the United States called for an "Open Door" policy vis-à-vis the underdeveloped regions of the world and used its growing economic might to penetrate the markets and societies in these regions. Subsequently adopted by other imperial powers, this system of domination has been characterized as a "neocolonial system," one in which a metropolitan country holds sway over a formally independent country and extracts economic and political benefits from this arrangement.

It was in the Caribbean Basin that the United States first consolidated its informal empire. Although the United States had staked out its claim to the region with the enunciation of the Monroe Doctrine, it was not until its victory in the Spanish-American-Cuban War of 1898 that its dreams of empire in the region became a reality. After the war, U.S. direct investments in Central America and the Caribbean mushroomed, concentrating in banana and sugar plantations, public utilities, and transportation facilities, virtually the only areas where lucrative profits were to be made.

While eschewing direct colonial rule (with the exception of Puerto Rico), the young empire often resorted to military force to assure its informal political control. Between 1900 and 1930, the United States carried out twenty-eight military interventions in the Caribbean basin.[1]

---

*Great Britain actually exercised informal control over some countries in the early twentieth century (particularly in South America), but the heart of its empire was built on direct territorial control.

The interventions had a variety of motives—ensuring that the governments paid their debts to U.S. bankers, protecting U.S. investments, and generally guaranteeing that no governments came to power in the region which would challenge U.S. prerogatives. Political control may not have been formal, but it was virtually complete. Indeed, the two most infamous characterizations of U.S. foreign policy—"Gunboat Diplomacy" and "Dollar Diplomacy"—aptly described U.S. activities in Central America and the Caribbean during this era.

This early period of U.S. dominance in the region laid the basis for the special role which it plays in the U.S. global empire up to this day. This is the region where the sun first rose on the U.S. informal empire, and any challenges in the region strike at the underpinnings of the entire U.S. imperial system.

The U.S. Economic Stake

With the post-World War II expansion of the United States as a world power, the Caribbean Basin seemingly receded in importance. U.S. military bases were established in Western Europe and Asia, and U.S. trade and investments burgeoned around the world. Furthermore, U.S. disinvestments in plantations and public utilities in the region made it appear that the region was of only marginal economic importance to the United States.

But the expansion of U.S. power abroad did not really diminish the importance of Central America and the Caribbean. U.S. business actually expanded in the Basin, diversifying into new areas of production. As we point out in Chapter 6, "The U.S. Corporate and Economic Stake in the Caribbean Basin," U.S. corporate holdings in the region became quite substantial. Today, agriculture, manufacturing, commerce, mining, and tourism account for $6.2 billion in productive investments, and another $16.9 billion is tied up in banking and financial operations in the Caribbean Basin. (These investment totals do not include Puerto Rico.) This $23.1 billion constitutes 9 percent of total U.S. investments abroad. When compared to other third world regions, these figures put the Caribbean Basin in second place in economic importance to the United States, surpassed only by the rest of Latin America. (i.e., South America and Mexico).

Virtually every major corporate sector in the United States has a significant stake in the Caribbean Basin. Among the big corporate interests in Central America and the Caribbean, the Rockefellers clearly predominate, with sizeable holdings in tourism, petroleum, and banking. In addition, a very large number of small firms and investors, particularly from the southern and western United States, have holdings there. For these firms, the Caribbean Basin is of singular importance. Geographic proximity enables them to use the region to test their foreign investment strategies and to lay plans for further international expansion.

Do these substantial holdings mean that the U.S. corporate community is a fundamental obstacle to the revolutionary process in the region? In Chapter 3 we point out that one school of U.S. policymakers and analysts called "neorealists" advocate a kind of "peaceful coexistence" as the best survival strategy for capitalism in the third world. They argue that U.S. corporations should be able to operate profitably even in revolutionary and socialist countries.[2] While the neorealists are correct in pointing out that the multinationals have made profitable investments in established socialist countries, it is also true that historically those same corporations have consistently tried to stop revolutions in countries where existing U.S. investments might be threatened. One need only recall the role of U.S. corporations in overthrowing Jacobo Arbenz in Guatemala or Salvador Allende in Chile to recognize this reality.[3]

The same counter-revolutionary instincts shape the behavior of U.S. corporate interests in Central America and the Caribbean today. While some U.S. transnationals have remained in Nicaragua after the Sandinista victory, they have made virtually no new investments (and even some disinvestments) despite Nicaragua's relatively liberal foreign investment code. This is certainly not a favorable omen for those who maintain that U.S. economic institutions can or will remain neutral in the midst of the revolutionary upheaval that is gripping the region.

In Central America and the Caribbean, U.S. corporations are, in fact, actively involved in trying to stop the revolutionary movements and to preserve what they regard as the best climate for investment— free market economies. The major business organization spearheading this effort is Caribbean/Central American Action (C/CAA). Founded during the last year of the Carter administration and initially led principally by southern and western capitalists, the organization has grown rapidly in the past two years. Today it is supported by over one hundred big corporations and is headed by David Rockefeller, the old stalwart of the eastern financial establishment. The C/CAA is a fervent supporter of Reagan administration policies, having endorsed the Caribbean Basin Initiative and the report of the Kissinger Commission on Central America, which called for massive economic and military aid to the region.

What these and other programs by the business community demonstrate is that U.S. corporations are clearly an integral part of the U.S. effort to maintain capitalism in Central America and the Caribbean and to stop the revolutionary threat to that system. They want to preserve the region for capitalism in general, and as an outlet for U.S. investments in particular. Corporate capital abhors revolutionary upheaval: it disrupts the local economies and throws investment planning into chaos. Nationalist and social democratic governments are also generally opposed by corporate capital, as was demonstrated by the antagonistic behavior of many U.S. multinationals toward the Manley government in Jamaica in the mid and late 1970s.

Central America and U.S. National Security

In defending their aggressive actions in the region U.S. leaders do not, of course, assert that they are protecting U.S. economic interests, or that the Caribbean Basin plays a special role in the U.S. imperial system. Presidents from Eisenhower to Reagan have ultimately justified U.S. intervention in the Caribbean Basin by asserting that "it is the U.S. national security that is at stake."[4]

Why has national security become the cornerstone used to justify U.S. actions in the region? The answer lies in the way in which the needs and interests of the U.S. empire have been wedded to the concept of national security. The merger of national and imperial interests, while characteristic of most empires, achieved a particular thrust in the United States after World War II, when the United States began a policy of systematic opposition to the Soviet Union in particular, and toward communism and revolutionary movements in general.

In National Security Council Document No. 68, or NSC-68, drawn up in 1950, U.S. national security was explicitly tied to the demands of maintaining the U.S. system abroad. This document remains a central pillar of U.S. foreign policy to this day. As the document notes on the first page, wars and revolutions led to the collapse of five empires in the past century—the Ottoman, the German, the Austro-Hungarian, the Italian, and the Japanese— and to the drastic decline of the French and the British systems. To ensure that the United States does not meet a similar fate, the document argues that the United States cannot accept "disorder" in the world at large. Viewing the Soviet Union as the primary obstacle to U.S. interests, NSC-68 asserts that the United States must "foster a fundamental change in the nature of the Soviet system." Only by using "any means, covert or overt, violent or non-violent" to achieve its global objectives could the United States create "a successfully functioning political and economic system."[5]

This is the doctrinal basis for the East-West conflict and U.S. national security. The entire world, developed and underdeveloped, is viewed as an arena of competition between the United States and the Soviet Union. Revolutionary movements in the third world are consistently seen as part of the "Soviet challenge," even though the Soviet Union in most cases has little to do with the movements.

This vision of U.S. national security has been applied with particular ferocity in the Caribbean Basin. Here, next to the U.S. shores, any efforts to break away from the U.S. orbit have been resisted and when breaks have occurred, as in the case of Cuba in the 1960s, the United States has conducted an incessant campaign—with military, economic, and political components—to contain or reverse these challenges to the U.S. system. U.S. presidents as diverse as Harry Truman, John F. Kennedy, and Ronald Reagan have all acted on the explicit assumption that in order to wage the global struggle against communism, the Caribbean Basin had to be made as secure as possible. A southern ring of "hostile or nonaligned states" (the two being considered virtually synonymous) was simply unacceptable to the leaders of the United States.

The special importance of the region since the Cold War was launched is revealed by the frequency of U.S. military interventions. While the United States has not yet waged a massive war in the Basin on the scale of the Korean and Vietnamese conflicts, it is notable that no other region has suffered as many U.S. interventions in the postwar era as the Caribbean Basin. The CIA's overthrow of the government of Jacobo Arbenz in 1954, the invasion of Cuba at the Bay of Pigs in 1961, the naval blockade of Cuba during the 1962 missile crisis, the use of U.S. troops in the Canal Zone to quell political unrest in Panama in

1964, the dispatch of the U.S. marines to the Dominican Republic in 1965, the U.S.-backed counterinsurgency wars in the 1960s (particularly in Guatemala), the U.S. invasion of Grenada, the present intervention in El Salvador, and the clandestine war against Nicaragua—these are the most well-known overt or covert U.S. military operations in the Caribbean Basin. The fact that U.S. interventions of one form or another have occurred approximately once every three years reveals that the United States has actually been involved in a protracted conflict in the region, for the past three decades.

In sum, a constellation of forces are at work which make it impossible for the United States to calmly accept revolutionary governments in Central America or the Caribbean. The fact that the region has historically been at the center of the U.S. informal empire, the extensive U.S. investments in the region, and the reality that counter-revolution has been at the core of U.S. national security thinking—all these factors lock the United States in a prolonged period of conflict with the revolutionary movements and governments in the region.

The Fundamental Challenge of Central America and the Caribbean

The U.S. dominance of most facets of life in Central America and the Caribbean has dramatic consequences for the revolutionary movements in the region. These movements have all been strongly conditioned by the overwhelming presence of the United States in the Basin. It is no accident that the most significant and sustained challenge to the U.S. informal empire should emerge in this region. This is where the links of informal empire are strongest, and consequently the area where contradictions between the United States and the revolutionary movements are deepest. Even more so than in Vietnam—where the historical anticolonial struggle against the French was directed against the United States only because of its military intervention relatively late in the game—the Central Americans are rebelling against decades of U.S. domination over all aspects of their society (military, economic, political, and cultural).

A brief look at the economic and social realities of the region reveals just how deep-seated the contradictions are. Economically, the countries and territories are more tightly tied to the U.S. economy than any other third world region. While other economies in Latin America, such as Mexico's and Brazil's, are also linked to the U.S. system and even have a larger absolute quantity of U.S. investments, the diversity and extensiveness of their economies gives them more room for maneuver vis-à-vis the United States.

Due to the overwhelming economic dominance of the United States, the economies in the Central America and the Caribbean have never been able to develop an effective plan for regional economic integration which could have given them more clout in the global capitalist system. The consequences of this extreme dependency on the United States have been severe— the failure of the region to develop heavy industries, the reliance on U.S. imports and technology for the limited industries that did develop, and the lack of significant regional markets and regional transportation and communications systems (all of which are discussed in depth in Chapter 7). This legacy of dependency means that efforts to achieve balanced economic development that responds to the internal needs of the countries in Central America and the Caribbean have inevitably come into head-on conflict with the United States.

The total U.S. economic dominance of the region in turn has had profound repercussions for the social and cultural development of the region. In many ways, the Caribbean Basin is one of the most diverse regions of the world: the array of cultures, the different colonial roots of the countries, the presence of all the major ethnic groups of the world— these factors and others have combined to create a tremendous cultural diversity.

While these diverse cultures remain, they have all been strongly affected by U.S. penetration. A prolonged assault on the region's cultures has come from an array of U.S. groups ranging from U.S. evangelical missionaries and businessmen to droves of American tourists and pop music artists. Today, in fact, if there is one characteristic that unifies the region culturally, it is the penetration of the "American way of life."

The Ideological Roots of Conflict

Given U.S. economic and cultural domination, it is not surprising then that the revolutionary forces say their main objective is self-determination—the right of even small countries to choose their own social, economic, and political systems, and the international relations which respond to their respective needs. They intend to rupture the neocolonial system in which the United States determines the political and economic destinies of third world countries.[6] The revolutionary forces, in fact, enunciate political principles that conflict with many of the premises that guide the U.S. system. The diverse revolutionary movements and governments that have developed in such countries as Cuba, Nicaragua, and El Salvador draw their inspiration from a political worldview which is very different from that which has shaped the United States throughout its history. The United States emerged in the era of the great bourgeois democratic revolutions of the late eighteenth and early nineteenth centuries. Drawing heavily on the political philosophy of John Locke, the U.S. revolution and its founding documents stressed individual initiative and individual rights in the economic and political spheres as the basis of its political system. These "rights" were essential for the development of the new capitalist societies in the United States as well as in Western Europe. To the extent that the United States has supported revolutionary movements in other parts of the world, in Latin America in the early nineteenth century or in Africa after World War II, it has always been in an effort to encourage or to compel them to incorporate these principles in their political systems.[7]

The movements in Central America and the Caribbean, on the other hand, are rooted in the revolutionary traditions of the twentieth century. Driven by the most dispossessed and exploited social sectors, and heavily influenced by the political philosophies of Marx and Lenin, these revolutions seek to establish political systems based on the mobilization of the masses and the redistribution of the material wealth to the most impoverished sectors of society. These revolutionary movements clearly do not intend to recognize the individual's rights to accumulate economic wealth on an extensive scale, and they want to set up political systems that redefine U.S. concepts of democracy and freedom.

Terms such as "democracy" and "freedom," in fact, have an entirely different meaning in each of these social orders. In the contemporary revolutionary societies, for example, democracy is often prefaced by the word "popular," meaning that participation in the direction of society can occur in various forms and at different levels—in the factories and the fields, in the communities, in the schools, and in the government itself. The local organizations that exist in these and other areas enable people to participate in decisions that affect their daily lives. While bourgeois democratic societies, on the other hand, do have some organizations that influence local decisions (school boards, community groups, etc.), the term "democracy" is predominately identified with electoral politics: it means the right of everyone to go to the ballot box every few years, even if the majority of the populace finds it irrelevant to exercise that right. This concept of democracy is what enables U.S. interventionists to proclaim that they are protecting the "democracies" in Central America while they prop up murderous regimes that hold formal elections and tyrannize their populations.

These are the fundamental differences over political philosophies between the United States and the Central American and Caribbean liberation movements. They explain, at least on the ideological plane, why it is often as difficult for liberal Democrats as it is for Reaganite Republicans to accept the revolutionary movements. Even some of the most ardent Democratic critics of Reagan's Central American policies refer to the revolutionary movements as "totalitarian" or as "anti-democratic" in nature. These characterizations are not simply political rhetoric designed to win elections in the United States—they are terms that indicate profound differences with the political philosophy of the contemporary revolutionary movements.

The Special Characteristics of the Revolutionary Movements

The rebellion against U.S. dominance in the heart of its informal empire (the Caribbean Basin) is perceived as even more profound a challenge to the foundations of the U.S. global power than was the Vietnam conflict. President Reagan, in spelling out the U.S. stake in the Caribbean Basin in his address to the Joint Session of Congress (April 27, 1983) asserted that if the United States lost this region, "we cannot expect to prevail elsewhere. Our credibility would collapse, our alliances would crumble, and the safety of our homeland would be put in jeopardy."[8] What in fact is being challenged is the U.S. commitment to a particular type of society and social formation which the United States and other dominant capitalist nations have imposed on large parts of the third world.

U.S. determination to hold onto the region explains why during much of this century the insurgencies have perforce been directed as much against the United States as against the local ruling classes. To be successful, the movements for self-determination in the region must be anti-imperialist, armed, militant, and capable of mobilizing the be anti-imperialist, armed, militant, and capable of mobilizing the majority of the population to resist U.S. intervention (whether overt or covert, economic or military).

Here, even more than in other parts of the world, there is no reformist path which will enable the countries to escape from U.S. control. Governments that have challenged U.S. dominance by adopting reforms within a capitalist framework, and that have not mobilized and armed their people to resist the inevitable U.S. intervention, have had to pay the ultimate consequence, i.e., the loss of power to U.S.-backed right-wing regimes. Two striking and somewhat disparate examples of this reality are the governments of Jacobo Arbenz in Guatemala in the 1950s and of Michael Manley in Jamaica in the late 1970s.*

The genius of Fidel Castro's July 26th Movement is that it recognized from the moment it took power that the support of the Cuban people was central to the revolution and that the United States would be its implacable enemy. The old debate over whether or not Fidel Castro was a Marxist when he came to power is actually misleading.[9] The key factor to understanding the initial stages of the Cuban revolution is that the leadership of the July 26th Movement recognized that the United States would oppose its economic and political platform because it challenged U.S. dominance of the island. Accordingly, the leadership began very early on to mobilize the country's population, and to seek international alliances that would give it the capacity to thwart U.S. efforts to destroy the new government. This reality, that the United States will move directly against any government which alters the status quo and challenges its prerogatives, was mastered by the Sandinistas when they took power and it is a central lesson that all future revolutions must act upon.

Zimbabwe and Nicaragua: Exceptions that Prove a New Rule?

The pervasiveness of the antirevolutionary thrust of the United States is obvious when one looks at the global U.S. response to revolutionary movements throughout the twentieth century. In countries as

---

*A bitter lesson of the 1983 Grenadan experience is that the revolutionary forces must also maintain total unity. Any divisions or splits within the revolutionary leadership will cost them popular support, which among other things will leave them immediately vulnerable to the hostile actions of the United States, with dire consequences for the revolutionary movements.

diverse as the Soviet Union, Cuba, China, Angola, and Vietnam, the United States not only tried to prevent the revolutions from seizing power, but once they did attain power, the United States used a variety of measures and tactics in an effort to undermine or destroy the revolutionary processes. In the case of the older revolutions (the USSR and China), only after a period of a decade or two, when the new revolutionary governments had demonstrated that they were firmly in power, did the United States finally accept the new reality and begin to search for ways to accommodate itself to the new governments. And as we know in the cases of Vietnam, Cuba, and Angola, the United States has yet to even recognize the existence of these revolutionary governments.

However, with the triumph of the Nicaraguan and Zimbabwean revolutions in 1979 and 1980, there were signs that the United States might break with its past policies. In each case the United States (specifically the Carter administration) moved quickly to recognize the new governments and to extend significant amounts of bilateral assistance. Do these cases demonstrate that at least one sector of the U.S. ruling class may be willing to enter a new epoch in its relations with revolutionary governments?

A review of specific developments in the cases of Zimbabwe and Nicaragua provides little hope that the United States is on the brink of a major shift in its historic counter-revolutionary politics. As regards Zimbabwe, the principal reason why the United States has not opposed the revolutionary process is because sub-Saharan Africa in general, and Zimbabwe in particular, are not in what is recognized as the U.S. sphere of influence. U.S. interests, both historic and contemporary, have been quite limited in that region. Even more importantly, the United States recognizes Great Britain as the major European power when dealing with Zimbabwe. Thus when Great Britain worked out the Lancaster Agreements, which were the basis for the subsequent elections in Zimbabwe and the extensive economic aid given to the country, the United States had no real alternative but to support the results of the elections, even though the openly avowed Marxist candidate, Robert Mugabe, became the prime minister.

The case of Nicaragua is obviously more relevant for the projection of future events in the Caribbean Basin. But this case offers even less basis for hope; in fact, it demonstrates that there are irreconcilable differences between the United States and the revolutionary movements in Central America and the Caribbean. As is well known, the Carter administration extended emergency relief to the new Sandinista government, and it persuaded Congress to approve a special program for $75 million in economic assistance.

However, the main problem with viewing this as a sign that the United States will not oppose future revolutionary processes in the region is that the Carter administration was clearly trying to coopt the Sandinista revolution: it wanted to create a Nicaraguan political system in the mold of the bourgeois democratic revolutions of the eighteenth and nineteenth centuries. U.S. aid was in no way designed to facilitate a transition to socialism. Over 60 percent of the assistance went to the private sector in Nicaragua, and the Carter administration in its official statements as to why it was providing the assistance repeatedly declared that it was trying to encourage a "pluralist society," i.e., a society in which private business would have a leading role and in which there would be periodic elections similar to those in Costa Rica or Venezuela.

This program of trying to coopt the Sandinista revolution was clearly doomed to failure. Even before the Reagan administration assumed power, there were signs that relations were souring between the United States and Nicaragua. The reason for this was simple—the Nicaraguan revolution, for all its uniqueness, was cast in the general mold of the twentieth century social revolutions. The decline of the private business sectors, the growing prominence of the militant peasant and trade unions, the clear anti-imperialist stance of the Sandinista Front, and the reality that the Sandinistas politically supported the revolutionary forces in El Salvador—these were the major reasons why the Carter administration in its waning days found it increasingly difficult to accept the Sandinista government and why it even began to prepare a legal brief for the incoming Reagan administration to end U.S. aid to the Sandinista government.[10]

The "Third Way"

Facing U.S. belligerency on the military and economic fronts, and given the overwhelming preponderance of the United States in the region, must the postrevolutionary societies inevitably join the socialist bloc countries in order to survive? Or are there important limits and restraints placed on U.S. intervention which make it possible for the countries in Central America and the Caribbean to find a "third way," a way in which the societies will not be dependent on the Soviet Union?

Due to the particular nature of the economic system it has helped develop in the region the United States has ironically created the conditions which facilitate the process of transition there. While U.S. capital (whether through transnational corporations or bilateral aid programs) has caused severe economic and social dislocations discussed elsewhere in this volume, the U.S. economic penetration of the region has also been a major force in developing a relatively modern economic infrastructure. Some of the countries in the region may be among the poorest in the Western Hemisphere but compared to other countries in the third world (particularly many Asian and sub-Saharan African societies) even these societies are in a far better position to develop their economies.

The process of imperialist-led development has also brought into existence new social forces. The emergence of urban and rural proletariats, the fact that these working classes are generally literate and have achieved a certain degree of education, the existence of peasant populations which in many cases have ample contacts with the major urban centers and are not as isolated and politically conservative as in more traditional peasant societies, and the emergence of substantial middles classes from which key leadership has emerged for the revolutionary movements—these are the social forces the United States has helped create through its economic penetration of the region, and which place the Caribbean basin in a much better position than other third world regions to try to build a socialist society.

The International Context

These developments combined with changes in the global economy could enable the countries in the region to deal with the economic obstacles to building socialist societies without totally transforming their economic infrastructure and becoming dependent on the Soviet Union. During the past twenty-five years, and particularly in the last decade, the capitalist world has, in fact, become multipolar. As U.S. hegemony and the "American Century" draws to an end, the United States is no longer able to impose its will on the other capitalist countries. Specifically, the United States cannot dictate international trading patterns, nor is it even able to control the trade of its own multinational corporations.

This is a very significant development, which gives the new revolutionary societies in the Caribbean Basin much more room to maneuver than the Cuban revolution had when it came to power in 1959. Even leading third world capitalist countries have more flexibility vis-à-vis the United States. While such countries as Brazil and Mexico are still linked economically to the United States, they, along with more maverick countries such as Libya and Algeria, have been able to exercise considerable autonomy in the international political sphere and to adopt commercial and economic policies that are opposed by the United States.

The Sandinista government during its first half decade in power has fully understood this reality. This explains why it has sought and continues to receive vitally needed international development assistance without moving into the socialist bloc. Not only have Western European countries provided aid, but third world assistance has been just as critical. Import loans from Brazil, subsidized oil from Mexico, hard currency aid from Libya—these are some of the more important and critical forms of aid Nicaragua has received from the third world. There is clearly flexibility in the global capitalist system, a flexibility and multipolarity which will facilitate the development of socialist societies in the Caribbean Basin even if the United States maintains a generally antagonistic stance toward them.

U.S. Society and the Transition Process

While the United States is clearly the main threat to the revolutionary movements in the Caribbean Basin, it would be simplistic to write off all of U.S. society as an obstacle to the revolutionary process. Within the United States there are social forces at work which have the capacity to significantly influence the U.S. role in the Caribbean Basin. The U.S. ruling class, left to its own devices, would no doubt use every means possible to destroy the revolutionary movements and governments in the Basin. But it operates under severe constraints, not only internationally, but most importantly from within the United States. Opposition from the U.S. public and from Congress, for example, has been a major force limiting the Reagan administration's interventionary plans in Central America.

Public opposition to U.S. intervention in the region is not simply a transitory phenomenon which Reagan or any other president will be able to purge from the U.S. body politic by manipulating the media or by mounting an anticommunist campaign. The opposition to interventions in third world countries now has a substantial social base, particularly within the Black and Latin communities, churches, the women's movement, the intellectual community, some trade unions, and peace, environmental, and third world solidarity activists. These movements and organizations are firmly opposed to U.S. intervention in the third world. Some have been mobilized by the fact that they are directly victimized or outraged by the injustice and irrationality of the capitalist system; others are more strongly motivated by the blatant contradictions they see between the democratic rhetoric of the United States and the actual impact that the U.S. system has on many third world countries striving for their economic and political independence.

While most of these social sectors do not articulate an anticapitalist or prosocialist perspective, they nonetheless do question the prevailing economic and political system and are groping for some new alternatives to present U.S. policies, both at home and abroad. These forces are the natural allies of the liberation movements in Central America and the Caribbean. While they will not obtain control of the U.S. government apparatus in the foreseeable future, they do have sufficient (and growing) political clout in the U.S. system to undermine the more interventionist thrusts.[11] The existence of these internal forces will, in fact, cause U.S. policies toward the Caribbean Basin to be fairly volatile during the next decade. While the inherent tendency of the U.S. state is to destroy the revolutionary forces, the social forces mentioned above are continually operating to undermine or check that tendency. In fact, the existence of these forces explains why under a future Democratic president, there will at times be serious attempts to search for a truce with the revolutionary forces in the region. Most of the social groups listed above have historically had some influence within the Democratic Party; if that party takes power, these groups will pressure the party leadership and the executive arm of the government for real changes vis-à-vis the revolutionary movements, even though they obviously will in no way be strong enough to compel the U.S. government to come to a permanent accommodation with them.

In the coming years, however, there will be a deepening interaction between the revolutionary processes in Central America and the Caribbean and political developments in the United States. The strong cultural, social, and economic ties that exist between this country and those in Central America and the Caribbean mean that there will indeed be a "spill over" effect as the revolutions in the region gain momentum. Revolutionary successes will create new problems for the U.S. ruling elites and give new momentum to the social sectors opposed to many aspects of U.S. policies at home and abroad. Minimally, the successful revolutionary movements there will have an effect on third world peoples in the United States, particularly those whose origins are in Central America and the Caribbean. At the same time, the local ruling classes in the region, once they lose power, will continue their migration to Miami and other parts of the United States, adding to the strength of the reactionary forces in this country. In effect, successful revolutionary movements in the region will increasingly polarize the political process in the United States.

Ultimately, the successful transformation of Central America and the Caribbean is linked to a major political transition in the United States, a transition in the U.S. ideology of empire. Other, older imperial powers finally had to adjust, however involuntarily, to anticolonial movements and to a new concept of empire.

The United States has not yet reached this point; the fundamental concepts that drive its imperial system, however unviable, still dominate the foreign policy elites as well as the Republican and Democratic parties. The United States will have to go through a period of extended conflict with the revolutionary forces in Central America and the Caribbean before these concepts are discarded in favor of a new worldview.

Notes

1. William Appleman Williams, *Empire as a Way of Life* (New York: Oxford University Press, 1980), pp. 136-42.
2. Richard E. Feinberg, *The Intemperate Zone: The Third World Challenge to U.S. Foreign Policy* (New York: W.W. Norton, 1983).
3. Richard H. Immerman, *The CIA in Guatemala: The Foreign Policy of Interven- University of Texas Press, 1982), and NACLA, New Chile* (New York: NACLA, 1973).
4. State Department documents released in 1984 show that President Eisenhower asserted in a National Security Council meeting in 1954 that the United States is not merely "doing business in Latin America but is fighting a war there against communism." This pronouncement was made after the CIA-sponsored invasion of Guatemala. "Latin Communism Worried Ike in 1954, Documents Reveal," *San Francisco Chronicle*, January 4, 1984.

5. National Security Council, "A Report to the National Security Council by the Executive Secretary on United States Objectives and Programs for National Security," April 14, 1950, Naval War College Review 27 (May-June 1975).

6. For an in-depth understanding of what self-determination means for many revolutionaries in the region see *Listen, Compañero: Conversations with Central American Revolutionaries* (San Francisco: Solidarity Publications, 1983).

7. Gene Bell-Villada, "Two Americas, Two Worldviews," *Monthly Review* 34, no. 5 (October 1982): 37-43.

8. President Reagan, "Central America: Defending Our Vital Interests," U.S. Department of State, Current Policy No. 482, April 27, 1983.

9. The U.S. State Department under the Reagan administration has given a new twist to this debate. It argues that it was principally Fidel Castro's quest for personal aggrandizement which led him to adopt Marxism-Leninism. This supposedly occurred after the revolutionary victory in 1959, when Castro was looking for a system that would enable him and his "tiny elite" to remain in power indefinitely. See Elliot Abrams, Assistant Secretary of State for Human Rights, "The Cuban Revolution and its Impact on Human Rights," U.S. Department of State, Current Policy No. 518, Washington, D.C., October 6, 1983.

10. Author's interview with State Department official, mid-1981.

11. See Policy Alternatives for the Caribbean and Central America (PACCA), *Changing Course: Blueprint for Peace in Central America and the Caribbean* (Washington, D.C.: Institute for Policy Studies, 1984). This is a policy blueprint developed to provide the anti-interventionist forces in the United States with an alternative perspective for U.S. policy.

1. Central America: The Roots of Revolt

Patricia Flynn

*Those who make peaceful revolution impossible make violent
revolution inevitable.*
                              —*President John F. Kennedy, 1962*

*For more than forty years the popular movement in El Salvador
fought for the enforcement of legal rights, participated in
elections, and tried to elect mayors and deputies. . . . The
people of El Salvador finally realized that they had been
spinning and unraveling, like spiders, for over forty years.*
                              —*Salvador Cayetano Carpio,
                              Salvadoran guerrilla leader, 1982*

The Nicaraguan revolution marked a watershed for Central America and U.S. policy in the region. For the people in neighboring countries, the defeat of Somoza was both a hope and an inspiration. The old political order—brutal and unpopular dictatorships, nurtured and sustained by the United States—no longer appeared invincible. This lesson was not lost in Washington. Even long-time supporters of Somoza recognized the handwriting on the wall: popular discontent had burst into open rebellion in both El Salvador and Guatemala, and time was running out.

To avoid another revolutionary victory the United States developed a new political formula for the region: electoral democracy and governments of the moderate center. Under presidents Carter and later, Reagan, the United States promoted this formula as the only alternative to the "extremes" of both right and left. The real target was the revolutionary left, denounced as agents of Soviet totalitarianism. This democratic formula was only one element in a two-pronged strategy, political and military, to contain revolution in the region. While seemingly contradictory, the political and military strategies were in fact intimately linked. To achieve its principal goal—destroying the revolutionary alternative in Central America—the United States had to rely increasingly on military means. But to win political backing at home and abroad for its growing intervention in the region, it had to offer an alternative to the discredited regimes of the old order, almost universally recognized as guardians of a brutally unjust social and economic order.

The political strategy came too late, however. By the time of the Sandinista revolution, the so-called centrist solution had been choked off as a viable political force in all but Costa Rica. The local elites correctly viewed any social and economic reforms as incompatible with their own power and privilege. And the United States, jealous of its own political and economic interests in the region, had helped snuff out any serious attempts at reform, much less revolution. In the process, they also stifled the centrist political forces who supported democratic reforms and espoused moderate rather than revolutionary change.

By the time of the Sandinista triumph, those who opposed dictatorship and social injustice had learned from history that few options remained. Decades of frustration with the impossiblity of peaceful change had driven the opposition—ranging from the moderate center to the radical left—to armed revolt. The "democratic" solutions being proposed by the United States bore little relationship to reality. Ironically, it was largely the historic success of U.S. counter-revolutionary policies in closing off other avenues for change that made the revolutionary upsurge of the 1980s inevitable.

The Revolution Brews

Colonial Pyramid

Like all popular revolts, the Central American revolution has been a long time in the making. Even before the young U.S. empire turned its sights on Central America at the turn of the century, the region's social and political topography had been molded by centuries of Spain's colonial domination. Land was the key to wealth in these predominantly agricultural societies, and the best of it was controlled by a handful of families. The vast majority of the population eked out a living as subsistence farmers and occasional laborers on large estates, where they were often treated more as beasts of burden than as human beings. The gap between the wealthy few and the impoverished many was enormous, and there was virtually no middle ground. Only Costa Rica escaped this pattern. There, the Spanish landholding system never took as firm a hold as in the rest of the region, opening the way for small farm settlement by European immigrants. Their descendants are the backbone of that country's middle class today.[1] Even after independence in 1821 the pyramidal colonial structure remained intact. But there were some important changes at the top. The traditional landowning aristocracy was overshadowed by a new elite, many of whom made their wealth in the nineteenth-century coffee boom. Coffee transformed Central America's agriculture in all but Honduras and in so doing created a new oligarchy.

Modernizers in their time, the coffee oligarchy branched out into other areas of the economy, using their growing political influence to stimulate economic development. But it was development narrowly defined in their own interests. The road-building and export-financing programs that were the hallmark of their development scheme brought no benefits to the majority of Central Americans. Indeed, the coffee boom took place at the expense of the rural poor, as governments in Guatemala, Nicaragua, and El Salvador confiscated Indian and peasant lands to make way for expanded coffee production.

There was sporadic resistence and local revolts by some of the dispossessed—particularly in the small country of El Salvador, where landlessness was a severe problem. But the isolated and unorganized peasantry was no match for the oligarchy, who had created national armies to protect their privileged rule.[2] Already the pattern of modern politics in the region was firmly established: force was the ultimate guarantor of power. What passed for constitutional democracy was actually a system for settling squabbles between factions of the elite.

When the United States entered the picture, it threw its weight behind the elite factions willing to kowtow to U.S. demands for unchallenged economic and political dominance. After President Theodore Roosevelt's enunciation of his famous corollary to the Monroe Doctrine, claiming the right to intervene to restore "order" and stability in the region, the United States did not hesitate to use military force to guarantee pro-U.S. stability. By 1926 U.S. forces had intervened six times in Honduras and Nicaragua suffered continuous occupation by U.S. forces from 1912 to 1925. In other cases the United States simply used its political and economic clout to guarantee the rise and fall of Central American governments.[3]

Until the 1920s, threats to "stability" came mainly from recalcitrant elites who incurred U.S. wrath by defaulting on debts or flirting with rival imperial powers. The desperate plight of the rural masses—potentially the most explosive threat to stability—had not yet found organized political expression. In the countryside especially, legal restraints on organizing were reinforced by open repression.

The 1920s saw the first stirring of organized opposition, though the movement remained weak and marginal for decades to come. Opposition was centered mainly in the urban areas (where small industries began to spring up) and in the large U.S. enterprises, especially the banana plantations—all places where the isolation of rural peasants and semi-feudal traditions had broken down. Strikes hit U.S. banana companies in Honduras, Nicaragua, and Guatemala throughout the 1920s; they were often put down by force of arms. In El Salvador the trade union movement became remarkably active in the 1920s, carrying out strikes to improve members' wages and working conditions and growing to represent 10 percent of the economically active population. Costa Rica had its first general strike in 1921, becoming the only Central American country where workers won the right to an eight-hour day.[4] An incipient class consciousness was reinforced by the influence of radical currents of thought, and by the end of the 1920s Guatemala, El Salvador, and Honduras had their own small socialist parties.

Sandino's Rebellion

The first significant revolt against U.S.-backed elite rule was in Nicaragua, the country which had suffered years of humiliating submission to U.S. dictates. In 1926 the United States had once again sent in the marines (over 6,000 of them) to back up its side in an internecine dispute between warring factions of the Nicaraguan elite— the Liberal and Conservative parties. This time a major justification for the intervention was the threat of "Mexican Bolshevism"—an early expression of U.S. tendencies to see communist threats where, in fact, none existed.

When the United States forged a pact between the two parties, the young Augusto César Sandino refused to capitulate to the U.S.-imposed government. Though far from being a "bolshevik," Sandino was staunchly nationalist, anti-yanqui, and sympathetic to the unmet needs of the exploited classes. He assembled an army of peasants and mineworkers and fought a seven-year guerrilla war against the invading U.S. marines and aerial bombardment from U.S. airplanes.

In 1933, the marines gone, Sandino began negotiating with the government. In the midst of these talks he was gunned down by the National Guard, headed by Anastasio Somoza García. His followers were quickly and brutally repressed.[5] The defeat of Sandino's movement was a watershed in Nicaraguan politics and a warning to other countries. It demonstrated U.S. resolve to resist popular challenges to the status quo, and marked the rise to power of the Somoza family, which used its control over the National Guard to stifle opposition for the next four decades. In spite of their antidemocratic and unpopular rule, the Somoza family won unflagging support from Washington for effectively maintaining stability.

El Salvador's Peasant Uprising and the Era of the Dictators

The same desperate economic conditions that motivated Nicaraguan peasants to support Sandino were also creating mass unrest in other Central American countries hard hit by the Great Depression. In El Salvador, for example, the wages of rural coffee workers (many of them former peasant farmers whose lands had been swallowed up by the coffee oligarchy) were cut in half after the collapse of the world coffee market.[6] In 1932 discontent broke into open revolt in the coffee growing region, where the newly formed Salvadoran Communist Party, led by

Agustín Farabundo Martí, had won some electoral victories. Prevented from taking office by the country's military rulers, the party decided the time was ripe for an uprising, and the peasants were willing to join in.

The ill-planned rebellion, discovered by the government, was easily crushed. And then the army and civilian guards moved in for the slaughter. In a wave of reprisals that reverberated in the national consciousness for decades to come, an estimated 30,000 peasants were killed in the name of anticommunism. Martí was executed and the Communist party was decimated. Although the United States played no direct role in these events (a reflection of both its limited economic role in the country and the Salvadoran oligarchy's traditional independence), it was clearly pleased with the outcome. U.S. warships were stationed off the coast at the time in apparent readiness to lend support.[7]

As in Nicaragua, the defeat of the rebellion brought to power an iron-fisted dicatator, General Maximiliano Hernández Martínez. For the next thirteen years, Martínez ruled El Salvador on behalf of the coffee oligarchy, making any kind of opposition or popular organizing impossible, except in clandestinity. In the same way the lid was kept on volatile social tensions created by the Great Depression in Honduras and Guatemala. Guatemala's dictator, General Jorge Ubico (1932-1944) ruthlessly silenced all opposition and disbanded the Communist party and trade unions alike, executing or exiling their leaders. Once the purge was completed, he launched an economic modernization plan which included an open door policy for foreign investors and repressive labor laws—unwittingly spawning the forces that would bring his downfall.

In Honduras, dictator Tiburcio Carias Andino (1932-48), a friend of the U.S. banana companies, gave the country sixteen years of martial law. Although using somewhat less brutal methods than his neighbors, he too repeatedly crushed revolts by his political opponents.[8] In every case, the U.S. government threw its weight behind these unpopular dictatorships. The unholy alliance between the military and the oligarchy, after all, performed the job the marines had previously been called in to do: protecting U.S. political and economic interests and providing stability to a skewed social structure, where 2 percent of the population controlled 98 percent of the land.[9] The attempt to impose stability through repression, however, only delayed the inevitable explosion.

The United States Turns Back Reform

However iron-fisted their rule, the Central American dictators could not halt the emergence of new social forces created by modernization. Pressures for change came to a head after World War II. A strong coalition arose in opposition to the exclusive rule of the traditional oligarchy. It was drawn from the growing professional and middle class, a newly politicized student population, an expanded working class, young military dissidents, and a new faction of the economic elite whose wealth came from industry and new crops such as cotton and sugar. The demands of this coalition included political democracy, economic reforms, and an end to subservience to foreign interests.

By 1948 the postwar political explosion had brought the demise of the old dictatorships in all but Nicaragua. But when the dust finally settled, the system of oligarchic rule remained intact. The United States played a decisive role in the outcome. Instead of welcoming the opportunity to encourage democracy and reform, the United States branded those who advocated moderate changes "radicals" and "communists." The U.S.-sponsored crusade against communism was under way.

Guatemala: The Democratic Revolution Undone

The decisive showdown came in Guatemala. In 1944 the Ubico dictatorship was overthrown by a broad coalition led by the middle class and supported by virtually every sector of society. United in their desire to overturn the archaic rule of the oligarchy, over 85 percent of the electorate voted for Juan José Arévalo, who opened a ten-year interlude in Guatemalan politics known as the "democratic revolution." Arévalo and his successor Jacobo Arbenz (elected in 1950) introduced reforms designed to bring Guatemala into the twentieth century. They guaranteed democratic rights, initiated social welfare programs and progressive labor legislation, and began an ambitious economic modernization program with a strong nationalist component.

U.S. fears that these reforms were communist-inspired turned to alarm when Arbenz succeeded to the presidency. Although a moderate who hoped to strengthen Guatemalan capitalism, Arbenz went further than his predecessor in challenging the basic assumptions of elite rule and U.S. prerogatives. His land reform program targeted only idle lands, but it enraged the United States and even members of the elite who had helped oust Ubico. To make matters worse, peasant organizations were put in charge of local administration of the law—a move which began to unleash the energies of the peasantry, long held in submission. Just as bad, Arbenz was not anticommunist: his government legalized the Communist party and allowed party members to work in the government. The last straw for the United States was the expropriation of the idle lands of the United Fruit Company. U.S. officials, responding both to pressure from investors and their own calculations, decided that the democratic revolution had to be destroyed. The Central Intelligence Agency organized a successful invading force of Guatemalan exiles led by Colonel Carlos Arana, a staunch anticommunist hand-picked by the United States. The new government, headed by Arana, immediately unleashed a fierce wave of repression, targeting trade union and peasant leaders with particular ferocity. And the country's leading moderates, like Arbenz, were forced into exile or retirement. Guatemala once again became the province of the generals.[10]

Costa Rica: Another Alternative to Radicalism

For many in Guatemala, as well as the rest of Central America, 1954 was a bitter first lesson in the impossiblity of democratic and peaceful change. Yet U.S. postwar policy in Costa Rica provided what appeared to be a counter-example. There the United States actually helped bring to power a reformist government, led by José Figueres Ferrar. Figueres was a social democratic politician whose party became the most important force in Costa Rican politics for the next decade. He was also a willing ally in U.S. efforts to counter what it saw as a growing threat of communism in the region.

Historically, Costa Rica had always been the exception to the rule in Central America—more stable, more democratic, and more egalitarian. The prevalence of family-sized farms, the existence of unsettled lands as an escape valve for dispossessed peasants, the lack of a large indigenous population, the overwhelming influence of European immigrants and earlier manufacturing development—all these factors meant the poles of wealth and poverty were less extreme than in the rest of Central America. Costa Rica had its wealthy coffee elite, but there was also a sizeable urban and rural middle class which was literate, educated, and an active participant in political life. The ruling elite had also demonstrated greater flexibility than in other Central American countries, using state revenues to finance extensive social welfare programs.[11]

But Costa Rica too had its share of social problems, including landless peasants, malnutrition, poor working conditions and lack of sanitation, and in the 1940s it also felt the pressure for more radical approaches to these problems.[12] These pressures came primarily from the small but militant labor movement and the Communist party. By 1943 the party had achieved enough influence to become part of a governing coalition led by a political moderate, Rafael Angel Calderón Guardía, and joined by the Catholic Church. The government's reform programs (including social security, an eight-hour workday, and the right to unionize) sparked an immediate anticommunist backlash and mounting concern in Washington.[13]

One of the leading anticommunists was Figueres. When the ruling coalition refused to recognize an electoral victory by the opposition in 1948, he led an armed revolt, supported by the United States. U.S. troops in Panama were placed on alert, ready to intervene if Figueres' forces faltered.[14] A U.S.-engineered mediation effort then resulted in the exile of radical leaders and the installation of Figueres as president. Figueres was enough of a maverick to occasionally worry U.S. officials: he continued to support efforts to overthrow the Somozas, whom he regarded as unacceptably dictatorial, and he developed a nationalist policy that gave the state a prominent role in the economy. But he did not fundamentally challenge the prerogatives of U.S. investors, and he remained staunchly anticommunist, outlawing the Communist party and its trade unions. Under his party's rule, workers won a minimum wage law, but it was not enforced, and nearly every collective bargaining contract was lost.[15] Though Figueres at first aroused the opposition of the country's coffee elite, the gradual moderation of his policies eventually led to a modus vivendi. Far from threatening stability, Figueres' social reforms were a major factor allowing Costa Rica to escape the social turmoil that gripped the rest of the region in later years.

Stemming the Tide:
Nicaragua, Honduras, El Salvador

Somoza was the sole survivor of the Great Depression dictators. But even Nicaragua did not escape the postwar social ferment, however brief its duration. A wave of worker militancy followed the founding of the Nicaraguan Socialist Party in 1944, but was suppressed by the National Guard. Within two years the party and militant trade unions were banned, and Somoza set up a series of progovernment unions.[16] More threatening was the opposition from members of the Nicaraguan elite, disgruntled at the Somoza family's concentration of economic and political power in its own hands. This opposition was variously contained by political deals and brute force, but never by granting it any real power in running the country. Even though it occasionally balked at the brutal methods of the National Guard, the United States found the immediate stability provided by the dictatorship too attractive to abandon. But the narrowness of its political rule and the ruthlessness of the Guard were ultimately the source of the dynasty's downfall.

In Honduras, the Carias dictatorship was ended, but without the same social turmoil that afflicted its neighbors. Honduras was still the least modern society in the region, partly because it was so thoroughly dominated by the U.S. banana companies. But the 1950s brought some important changes: a spurt of economic modernization (making coffee production important for the first time) and the rise of an organized and militant trade union movement in the banana industry. When 25,000 banana workers went on strike in 1954, the government sent troops to the plantations; but instead of using force to crush the strike, it allowed U.S. labor advisers to mediate the crisis and installed a conservative, procompany union. This approach to controlling the workers' movement by imposing a docile leadership was a forerunner of things to come in the rest of the region.[17]

In the wake of the strike upsurge, the Honduran military stepped to the center of the political stage. After a series of coups, it allowed Ramón Villeda Morales to be elected on a reform platform, extracting a guarantee that the army could contest the president's orders. Villeda, who was an admirer of Arbenz and Figueres, began to enact some moderate reforms. But his 1961 agrarian reform law went too far for the United States. The U.S. ambassador objected to the law, but it was finally the United Fruit Company which forced Villeda into an agreement that the law would not be enforced.[18] Together with the army, the United States was still the most influential political force in the country.

In El Salvador, the Martínez dictatorship was swept away by a coalition similar to the one that emerged in Guatemala in 1944. The immediate result was another military government, albeit one that was tied to the modernizing sector of the oligarchy interested in promoting industry and diversifying agriculture. There was some political liberalization, but increasing trade union activity and student militancy inevitably sparked repression in the name of anticommunism.

A particularly severe wave of repression in the late 1950s provoked an uprising by young military officers (supported by the university community) who promised free elections and reforms. In one of the first instances of direct U.S. involvement in Salvadoran politics, the United States used its influence against the new government, which it considered procommunist, refusing to recognize the coup. U.S. policy once again condemned the moderate reformers to the sidelines, as a right-wing military government came to power.[19]

The Alliance for Progress: Counterinsurgency in Disguise

After this long history of resisting reforms and defending elite rule, Washington began to worry that social inequality and dictatorial rule were the breeding ground of revolution. The success of the Cuban revolution, which reverberated throughout the region, spurred the United States to action. Warning that "those who make peaceful revolution impossible make violent revolution inevitable," President John F. Kennedy launched the Alliance for Progress in 1961. Openly anticommunist in its aims, the Alliance was a multifaceted political, economic, and military intiative designed to contain social revolution in Latin America.

As orginally conceived, the Alliance was to promote governments of the democratic center—governments that would allow political liberalization and support reforms. But the same fate befell the program in Central America as in the rest of Latin America. Before long the army virtually held power in every country but Costa Rica. Honduras suffered a military coup in 1963, at first frowned upon by the United States but recognized within six months. The new government immediately halted the land reform initiated the previous year—the only serious attempt at reform in Central America during the Alliance. The same year right-wing army officers in Guatemala staged a coup; this time the military was actually encouraged by the United States, who feared an electoral victory by its old nemesis Arévalo (who had returned from exile).[20] In El Salvador, the colonel who took power in the U.S.-backed coup in 1960 allowed opposition parties to operate for the first time; he also helped institutionalize the power of the oligarchy by forming an official party, the Party of National Conciliation (PCN). El Salvador soon became the showcase of the Alliance in Central America, but there was no land reform.

Throughout Central America, the foundations of elite rule were untouched by the Alliance. U.S. officials said they wanted a revolution by moderate reformers, but in practice they still viewed true reformers as too radical and too threatening. In the end, Kennedy's warning was forgotten, and the United States fell back on supporting the old right-wing alliance of oligarchs and military men.

Militarism and Armed Challenges

As the reform side of the Alliance fell by the wayside, the military side of the program came to the fore. In the name of "internal security," the United States beefed up the military aid programs it had launched in the 1950s. U.S. military advisers began to teach Central American armies counterinsurgency methods, their officers were trained at U.S. army schools in such places as Panama and Fort Benning, and the Pentagon began to step up military assistance programs. In Guatemala, Honduras, and Nicaragua, U.S. military aid from 1964 to 1967 was almost twice what it had been from 1950 to 1963.[21] Washington also helped establish a regional military alliance in 1964, the Central American Defense Council (CONDECA), meant to coordinate joint actions to protect "internal security."

The concern that Central Americans might take up arms against unresponsive governments was soon borne out, and precisely in those countries where legal channels for political opposition had been most systematically closed off: Nicaragua and Guatemala.

In Nicaragua, now in the second generation of Somoza rule, many had abandoned hope that the dictatorship could be ousted through legal channels. A group of dissidents (led by students and intellectuals) formed the Sandinista Front for National Liberation (FSLN) in 1961, taking inspiration from Sandino's earlier struggle. Influenced by the success of the Cuban revolution, the FSLN initially set up a guerrilla *foco*—an armed base in the countryside which it hoped would eventually spark a mass uprising. But this first effort was crushed by the National Guard. The FSLN then returned to legal forms of struggle before taking up arms again in the late 1960s.[22] Still lacking a mass following, the Sandinistas did not represent a real threat to the Somoza dynasty until more than a decade later. Their appearance, however, provided the rationale for a ruthless crackdown by Anastasio Somoza Debayle's security forces, with the United States providing 13 percent of his defense budget.[23]

As in Nicaragua, the armed movement in Guatemala was fed by dis-illusionment with the possibilities for peaceful change. Members of the coalition that had supported Arbenz—students, intellectuals, the Com-munist party, workers, and reform-minded military officers—grew in-creasingly unhappy with the right-wing governments that followed Ar-benz. Strikes and protest broke out, demanding restoration of some of the political and economic reforms of the Arbenz period. After a refor-mist coup was successfully put down in 1961 (with U.S. naval ships sta-tioned off the coast), some opposition members (led by the reformist military officers) decided to turn to guerrilla warfare. By 1963 several guerrilla *focos* were operating in the countryside. While not an im-mediate threat to the power of the oligarchy, the guerrillas had won sympathetic support from some peasants and managed to hold their own against the Guatemalan army.[24]

U.S. aid was decisive in defeating the insurgency. In 1966 U.S. coun-terinsurgency experts were given a free hand by the Guatemalan gov-ernment (headed by a civilian president, Julio César Mendez Mon-tenegro) and U.S. military aid dollars poured into the country. Al-though the extent of U.S. participation was a highly guarded secret, 1,000 Green Berets were reportedly sent to Guatemala.[25] Within three years a massive counterinsurgency campaign had savagely crushed the guerrilla movement and taken an estimated 8,000 civilian lives.

Systems of Control: AIFLD and Death Squads

The containment of the Central American guerrilla movements was due not just to the military superiority of the U.S.-backed regimes, however. It also reflected the failure of the armed opposition to build a mass following. The premise of the *foco* theory was roundly disproven: a popular rebellion could not simply be sparked by armed actions. One obstacle to building a mass-based movement was the weakness of popular organizations such as trade union and peasant groups, held back by years of repression. While unions had been formally legalized by the 1950s, active trade unionists were often labeled communists and treated as subversives. Strikes were routinely declared illegal. In El Sal-vador, where a relatively liberal labor law existed on paper, only three strikes were recognized between 1945 and 1977 and rural unions were banned entirely.[26]

To complement government repression, a semiofficial network of ter-ror also emerged in the 1960s to dampen any popular organizing—the death squads. The head of the Salvadoran State Intelligence Agency founded the Democratic Nationalist Organization—known as ORDEN—in 1966, inspired, he said, by John Kennedy and the Alliance for Progress.[27] Although ostensibly a grass-roots peasant organization set up to organize support for the PCN, ORDEN became an instrument of terror in the countryside.

In Guatemala some twenty clandestine anticommunist organizations were formed in the 1960s, many of them as special commandos of the state security forces.[28] In the service of the oligarchy and the military (from whom they often took orders), the Salvadoran and Guatemalan death squads became an effective instrument for suppressing dissent. But their activities also fed the growing polarization that occurred during the 1960s.

Besides open intimidation and terror, more sophisticated methods were used to stifle militancy within trade unions and peasant organizations. The Inter-American Regional Organization of Workers (ORIT), an openly anticommunist labor organization set up in 1951 with help from the AFL-CIO, worked throughout the region to undercut independent trade unions. ORIT helped organize progovernment trade unions in Guatemala during the Castillo Armas counter-revolution. And in Honduras, ORIT played a similar role after the militant strikes by banana workers in 1954.[29]

These efforts to channel and de-fuse class struggle were redoubled with the founding of the American Institute for Free Labor Development (AIFLD) in 1962. Backed by the AFL-CIO, the U.S. government and major corporations, AIFLD was designed to promote docile and compliant unions. Its mission was militantly anticommunist. It trained union leaders in procapitalist ideology and offered social welfare benefits to win workers' loyalty. As conditions became more explosive in the countryside during the 1960s, AIFLD targeted Central American peasant organizations. In Honduras, where peasants displaced by agricultural modernization developed a militant movement in the 1960s, AIFLD was called in to support the more conservative peasant organization, the National Association of Honduran Peasants (ANACH), which had been created by ORIT. Nurtured by AIFLD, ANACH helped provide the government with a base of support in the countryside. With similar ends in mind, AIFLD trained union leaders in El Salvador and set up the Salvadoran Peasants Union (UCS), later promoted by the U.S. government as an alternative to the more radical organizations that became active in the 1970s.[30]

The Revolution Explodes

Crisis of Modernization

The multifaceted program to counter revolution in Central America looked to its sponsors in Washington like a great success. Secure in the knowledge that the danger of another Cuba had subsided, Washington abandoned its earlier concern about social reform and political democracy. As the 1970s dawned, the fear of revolution had given way to the euphoria of economic growth. Central America looked like a model of capitalist success in the third world. Economic growth rates averaged above 5 percent during the 1960s in every country, fueled by the dramatic expansion of new export crops (such as sugar and cotton, introduced in the 1950s) and by the spurt of industrial growth set off when the Central American Common Market was founded in 1961. The United States was complacent.

But the very modernization U.S. officials saw as a sign of success was creating the conditions for revolutionary upheaval. Economic development took place at the expense of the already impoverished majority. In the countryside, for example, every time a large cotton or sugar plantation expanded its acreage, another group of peasant farmers lost their lands. In El Salvador, the most densely populated country in the region, approximately one out of every ten agricultural workers was landless in 1961; by 1975 the number was four out of ten. In Guatemala, the average size of the farm of a highland Indian was cut in half between 1955 and 1975.[31]

The situation was hardly better in the cities, flooded by dispossessed peasants looking for work and winding up more often than not unemployed slumdwellers. In spite of industrial growth, jobs were scarce. In both cities and countryside, economic growth was sustained by a near total disregard of workers' salaries, benefits, and working conditions. The urban and rural poor bore the brunt of this model of growth without redistribution. But the worldwide recession and inflation of the early 1970s also began to affect a growing middle class, such as teachers, bank workers, and public employees. Living standards dropped precipitously. Real wages in Nicaragua fell by 25 percent from 1967 to 1975 and by 30 percent in Honduras between 1972 and 1978. In Guatemala the average per capita income of two-thirds of the population dropped from 1950 to the mid-1960s.[32]

Once again, pressures for change built. And once again the oligarchy and the military remained unresponsive. Only this time, pressures reached the exploding point. By the end of the decade, Nicaragua, El Salvador, and Guatemala were on the brink of revolution. The crisis came to a head because the existing political and economic system proved itself incapable of accommodating to massive and widespread demands for peaceful reform. An unprecedented outpouring of social protest and organizing met with violent repression. Hopes for finding a moderate solution through the electoral process were dashed. At the same time revolutionary organizations were reaching a new level of political and military maturity, becoming for the first time a real alternative.

The Mass Movement Takes Shape

The first stirrings of what was to become a massive, popular movement came in the early 1970s. It began with the largely spontaneous protests by those who bore the brunt of modernization—peasants, industrial and agricultural workers, shantytown dwellers, and even white collar workers. Growing numbers of people began to take to the streets to demand the right to a decent standard of living, challenging the fear of government repression and the death squads. The examples were many. In 1973, Guatemalan school teachers went on strike for six months; their protests against increases in the cost of living were joined by students, industrial workers, public employees, and slumdwellers. It was the first time in a decade that people marched in the streets of the capital. Nicaragua experienced a wave of protest, including labor strikes, land occupations, and demonstrations on behalf of political prisoners. In El Salvador's cities, the teachers union, industrial workers, and students were increasingly militant; in the countryside members of the Farmworkers Union (UTC) and the Christian Peasants Federation (FECCAS) defied the legal ban on rural organizing to become two of the largest popular organizations in the country.[33]

The demands of the popular organizations were hardly radical: better lighting for their communities, lower prices for fertilizer, higher wages, improved housing. But the demands were met with reprisals, and as the reprisals grew increasingly violent, the protest movement grew more militant. It was emboldened by its own sense of strength in numbers and common purpose, politicized by contact with the emerging revolutionary organizations, and radicalized by the realization that even the most moderate demands would be resisted by the ruling elite.

Since the late 1960s, the grass-roots organizing work of the Catholic clergy had also been an important factor in this process of radicalization. Catholic priests and nuns, influenced by their own experience in Central America and by the progressive pronouncements of Vatican II, began to live and work alongside the poor in urban slums and rural communities, preaching the gospel of Christian equality and social justice. But they did more than preach. They also encouraged the organization of "base communities." Led by local lay preachers (known as "delegates of the word"), these discussion and action groups provided forums where people could discuss and analyze their own plight in the light of Christian teachings. The guiding principle was a simple one: the poor, too, have rights and dignity. Awakened by this realization, the poor began to organize for their rights, demanding a schoolhouse in their community or a paved road. Invariably the school did not come and the road was not built. And eventually they learned that the Christian principles of equal rights and dignity for all would never be fulfilled within the existing system. The effect was truly revolutionary.[34]

Groups such as FECCAS in El Salvador and the Commmittee for Peasant Unity (CUC) in Guatemala were products of this grass-roots Christian movement. They were also among the leading forces in the broad coalitions of popular organizations that emerged in the mid 1970s. The prototype was the United People's Action Front (FAPU), first founded in 1974 in El Salvador. It brought together church groups, labor unions, the student movement, and teachers. The People's Revolutionary Bloc (BPR), formed the following year, soon became the largest popular organization in the country.

In Guatemala, a similar broad umbrella group, the National Committee of Trade Union Unity (CNUS) was formed in 1976. Nicaragua's equivalent was the United Popular Movement (MPU), founded just a year before the revolution and closely linked to the Sandinista-led struggle against Somoza. All of these mass organizations continued to work on the daily survival issues of their members and to present a united front against the escalating repression. They also became open supporters of the revolutionary alternative.

The Oligarchy Strikes Back

The oligarchy correctly viewed the mushrooming popular movement as a real threat, and repression became increasingly ferocious. In 1977 the Salvadoran army swooped down on peasants carrying out a peaceful land occupation, leaving at least fifty dead. The Church was blamed for "subversive" organizing, and in both Salvador and Guatemala, priests were targeted for assassination. "Be a patriot, kill a priest," read a leaflet issued by a Salvadoran death squad. Later that year, the Salvadoran government issued the Law for the Guarantee of Public Order, making it a crime to criticize the government and greatly restricting freedom of association and information. Several months later when peasants marched in the capital to protest the refusal of government officials to discuss their request for lower interest and rent, the army killed at least nine.[35]

In Guatemala the toll also mounted. In May 1978 over 100 Indian men, women, and children were gunned down in the town square of Panzos, where they had gathered for a public meeting with officials to protest the seizure of their lands by a local landowner. Several months later a massive popular demonstration led by trade unions in Guatemala City against the doubling of bus fares ended with thirty-one persons killed by the army.[36] In Nicaragua, the government cracked down on peasants involved in land takeovers and suspected rural sympathizers of the increasingly active Sandinista Front. During the thirty-three months the country suffered under martial law (declared by Somoza in 1974), an estimated 3,000 peasants died at the hands of the National Guard.[37] Even in Honduras, where social tensions were less acute, an increasingly militant wave of peasant land occupations met with harsh reprisals. When the National Peasant Union (UNC) staged a "hunger march" on the capital in 1975 to protest government unresponsiveness, they were attacked by the army. The toll was fourteen dead.[38]

Repression: Choice or Necessity?

Some have argued in retrospect that the Central American oligarchy, due to short-sighted stubbornness and the unflagging support of the United States, made a bad decision in refusing to accede to the demands for reform in the 1970s. If only they had opted for a Costa Rican type solution—liberal democracy and social reforms—political pressures could have been diffused and the present crisis averted. In fact, as the ruling elites instinctively recognized, such a solution was impossible if the basis of their power and wealth were to be kept intact.

As we have seen, the Costa Rican "solution" was based on the country's distinct social and economic realities. Unlike neighboring countries, Costa Rica had a social base that lent itself to a centrist political formula and liberal democracy. Though not isolated from the impact of rapid capitalist development that swept the region in the 1970s, it was not convulsed by these changes in the same way as its neighbors. The locus of Costa Rica's agricultural modernization in the 1970s was the cattle industry. While the boom crops of neighboring countries, cotton and sugar, relied on a huge and highly exploited labor force, cattle was not labor intensive. In fact, the lack of a large and highly exploitable landless peasantry made Costa Rica a far less attractive site for labor-intensive agriculture. While beef production displaced some Costa Rican peasants, the increase in landlessness was not as dramatic as in neighboring countries. Most of the cattle expansion in Costa Rica occurred on traditional haciendas which modernized their operations rather than taking over peasant lands.

The existence of government social programs also provided a certain cushion against economic adversity for most Costa Ricans. When these programs were threatened by the economic downturn of the early 1970s, massive loans from U.S. and international aid agencies helped sustain them. By the end of the decade, however, the country's huge debt and other economic problems brought a reduction in government social spending. The cutbacks contributed to the rising social unrest which threatened this model of social democratic stability.

By contrast, the neighboring countries of Nicaragua, El Salvador, Guatemala had neither the economic nor social base for a Costa Rican type solution. They had also experienced a different kind of development since 1960, one based on labor intensive agriculture (primarily cotton and sugar) and manufacturing industries (described in detail in Chapter 7). Given acute land pressures, agricultural expansion could not take place without driving peasants off the land. With low labor costs the cutting edge of profitability, keeping wages and working conditions at bare subsistence levels was the basic ingredient of economic growth. It was the logic of the system then, not simple recalcitrance, that led the oligarchy down the path of brutal repression rather than conciliation and reform.

Demise of the Center

For many Central Americans, the lesson that change would not come within the system was learned through peaceful protests that turned into government massacres. For others it was learned in a final futile attempt at electoral politics. Though free elections in Central America had been few and far between, in the early 1970s "democratic" channels still tempted some centrist opponents of the oligarchy. Even the left was engaged in intense debates about participation in elections.

El Salvador. During the 1960s El Salvador witnessed a carefully controlled political liberalization. Relatively free municipal and legislative elections were permitted, on the implicit assumption that oligarchic power would not be challenged. Surprisingly impressive gains were made by the newly formed Christian Democratic party, whose main support came from well-to-do and middle-class urban professionals. As mayor of San Salvador, Christian Democrat José Napoleon Duarte also developed a certain following among the urban poor. When the 1972 presidential elections approached, hopes were high that some real changes might be in the offing.[39]

The Christian Democrats joined with the Communist party and the National Revolutionary Movement (MNR, the social democratic party led by Guillermo Ungo) to present a reform ticket, with Duarte as president and Ungo as vice-president. Though the vote went in favor of the Duarte/Ungo ticket, the official election board declared the military-backed candidate the winner. Salvadorans were outraged. One month later, progressive military officers attempted a coup to restore the rightful victors. The army acted swiftly and brutally, squelching the coup with military assistance from Guatemala and Nicaragua—an intervention that many believe the United States had a hand in.[40] Two hundred people lay dead.

The tiny political opening was permanently closed down as the new president, Colonel Arturo Molina, launched a new wave of repression. The political center fell into disarray. Many Christian Democratic leaders, including Duarte, went into exile, and disputes broke out over the meaning of the electoral fiasco. Many disillusioned rank-and-file party members abandoned electoral politics, turning to the popular organizations to channel their grievances.[41]

In 1977 the military staged another election so fraudulent that the vote totals were not even announced publicly. Some 50,000 outraged citizens demonstrated against the rigged elections, and on the fifth day of protests the army fired on the crowd, leaving an unknown number of people dead.[42] El Salvador had a new military strongman as ruler, General Carlos Humberto Roméro, and the repression worsened.

Guatemala. A similar result was achieved in Guatemala by a somewhat different path. After 1954, right-wing military officers managed, with U.S. backing, to keep tight control over the reins of power. The army overturned elections in 1958 and 1963, entering into a U.S.-engineered pact with a civilian president in 1966, and fielded its own candidate on a right-wing party ticket in 1970. The small social democratic party (FUR) and the Christian Democrats emerged from the shadows of semi-legality in 1974 to support their own military candidate for president, General Efraín Ríos Montt, who ran on a reform platform. His surprising victory led to an official recount and a new victor—the official military candidate, General Kjeill Laugerud. The military once again made clear that even talk of reform would not be tolerated. The result, as one writer noted, "never again would significant numbers of voters place their faith in peaceful reform through the ballot box."[43] As the decade wore on, the leaders of the two centrist parties were gunned down by right-wing death squads, who systematically set out to destroy the moderate opposition.

Nicaragua. In Nicaragua, the unchallenged power of the Somoza family had already stretched the facade of electoral democracy thin. Even the Conservative Party, which represented members of the elite edged out of power by the Somozas, found elections so futile that they turned occasionally to armed actions in the late 1950s and 1960s. As the 1967 presidential elections approached, the Conservatives once again spoke of armed opposition, and called a major protest demonstration. But the people were not armed, and when the National Guard fired on demonstrators an estimated 600 were killed. The incident discredited both sides—the Somozas for their brutality and the Conservatives for their ineptness.[44] The son of the dynasty's founder, Anastasio Somoza Debayle, the head of the National Guard known for his hard-line methods, became president.

In 1974 all major opposition parties boycotted the elections and Anastasio Somoza again became president. But the regime had never been weaker or more isolated. The bourgeois opposition to the Somoza dictatorship mushroomed after Somoza used 1972 earthquake relief funds to further enrich his family's fortune. In addition, the revolutionary alternative proposed by the Sandinistas was rapidly becoming a force to be reckoned with.

Some members of the opposition, however, still stubbornly insisted on an electoral path to power. A new electoral coalition was formed, the Democratic Union of Liberation (UDEL). Led by Pedro Joaquín Chamorro, the prominent editor of the daily *La Prensa*, UDEL included the Social Christian Party, dissident Conservatives and Liberals, the small pro-Moscow Nicaraguan Socialist Party, and a number of trade union groups. UDEL was essentially a centrist alternative to Somoza rule. It proposed reforms and moderation, and was quietly supported by the United States.[45] But the intransigent reaction of Somoza—culminating in the 1978 assassination of Chamorro—sealed the fate of the center. Many of the forces in UDEL became radicalized by the repres sion, and there was an explosion of mass protests against the Somoza dictatorship. As elsewhere, the alternatives were increasingly stark: the old order of brutal dictatorships or a new revolutionary order.

The Revolutionary Alternative

In 1970 the FSLN numbered only a few hundred men and women, and today's revolutionary organizations in Guatemala and El Salvador were embryonic groups without public names. Less than ten years later, nearly the entire Nicaraguan population backed the Sandinista-led struggle against Somoza, and hundreds of thousands of Guatemalans and Salvadorans openly supported the revolutionary alternative.

The remarkable growth of the revolutionary organizations both reflected and fed the parallel growth of the mass movement. In the late 1960s the Central American left had entered a period of difficult reevaluation, resulting in new organizations and strategies. Many rejected the Moscow-oriented Communist parties' continuing emphasis on electoral politics to the exclusion of armed struggle. The *focista* strategy for revolution, however, was roundly rejected. Instead, a new understanding of the revolutionary process began to emerge, one which stressed that slow and patient organizing among the people was an essential complement to armed struggle. Reflecting this new strategy, the guerrillas of the 1970s called their groups "political-military" organizations. They set out to win the political loyalties of the masses as the basis of their revolution.[46]

The revolutionary organizations borrowed variously from Marxism, Christianity, and from the experience of other countries (including Cuba and Vietnam). But the starting point was their own national realities. While advocating revolution, their programs were similar to those originally advocated by the Alliance for Progress—agrarian and tax reform, better housing and education, political democracy, respect for human rights. None of these could be achieved without the fundamental change in the system of elite rule so long resisted by the United States. Just as unacceptable to Washington was the demand for "self-determination"—the right to shape their own political and economic future without outside interference.

The Revolution Organizes

In El Salvador, the continual refusal of the Salvadoran Communist Party to develop a military strategy to challenge the oligarchy led to the resignation of party leader, Salvador Cayetano Carpio, in 1970. To-gether with his political followers Carpio founded a new organization, later to take the name Popular Liberation Forces (FPL), which pioneered in the work of mass organizing. Disaffection with electoral politics also led dissident Christian Democrats to join with radical clerics and other leftists to form the Popular Revolutionary Army (ERP) in 1971. Disagreement within the ERP on the issue of how polit-ical organizing related to armed struggle resulted in the formation of a third organization, the National Resistance (RN) in 1975.[47] Until late in the decade, the public face of the revolution was seen mainly in the mass demonstrations that began to take place in San Salvador; militar-ily, the guerrillas focused on small actions such as kidnappings or bank robberies, designed to make a political statement or raise funds.

In Guatemala, the remnants of the defeated guerrilla groups of the 1960s, as well as some newcomers, quietly regrouped.[48] The Revolu-tionary Armed Forces (FAR), the only organization that survived in-tact from the 1960s, finally abandoned its *foco* efforts in 1971 to begin a new attempt to build a mass-based political movement among urban and agricultural workers. A different approach was followed by a group of FAR members who left to set up the Organization of the People in Arms (ORPA). Pointing to the failure of the *focistas* to incorporate Guatemala's Indian majority into the revolutionary movement, ORPA members worked in virtual clandestinity for eight years organizing highland Indians.

Meanwhile, a group of exiles entered the jungles of northwestern Guatemala to set up the first armed nucleus of the Guerrilla Army of the Poor (EGP), where for years they worked patiently to organize the peasants and Indians. As in El Salvador, the guerrillas didn't begin to carry out major armed actions until the end of the decade.

The FSLN followed a similar course of patient organizing among both the rural and urban population during the 1970s.[49] But it re-mained small, isolated, and politically insignificant until December 1974, when a group of Sandinistas raided a party attended by Somoza officials. The dramatic action galvanized the country and ended in a spontaneous outpouring of public sympathy for the FSLN. Somoza de-clared a state of seige, and the National Guard stepped up repression, particularly in the rural areas where the Sandinistas were most active. The Sandinistas once again retreated to clandestine organizing.

Following the public reappearance of the FSLN in a nationally coor-dinated attack against Guard posts in late 1977, events moved rapidly to bring the country to the brink of revolution. As the Somoza regime was stripped of the last shred of political legitimacy by its unrelenting strong-arm tactics, the ranks of the opposition swelled to include virtually every sector of the population, from the common people to Catholic priests and bishops, to prominent intellectuals and business people. And increasingly, this opposition rallied behind the the FSLN, which hoped to bring down Somoza with a broad alliance of all democratic sectors.

With all other channels closed off, the Nicaraguan people turned to the last resort—open war against the regime. The fact that victory came relatively soon after an unsuccessful popular uprising in September of 1978 was both a tribute to the skillful leadership of the FSLN and a reflection of the total political bankruptcy of the Somoza regime. This last reality contributed to another crucial component of the victory: the inability of the United States to come up with a successful interventionary strategy.

The Failure of U.S. Maneuvers

As we have noted, the U.S. government kept a low profile in Central America during the 1970s, leaving the job of maintaining order and stability to the local dictators. In 1977 President Carter launched an ill-fated initiative—his "human rights" policy, maligned by the left for its ineffectualness and by the right as a sell-out. In fact, the policy was a rational attempt to stabilize the pro-U.S. regimes of the region. Recognizing that extreme repression made the ruling elites more vulnerable to political opposition, the Carter administration pushed for an improved human rights image to undercut criticism at home and abroad.

The commitment to human rights, however, was soon superseded by the fear of revolution. When it became clear in mid-1978 that the FSLN-led coalition posed a real threat to Somoza, the U.S. government once again threw its political and economic weight behind the regime rather than accept the "radical" alternative. This policy only strengthened the FSLN as members of the moderate opposition realized that hopes for U.S. support in forcing concessions from Somoza were futile.[50]

The U.S. refusal to abandon Somoza was not mere obstinacy, but a recognition that there was no viable centrist alternative which could keep the Sandinistas out of power. Hence Washington's last-ditch attempt to stave off a Sandinista victory by a "mediation" effort: the U.S. envoy offered an interim government of the bourgeois opposition and Somoza's party, keeping the National Guard intact. The United States was only offering what many opponents called "Somocismo without Somoza." Somoza refused.

By 1979 Somoza had become virtually indefensible as an ally in Washington—particularly after his air force bombed several cities to rubble in a futile attempt to crush the revolution—and that summer the Sandinistas swept to power. It was only in the final weeks before imminent victory that the United States finally asked for Somoza's immediate resignation.

The Revolution Spreads

After the Sandinista victory, events moved at breathtaking speed to bring both El Salvador and Guatemala to a state of open civil war. "If Nicaragua triumphed, El Salvador will triumph too," was the new slogan of the popular organizations, who thronged the streets of San Salvador and occupied government buildings.

An alarmed oligarchy virtually declared war on the popular organizations, and the catalogue of massacres grew.[51] When leaders of El Salvador's BPR disappeared, supporters demonstrated on the steps of the Metropolitan Cathedral. Their protests and songs were silenced by National Guard sharpshooters, who killed twenty-three. Still refusing to be intimidated, the popular organizations staged the largest demonstration in the country's history in January 1980. The army again retaliated: 67 dead and 250 wounded. That same month in Guatemala, the government's brutality was tragically spotlighted for the world. Peasants protesting loss of their farmlands staged a peaceful sit-in at the Spanish embassy in Guatemala City; the army responded by firebombing the building, slaughtering thirty-nine men and women.

By late 1980, it was clear that open opposition was suicidal, and the popular opposition was forced into clandestinity. Crowds of protestors no longer flooded the streets of San Salvador and Guatemala City; instead there was the eerie silence of the death squads and army security forces. Many members of popular organizations merged into the ranks of the revolutionary organizations.

In Washington, concern mounted over this growing polarization. Even Costa Rica and Honduras, up to now the bastions of "stability," were beginning to experience the stirrings of an incipient revolutionary opposition.[52] Determined to prevent the events of July 1979 from repeating themselves in other countries, the United States decided it could no longer withhold urgently needed economic and military support from its beleaguered allies, however repugnant their human rights abuses. Yet a central dilemma remained. While the region's military rulers shared U.S. goals, their heavy-handed means were counter-productive: right-wing extremism not only radicalized the opposition, it also made it difficult to obtain domestic backing for U.S. support.

Having failed to moderate the right through a human rights policy, the Carter administration made a feeble attempt to resuscitate what was left of the democratic center. But it soon became clear that the United States was unwilling to abandon the right-wing alliance of officers and oligarchs. The test case was El Salvador.

El Salvador's Coup: The Center's Last Gasp

On October 15, 1979, in a coup that was welcomed and perhaps encouraged by the United States, a group of young army officers overthrew the discredited regime of General Carlos Roméro.[53] Promising reforms and an end to human rights abuses, they assembled a government that included the Christian Democrats and the social democratic MNR (represented by Guillermo Ungo). But it also included representatives of the old-line military in several key positions—on the junta and as defense minister. By the end of the year, the centrist scheme had begun to unravel as the right wing took de facto control of the new government.

While maneuvering behind the scenes to prevent a rightist coup, the United States was in agreement with the conservatives on a key question dividing the junta: dialogue with the popular organizations. Once again, fear of the left won out over U.S. desires to promote reform and moderation. When it became clear that the military had no intention of seriously pursuing the promised reforms, Ungo and other moderates demanded that they leave the government. The colonels stayed, and Ungo and several of his supporters walked out, abandoning what they had seen as "the last chance for peaceful change."[54] By March 1980, virtually every progressive civilian in the government had abandoned the junta, including a large faction of the Christian Democratic party.

The United States stood firm on the side of the junta, even increasing its economic and military aid, as it watched the hopes for a centrist solution trampled. When the country's archbishop, Oscar Roméro, spoke out against the repressive character of the regime, asking the United States to withdraw its support, he was murdered.

In April the Democratic Revolutionary Front (FDR) was formed, bringing together virtually every organization that opposed the oligarchy—trade unions, Christian organizations, professionals, and the popular and revolutionary organizations. The center was officially dead and buried. Disturbed but undaunted, the United States redoubled its efforts to drape the right in a mantle of moderation and legitimacy. José Napolean Duarte, the Christian Democratic leader, had returned from exile. His frustrated presidential ambitions and a marked shift to the right made him responsive to U.S. overtures and he agreed to join the junta. For the next two years Duarte served as civilian figurehead for the military-dominated government.[55]

Duarte's presence, together with a highly touted but largely ineffective agrarian reform program (analyzed in Chapter 5), allowed the United States to perpetuate the fiction that its support for El Salvador represented a commitment to moderation and reform. In fact Duarte stood in silent complicity with the reign of terror unleashed by semi-official death squads controlled by military officials. In the year after he joined the junta, repression increased. Over forty officials in his own party were killed. But most of the victims were ordinary civilians accused of being sympathetic to the "subversives." As the death toll mounted, Washington forged ahead with the centerpiece of its political strategy: promoting "democratic" elections. The target was not just El Salvador, but also the military governments of Honduras and Guatemala.

The Election Charade

Elections were designed to accomplish a number of objectives, all of them aimed at undermining the revolutionary alternative. Most importantly, restoring electoral democracy was viewed as a key step toward opening the floodgates to U.S. economic and military aid. If centrists could be lured into the government, all the better; but even if the right continued in power, at least its image would be cleansed.

But elections were not just for external consumption. They were also part of U.S. counterinsurgency strategies, particularly in El Salvador. Washington hoped that restoring electoral democracy would isolate the left, who refused to participate, and curb the excesses of the far right, forcing them to operate within the confines of the electoral arena. Finally, elections might mitigate explosive political tensions by making people believe that voting gave them a voice in their country.

For the United States, elections were thus an alternative to the political dialogue proposed by the left. The same purpose was at work at a regional level. By forging a regional alliance of pro-U.S. "democratic" states, the United States hoped to isolate and discredit Nicaragua as undemocratic and totalitarian.[56]

Honduras: The Power Behind the Throne

On the surface, results in Honduras, rapidly becoming the key U.S. ally in the region, were most positive for the United States. Still somewhat shielded from the turmoil that gripped its neighbors, Honduras was slated to become the forward base of U.S. military intervention in the region (see Chapter 2). Washington was therefore anxious to promote Honduras as a democracy. The November 1981 elections, which installed the Liberal party candidate Dr. Roberto Suazo Cordoba in the presidency, accomplished just that. But there was another reality behind the democratic facade. While stepping into the background, the Honduran military increased its real power. Much of that power was concentrated in the hands of Gustavo Alvarez Martínez, a hard-line anticommunist, who in January 1982 became the first colonel appointed as defense minister. It was widely believed that U.S. support was decisive in the unusual appointment. Indeed, Alvarez collaborated closely with U.S. ambassador John Negroponte, who became known as one of the most powerful men in the country. Alvarez' assumption later that year of the title and powers of commander-in-chief, an authority that traditionally resided with the president, only formalized the reality of Honduran politics. The military was the undisputed power behind the figurehead civilian president.[57]

Despite this reality, the democratic strategy worked in the U.S. Congress. Economic and military aid to Honduras passed with little resistance, and Honduras became the site of a massive U.S. military build-up. Few Hondurans were fooled by the formal democracy. In the name of a crackdown on "subversion," the civil liberties of the democratic opposition were trampled and death squads began to operate. One of the few dissenting voices in Honduras, a leader of the ALIPO faction of the ruling Liberal party, predicted that U.S. policies were driving Honduras down the road to armed struggle.[58]

Guatemala: Changing of the Guard

Guatemala's exercise in electoral politics went less smoothly, exposing the divisions within the ruling elite. The 1982 election was a contest between parties of the right, with the small and conservative Christian

Democrats joining with the party of the oligarchy; no organized political force could even attempt to masquerade as the center. But U.S. officials heaved a sigh of relief: at least there were elections. Much to the
dismay of the United States, however, the military regime of General
Romeo Lucas García (whose disastrous human rights record had made
it impossible for Washington to resume badly needed economic and
military aid) made sure its candidate won the elections. Amid accusations of fraud by other parties of the right, a military coup installed
General Efraín Ríos Montt in power.[59] The United States warmly em-
braced Ríos Montt as a reformer and a protector of human rights. If it
couldn't have electoral democracy, the United States was willing to
have the next best thing: a masterful public relations campaign by the
new regime to convince international public opinion that Guatemala
had cleaned up its excesses.

The strategy worked briefly, but then the truth began to slip out.
While the death squads no longer roamed the streets of Guatemala
City, the army's counterinsurgency campaign wreaked havoc in the
countryside. Over ten thousand people were slaughtered by government soldiers, while many more fled to the mountains or across the border into Mexico.[60] Dozens of villages were destroyed, their populations
herded into Guatemalan versions of the strategic hamlets used in Vietnam.

However effective his military campaign in containing the guerrilla
threat, Ríos Montt soon lost favor with his rightist supporters. A fanati-
cal evangelist who believed he had a divine mission, the eccentric general alienated both the parties of the right and important sectors of the
military by keeping tight personal control over the reins of power.
Another military coup brought General Oscar Mejía Victores to power
in the summer of 1983. The death squads swung into action, and Mejía
Victores promised to "eradicate" the "Marxist-Leninists."

Although their political base of support had been severely damaged
by the army campaign, the guerrillas began to recoup and mount new
armed strikes against the army. The war was picking up again.
Guatemala could not face the insurgent threat indefinitely without U.S.
support, yet the recalcitrant generals refused to go along with the
democratic face-lifting urged by U.S. officials. Once again, the United
States was in a bind in Central America: as long as its goal was destroying the revolutionary alternative, it had no other allies to rely on but
the right wing, unrepentantly brutal and opposed to change. Congress
balked, but Reagan and his bipartisan commission on Central America

continued to push for U.S. aid to the regime. In Guatemala, noted one State Department official, "we have no options."[61]

El Salvador: The Plan Unravels

El Salvador was the most dramatic illustration of the failures and contradictions of the U.S. political strategy. The first round in the two-stage electoral process came in March of 1982 with elections for a constituent assembly. The elections were an important if fleeting propaganda victory for the United States. The impressive voter turnout was interpreted as a defeat for the left, which had boycotted but failed to disrupt the election. Though it was later revealed that up to one-quarter of the ballots were fradulent, the fraud was covered up at the time and the elections were hailed as fair and free.[62] But the aftermath of this first round set the stage for a deepening political crisis which the 1984 presidential election had no hope of resolving. Indeed, to salvage the political formula it sought to impose in El Salvador, the United States was driven to increasingly blatant intervention in the country's political life.

One problem for the United States was a growing polarization among the political forces it had hoped to marshal into a ruling alliance against the left. While Washington hoped to bolster the mildly reformist program of Duarte's moderate right Christian Democrats, the far right parties of the oligarcy also had to be included in the new "democracy." Washington's task was complicated when the far-right ARENA party emerged from the 1982 elections with control over a majority bloc in the assembly. ARENA naturally attempted to appoint its leader Roberto d'Aubuisson, known for his death squad connection, as interim president. It was only due to intense pressure from the United States and an ultimatum from the armed forces that Alvaro Magaña, who had historic links with the military, assumed the post instead.[63] But the rivlary between the far right and Duarte's party only deepened as the 1984 elections approached. Reflecting the deep divisions in its ranks, Magaña's "national unity" government was weak, some said paralyzed. The military continued to hold the real power in the country despite the facade of democracy.

While Washington was its main supporter, the military's power brought certain problems. Chief among these was the difficulty of controlling the rightist death squads, whose links with the military run deep. Reflecting the political polarization within the government, the death squads began to lash out with renewed intensity before the 1984 elections. Their targets were those even remotely linked to reforms— peasant leaders linked to the Christian Democrats, labor leaders, and even officials in the foreign ministry. As the death toll rose, the already tarnished image of El Salvador's democracy was further sullied.[64]

In an attempt to cleanse that image and justify its support for the regime before Congress, the Reagan administration issued a public warning to the Salvadorans: restrain the death squads, prosecute those responsible for the killings of American religious workers, and remove the military officials notorious for their links to the death squads. There were a few cosmetic changes as a result, but the fundamental demands went unmet.[65] The military protected its own, and the United States, impelled by its fear of the revolutionary alternative, had no choice but to continue its support to the government.

Despite all evidence to the contrary, the Reagan administration insisted that El Salvador was progressing along the path to democracy. By the time of the March 1984 elections, however, the prospects for an outcome that would provide political stability and legitimacy to the Salvadoran government appeared increasingly remote. Whether the far right managed to control the presidency or not, it would continue to shape the character of Salvadoran politics. And whether the moderate right or the far right emerged victorious, the animosity and divisions between the two only intensified in the contest for power. Meanwhile, the military continued as the ultimate political arbiter.

A few months before the March 1984 election, the Reagan administration made one last attempt to woo the centrist parties away from the FDR into the electoral arena. This futile effort only demonstrated that the center was firmly wedded to the revolutionary alternative. Although the Reagan administration refused to grant the left any legitimacy, and simply branded the revolutionary organizations as terrorists, any political formula that excluded the left was doomed to failure.

While continuing to pay lip service to its centrist policy, the United States was allying itself with the right in order to contain the left. It was the tried and tested formula Washington had used for decades in Central America, but it no longer worked.

Notes

1. For more on the colonial period in Central America see John P. Augelli and Robert C. West, *Middle America: Its Land and Peoples* (Englewood Cliffs, N.J.: Prentice Hall, 1976) and Ralph Lee Woodward, *Central America: A Nation Divided* (New York: Oxford University Press, 1976).

2. On the rise of the coffee oligarchy and the policies of the Liberal Party dictatorships of the late nineteenth century see Woodward, *Central America*, pp. 149-76. On El Salvador during this period see Liisa North, *Bitter Grounds: Roots of Revolt in El Salvador* (Toronto: Between the Lines, 1981), pp. 17-29.

3. On U.S. intervention during this period see Jenny Pearce, *Under the Eagle: U.S. Intervention in Central America and the Caribbean* (London: Latin America Bureau, 1981), pp. 11-20; and Walter LeFeber, *Inevitable Revolutions: The United States in Central America* (New York: W.W. Norton, 1983).

4. See Norma Stoltz Chinchilla, "Class Struggle in Central America: Background and Overview" in Latin America Perspectives, Spring-Summer, 1980, p. 12. On Nicaragua see George Black, Triumph of the People: The Sandinista Revolution in Nicaragua (London: Zed Press, 1981), pp. 15-16. On Honduras see Victor Meza, *História del movimiento obréro Hondureño* (Tegucigalpa: Editorial Guaymuras, 1981). On El Salvador see North, *Bitter Grounds*.

5. This account is based largely on Black, *Triumph of the People*, pp. 18-24.

6. LeFeber, *Inevitable Revolutions*, p. 64.

7. See Robert Armstrong and Janet Shenk, *El Salvador: The Face of Revolution* (Boston: South End Press, 1982). The most complete account of these events is Thomas Anderson, *Matanza: El Salvador's Communist Revolt of 1932* (Lincoln: University of Nebraska Press, 1971).

8. On this period see Woodward, *Central America*, pp. 216-22.

9. LeFeber, *Inevitable Revolutions*, p. 81.

10. See Suzanne Jonas and David Tobis, eds., *Guatemala* (New York: NACLA, 1974), pp. 44-51.

11. On Costa Rica as an exception see Woodward, *Cental America*, p. 215. For socioeconomic data see J. Edward Taylor, "Peripheral Capitalism and Rural Urban Migration: A Study of Population Movement in Costa Rica," *Latin American Perspectives*, Spring-Summer 1980.

12. LeFeber, *Inevitable Revolutions*, p. 100.

13. See Woodward, *Central America*, pp. 222-26.

14. LeFeber, *Inevitable Revolutions*, p. 102.

15. Ibid., p. 187.

16. Black, *Triumph of the People*, pp. 29-31.

17. Steve Volk, "Honduras: On the Border of War," *NACLA Report on the Americas*, November-December 1981, pp. 8-9.

18. LeFeber, *Inevitable Revolutions*, p. 178.
19. On this period in El Salvador see Armstrong, and Shenk, *El Salvador*, pp. 43-44; Lefeber, *Inevitable Revolutions*, pp. 172-73; and North, *Bitter Grounds*, pp. 54-56.
20. George Black with Milton Jamail and Norma Stoltz Chinchilla, "Garrison Guatemala," *NACLA Report on the Americas*, January-February 1983, p.7.
21. Aid to Nicaragua increased from $4.5 million to $7.5 million, to Honduras from $2.6 million to $4.6 million, and to Guatemala from $5.3 million to $10.9 million. LeFeber, *Inevitable Revolutions*, p. 151.
22. For more on FSLN during this period see Black, *Triumph of the People*, pp. 75-86.
23. LeFeber, *Inevitable Revolutions*, p. 163.
24. See Jonas, *Guatemala*, pp. 177-87 and Gabriel Aguilera Peralta, "Terror and Violence as Weapons of Counterinsurgency in Guatemala," *Central America Perspectives*, Spring-Summer 1980.
25. Jonas, *Guatemala*, p. 199.
26. Armstrong and Shenk, *El Salvador*, p. 98.
27. Shirley Christian, "El Salvador's Divided Military," *Atlantic Monthly*, June 1983, p. 83.
28. Peralta, "Terror and Violence," pp. 102-3.
29. For an overview of ORIT's role in the region see Hobart Spalding Jr., *Organized Labor in Latin America* (New York: Harper Torchbooks, 1977).
30. On AIFLD and the peasant movement in El Salvador see Phillip Wheaton, *Agrarian Reform in El Salvador: A Program of Rural Pacification* (Washington, D.C.: EPICA, 1980). On Honduras see Volk, "Honduras," p. 19.
31. Roger Burbach and Patricia Flynn, *Agribusiness in the Americas* (New York: Monthly Review Press, 1981), p. 147 and Phillip Berryman, *What's Wrong in Central America and What to Do About It* (Philadelphia: American Friends Service Committee, 1983), p.8.
32. *Latin America Economic Report*, May 4, 1979, p. 133; *Latin America Regional Report*, June 6, 1980, p. 8; and LeFeber, *Inevitable Revolutions*, p. 168.
33. On Guatemala, see George Black with Milton Jamail and Norma Stoltz Chinchilla, "Guatemala—the War Is Not Over," in *NACLA Report on the Americas*, March-April 1983, pp. 3-10; and Guatemala Scholars Network, *Guatemala: Dare to Struggle, Dare to Win* (Washington, D.C., 1980). On Nicaragua see Black, *Triumph of the People*, pp. 120-23. On El Salvador see Armstrong and Shenk, *El Salvador*, pp. 70-102.
34. For the best overview of the role of the church in the region see Penny Lernoux, *Cry of the People* (Garden City, N.Y.: Doubleday, 1980).
35. Armstrong and Shenk, *El Salvador*, p. 94.
36. See Scholars, *Guatemala*.
37. Black, *Triumph of the People*, p. 89.
38. See Mario Posas, *El movimiento campesino Hondureño* (Tegucigalpa: Editorial

Guaymuras, 1981), p. 34. The event, known as the "Horcones massacre," is still commemorated in an annual march sponsored by peasant organizations.

39. See North, *Bitter Grounds*, p. 68.
40. Armstrong and Shenk, *El Salvador*, p. 63.
41. North, *Bitter Grounds*, p. 77.
42. See Policy Alternatives for the Caribbean and Central America, *Changing Course: Blueprint for Peace in Central America and the Caribbean* (Washington, D.C.: Institute for Policy Studies 1984), p. 35.
43. On political developments in the post-1954 period see Black, "Garrison Guatemala," pp. 6-9.
44. Black, *Triumph of the People*, pp. 43-44.
45. On the period leading up to the revolution see Harold Jung, "Behind the Nicaraguan Revolution" in Stanford Central American Action Network, Revolution in Central America (Boulder, Col.: Westview, 1983), pp. 25-30 and Alejandro Bendaña, "Crisis in Nicaragua," *NACLA Report on the Americas*, November-December 1978.
46. See Chinchilla, "Class Struggle."
47. On the emergence of the revolutionary organizations in El Salvador see Armstrong and Shenk, *El Salvador*, pp. 64-73.
48. For more on this process see Black, "Garrison Guatemala," pp. 26-33; and Scholars, *Guatemala*.
49. For a detailed account of the FSLN's development through the 1970s see Black, *Triumph of the People*, pp. 86-140 and Bendaña, "Nicaragua in Crisis," pp. 19-27.
50. See Jung, "Behind the Nicaraguan Revolution" and William LeoGrande, "The Revolution in Nicaragua: Another Cuba?" in Stanford Network, *Revolution in Central America*, pp. 86-89.
51. An amply documented and highly personal view of repression in Guatemala is Shelton Davis and Julie Hodson, *Witness to Political Violence in Guatemala: the Suppression of a Rural Development Movement* (Boston: Oxfam America, 1982).
52. Three main guerrilla organizations emerged in Honduras after 1980: the Popular Movement of Liberation (Chinchoneros), the Morazan Front for the Liberation of Honduras, and the People's Revolutionary Forces "Lorenzo Zelaya." Though small and lacking a mass base, they carried out a number of dramatic actions in 1981-82 which gained them notoriety. In Costa Rica, which had no armed movement, several leftist parties and the trade union movement were the leading forces behind an increasingly militant opposition.
53. LeFeber, *Inevitable Revolutions*, p. 248; Armstrong and Shenk, *El Salvador*, pp. 115-18; and LeoGrande, "The Revolution in Nicaragua," pp. 101-12.
54. Armstrong and Shenk, *El Salvador*, p. 126.

55. LeoGrande, "The Revolution in Nicaragua," p. 104. Duarte was finally appointed president in November 1980, in a cosmetic facelift of the junta carried out at U.S. insistence.

56. Armstrong, "Beyond Elections," *NACLA Report on the Americas*, March-April 1982, p. 3.

57. On the military's role see for example Robert Allen White and Jarke Almuli, *Counterinsurgency War in Central America: the United States Tries it Again* (Mexico City: Centro de Estudios Económicos y Sociales del Tercer Mundo, 1982), ch. 7; and Washington Office on Latin America, "Honduras: Democracy in Demise," February 1984.

58. Interview in Tegucigalpa, October 1983.

59. On the coup and the Ríos Montt government see George Black, "Guatemala: the War Is Not Over," *NACLA Report on the Americas*, March-April 1983, pp. 14-21.

60. On the counterinsurgency campaign and its devastating impact see Nancy Peckenham, Guatemala 1983 (Philadelphia: American Friends Service Committee, 1983); Allan Nairn, "The Guns of Guatemala," *New Republic*, April 11, 1983; and Black, "Guatemala," pp. 22-24.

61. *New York Times*, December 16, 1981.

62. See *Washington Post*, February 25, 1984; and Armstrong, "Beyond Elections."

63. *San Francisco Examiner*, June 6, 1983.

64. For a good summary of the political context of the 1984 elections see "El Salvador 1984," *NACLA Report on the Americas*, March-April 1984.

65. See *Washington Post*, November 26, 1983; and *New York Times*, January 27, 1984.

2. U.S. Policy: Crisis and Conflict

Roger Burbach

Whatever other crisis may arise to claim the nation's attention the United States cannot afford to turn away from the threatened region. Central America's crisis is our crisis.
        —Kissinger Commission, January 1984

We need to ask questions about the very nature of the traditional foreign policy of the United States, not questions concerning merely the means *of putting it into operation.*
        —William Appleman Williams,
The Tragedy of American Diplomacy, *1972*

In Central America where governments were once made and unmade through gunboat diplomacy, the United States today confronts revolutionary explosions that could very well topple the U.S.-backed surrogate regimes that long dominated the entire Central American isthmus. In a desperate effort to stop this process, the United States has militarized the region. It has sent in hundreds of U.S. military advisers, rapidly expanded U.S. military assistance programs, initiated large-scale CIA operations, and built up U.S. military facilities in the region to handle U.S. troops and war planes. But these activities have not stopped the growth of the revolutionary forces, nor have they brought the United States any closer to victory.

Why is this so? Clearly one major reason is the growing sophistication and development of the revolutionary forces in Central America. But there are other critical factors at work, particularly those that relate to the dynamics of U.S. foreign policy. Fundamentally, the United States is experiencing two interrelated foreign policy crises that directly affect the Central American conflict. One crisis is over U.S. relations with the third world; the other stems from the growing divisions within the dominant U.S. foreign policy circles over just what U.S. policy should be toward the third world. To fully understand the thrust and the limits of U.S. intervention in Central America it is important to explore in depth each of these crises.

The End of Pax Americana

The crisis in U.S. relations with the third world stems from the breakdown in the system of informal control that the United States has exercised over much of the third world since the end of World War II. That system has been built on two interrelated objectives that have guided U.S. policymakers: (1) the determination to prevent communist parties or radical revolutionary movements from obtaining power, and (2) the insistence that underdeveloped countries maintain an "open door" to U.S. economic and political interests.

During the late 1940s and 1950s the United States was highly successful in pursuing these objectives in the third world. Most of the underdeveloped countries fell into line behind the United States, and except for the Korean war, the challenges that emerged did not require massive military intervention. The defeat of the Huk guerrillas in the Philippines, the overthrow of the Arbenz government in Guatemala, and the toppling of the government of Mohammed Mossadegh in Iran were all major victories for the United States, enabling it to solidify and expand its political and economic control in key areas of the third world. This was the era of Pax Americana: the United States was both the guardian and chief benefactor of postwar prosperity.

However, by the 1960s the United States found itself increasingly unable to control the social and political dynamics of the third world. In the Caribbean Basin, the success of the Cuban revolution and the failure of the Bay of Pigs invasion marked the first decisive defeat for the United States. Next came the long, costly war in Southeast Asia, followed in the mid-1970s by the victories of the liberation forces in the former Portuguese African colonies of Angola, Mozambique, and Guinea-Bissau. And then, in 1979, the United States suffered two more serious setbacks when the Shah of Iran was forced out by a massive popular upheaval and the Sandinista National Liberation Front led a victorious popular revolution in Nicaragua.

These setbacks, combined with other problems the United States faces—such as the growing economic difficulties of the capitalist world and the emerging differences between Western Europe, Japan, and the United States—have substantially reduced U.S. maneuverability in the world. The more benign methods used to keep the third world in line— political cajoling or economic pressures (aid cutoffs, trade embargoes, etc.)—are simply less effective than they used to be. As a result the United States has turned more and more to military force or the threat of military force in an effort to maintain its hold over key areas of the third world. Thus, the Reagan administration's policy of building up U.S. military power and of adopting a tough posture abroad is in large part a logical consequence of the fact that the United States finds itself in a weakened position in the world.

The End of Consensus

This deepening crisis in U.S. relations with the third world has fed into the second related crisis in U.S. foreign policy—the development of deep divisions within the dominant circles that shape U.S. policy. Before the Vietnam war, a bipartisan consensus had existed on major U.S. policy issues, with the leaders of both Democratic and Republican parties united in backing policies designed to keep the third world firmly under U.S. control. And the circles that shaped U.S. foreign policy (the State Department, National Security Council, elite foreign policy associations, academic think-tanks, etc.) generally had a unified view of the world. But the Vietnam conflict and other foreign policy setbacks shattered this consensus, and today foreign policy issues often become the center of heated partisan debates.

The divisions over U.S.-third world policy are clearly visible in the debate over how the United States should deal with the Central American conflict. The fundamental issues raised in this debate are: how much of a threat the revolutionary movements are to the United States; the dimensions of the Soviet and Cuban role in the region; and just what are legitimate U.S. interests in the region. At present three major positions have been staked out on these issues. They are (1) the "confrontationalist" approach; (2) the "liberal interventionist" approach; and (3) the "neorealist" approach.* The confrontationalist approach predominates in the Reagan administration. Most clearly articulated by President Reagan himself, this position views the situation in Central America as an extension of the global struggle with the Soviet Union and its "Cuban surrogate." The forces of subversion and revolution have to be confronted and ultimately defeated in Central America if the United States is to protect its "vital interests."

The liberal interventionist position is primarily argued by some former members of the Carter administration. They maintain that Reagan is relying too heavily on a military approach to Central America's problems. This, they contend, strengthens the right-wing forces in Central America and undermines those political forces in the center which have the potential for resolving the conflict in a way that will preserve U.S. interests. This position, while it downplays the use of military force, is nonetheless interventionist because it accepts as legitimate the use of U.S. power to determine the nature of the governments

---

* The terms "confrontationalist" and "liberal interventionist" are categories developed by this author. The term "neorealist" was first used by Richard Feinberg and Tom J. Farer, both of whom regard themselves as neorealists. They see themselves as following in the footsteps of an earlier group of foreign policy analysts called the "realists," which included Walter Lippmann, Hans Morgenthau, and George Kennan. For more information on this see Richard Feinberg, *The Intemperate Zone: U.S. Policy Towards the Third World.* (New York: W.W. Norton, 1983.)

in Central America and to prevent Marxist movements from obtaining power.

The neorealists have begun to coalesce relatively recently, drawing some support from members of Congress, ex-State Department officials, and liberal think-tanks in Washington. This position acknowledges that dramatic changes have taken place since the postwar years, when U.S. global powers and prerogatives were virtually unchallenged, and that the United States can no longer impose its political will on Central America. While taking the defense of U.S. global power as a legitimate objective, the neorealists maintain that the United States must sometimes accept revolutionary governments as the only viable alternative to the crumbling right-wing regimes. To continue to escalate U.S. military involvement, or to prop up the so-called centrist forces, only draws the United States deeper into a hopeless morass that will ultimately lead to defeat.

The Aftermath of Vietnam

These divisions over U.S. foreign policy reflect the lack of consensus over the meaning and lessons of the Vietnam experience. Though there was no national debate over what happened in Vietnam, influential sectors in the United States did draw their own particular lessons from the Vietnam war. Clearly the group most profoundly affected by the conflict was the so-called eastern establishment. This group, dominated by individuals who came from the elite educational and foreign policy institutions, had shaped U.S. policy under both Democratic and Republican administrations since the end of World War II. "The Best and the Brightest," as it was called by author David Halberstam, this group led the United States into the disastrous land war in Asia. The Vietnam conflict threw the eastern establishment into such disarray that in subsequent years it was unable to impose its vision on U.S. foreign policy. Though they lost their almost exclusive hold on power, individuals from the eastern establishment did continue to play prominent roles in U.S. policy (an example is Thomas Enders, who directed U.S. bombings in Cambodia under Nixon and later became assistant secretary of state under Reagan).

Even before the Vietnam war ended, however, two major cleavages had developed within the eastern establishment. One pole, focused around Henry Kissinger and members of the Nixon administration, was determined not to allow the erosion of U.S. global power as a result of Vietnam. They had no intention of accommodating the United States to radical or revolutionary regimes in the third world. But they did realize that the overwhelming popular sentiment in the United States against any involvement in another land war made it virtually impossible to use direct military force in the third world. As an alternative defense of empire they developed a strategy of using regional military bulwarks (Iran, Brazil, etc.) to protect U.S. interests and squelch any new revolutionary movements. Simultaneously, Kissinger and Nixon relied heavily on covert operations to deal with revolutionary challenges. This enabled them to circumvent public scrutiny and to evade most congressional controls.[1] In Chile, Angola, and Portugal the Nixon administration unleashed the CIA to deal with the threat posed by revolutionary movements.

U.S. weaknesses in the wake of Vietnam was one factor which led the Kissinger team to push for detente with the Soviet Union. The tremendous opposition to any major step-up in defense spending limited the scope of the arms race with the Soviet Union. Kissinger hoped that by holding out the plums of technological and trade concessions to the Soviet Union, the Soviet leaders would take part in an arms agreement permitting the United States to maintain its military edge. Detente was also seen as a way to entice the Soviet Union to refrain from supporting wars of national liberation at a time when the United States was in a weak position in many areas of the third world.

The other pole within the eastern establishment regrouped mainly within the liberal wing of the Democratic party. Cyrus Vance, Robert McNamara, Paul Warnke, and Clark Clifford—all of whom had served in the Johnson administration—came to view the Vietnam war as a "mistake" which required a reassessment of U.S. involvement in third world conflicts. *Foreign Policy*, a quarterly publication which was founded in 1970 by liberal intellectuals and junior foreign service officers, became a major organ for articulating this new perspective. In its premier issue the quarterly proclaimed that "in the light of Vietnam, the basic purposes of American foreign policy demand re-examination and redefinition."[2] Many members of this school believed that a major mistake of the United States in Vietnam was to see the war as an extension of the global competition with the Soviet Union and China. They argued that henceforth the United States should treat third world conflicts as separate from the challenges posed by the dominant communist power, the Soviet Union. There would be changes in the third world, and even possibly new radical revolutionary governments, but the United States would have to view these developments as distinct from the competition with the Soviet Union. While supporting the Nixon administration's move toward detente with the Soviet Union, this group clearly broke with the Kissingerian view of developments in the third world and, most importantly, over how to deal with them.

There was one more small but significant splinter in the eastern establishment, significantly to the right of the other positions. As articulated by Paul Nitze, this group argued that the United States could have won the Vietnam war if only the United States had used its full military might early in the war, instead of engaging in a gradual build-up which sapped domestic support for the war and gave the North Vietnamese time to build up their forces. The members of this group, many of whom later became known as neoconservatives, soon broke completely with the eastern establishment and began to forge alliances with right-wing organizations in the southern and western United States. They provided the foreign policy basis of the New Right coalition that brought Ronald Reagan to power in 1980.

In 1976 the New Right set up the Committee on the Present Danger to wage a political campaign for a massive new armaments program to confront what it saw as the growing Soviet threat. Indeed, it considered this threat to be the central foreign policy issue. Under the leadership of figures like Paul Nitze, Richard Pipes, and Eugene Rostow, the Committee asserted that the United States was in imminent danger of becoming "second best to the Soviet Union" and that the United States could soon find itself "isolated in a hostile world facing the unremitting pressures of Soviet policy backed by an overwhelming preponderance of power."[3]

While demanding a hard line toward the Soviet Union, the New Right also pushed for a tougher stance toward the third world—a stance motivated by its vehement anticommunism. The New Right's most notable campaign around a third world issue came when its political allies tried to block passage of the Panama Canal treaties, arguing that the treaties would give an unreliable third world ally control over an artery vital to the security of the United States.

While the New Right was making its move in the mid-1970s, the more moderate and liberal groups in the eastern establishment tried to reforge the old consensus in U.S. foreign policy. A major vehicle in this effort was the Trilateral Commission. Established in 1974, the commission included representatives from Western Europe, Japan, and the United States who believed that the leading capitalist nations had to strengthen their multilateral ties and forge a common front for dealing with global problems. The U.S. representatives on the commission included such prominent representatives of the Democratic and Republican parties as David Rockefeller, Cyrus Vance, and George Ball. The commission also drew into its circle a rising political star, then-governor of Georgia, Jimmy Carter. In its stance toward the third world, the commission maintained that the leading capitalist nations, by presenting a united front, could alleviate tensions with third world countries through the expansion of international trade and by trying to stabilize commodity prices. The commission also supported detente with the Soviet Union, and stressed the importance of trade and investment rather than military policies in dealing with the rest of the world.

Carter and the Foreign Policy Crisis

The Trilateral Commission reached the peak of its influence in 1977 when Carter became president. The secretaries of state and treasury and other cabinet officers came from the commission, as did Carter's national security adviser, Zbigniew Brzezinski. Coming on the heels of the final debacle in Vietnam in 1975 and the growing public concern about Kissinger's heavy-handed tactics in dealing with third world countries (notably the Allende government in Chile), it was hoped that the incoming administration could formulate a new U.S. foreign policy, one that took account of the changes in the global balance of power and of the inability of the United States to dominate the third world as it had in the past. In its early days the administration claimed it was open to a "North-South dialogue" (to address conflicts between the third world and advanced capitalist countries). However, instead of forging a new consensus in U.S. foreign policy, the Carter administration soon demonstrated that it was incapable of maintaining unity even in its own ranks.

Two camps emerged within the Carter administration. One was led by Cyrus Vance, the secretary of state who remained faithful to the trilateralist global vision that advocated detente with the Soviet Union and a more flexible, pragmatic response to change in the third world. The other camp was led by the national security adviser, Zbigniew

Brzezinski. Although Brzezinski publicly proclaimed that he repudiated Kissinger's policies, the reality was otherwise. He maintained an orthodox anticommunist position, and soon moved to a position of arguing that liberation movements in the third world must be checked, and that the United States should adopt a more confrontational stance toward the Soviet Union.

These divisions within the administration were most clearly manifested over human rights policy. Brzezinski and the more rightist elements of the administration saw human rights primarily as a means to regain the ideological offensive against the Soviet Union. They focused their supposed human rights concerns on developments in the Soviet Union and other countries in the Eastern bloc. The other position, articulated by Vance, also regarded the human rights issue as an ideological weapon against the Soviet Union. But he also insisted that a strong human rights policy should be implemented against right-wing dictators in the third world in order to compel these regimes, increasingly threatened by revolutionary upheavals, to change their political methods before the opposition mushroomed beyond control. Brzezinski and others, however, tended to see revolutionary movements as both cause and consequence of increasing Soviet influence in the world, a problem which could not be neutralized with a simple human rights approach. In its desire to contain the revolutionary forces, the Brzezinski group accepted the slightest hint of "reforms" by dictatorial regimes as sufficient excuse to extend U.S. aid.

This basic split in the ranks of the Carter administration undermined its ability to carry out a coherent foreign policy, and also made it impossible to resurrect the broader unity of the eastern establishment. Indeed, the in-fighting and contradictory views within the administration made it an easy target for the New Right. The apparent indecisiveness of the adminstration combined with its insufficiently bellicose reaction to the Soviet invasion of Afghanistan, the "hostage crisis" in Iran, and the Sandinista victory in Nicaragua, provided the grounds for Ronald Reagan's attack on the detente and human rights policies of the Carter administration.

The victory of the Reaganites in 1980 signaled the final demise of the eastern establishment as the chief architect of U.S. foreign policy, and the rise of the New Right as an influential force in Washington. The new think-tanks and conservative institutes effectively supplanted many of the old institutions of the establishment. No longer were positions of power in Washington filled exclusively by people drawn from the Trilateral Commission or the Council of Foreign Relations, but also by individuals from the Committee on the Present Danger, the Hudson Institute, and the Center for Strategic Studies at Georgetown. The few members of the eastern establishment in the Reagan government, such as Vice President George Bush, renounced their positions in entities such as the Trilateral Commission and proclaimed that they were opposed to detente. The Republican wing of the eastern establishment was clearly decimated and disoriented. The individuals associated with Kissinger's policies, including Kissinger himself, began to adopt positions that were indistinguishable from those of the New Right.

A realignment also occurred within the Democratic party in the wake of the Reagan victory. Some Democrats, particularly those identified with the neoconservative position, supported or even joined the Reagan administration. Most prominent among these was Jeane Kirkpatrick, a member of the Democratic National Committee in the early 1970s, who became Reagan's ambassador to the United Nations and one of his most influential foreign policy advisers. Other Democrats, while not publicly endorsing the Reagan administration's worldview, did join his camp in supporting huge increases in military spending. Only a few Democrats in Congress, led in large part by members of the Black Congressional Caucus, explicitly opposed the Reagan administration's policies with regard to the Soviet Union, the third world, and defense spending.

Emergence of the Three Positions vis-à-vis Central America

The realignment of forces on U.S. policy in the third world first clearly manifested itself around Central America. The three positions toward Central America—confrontationalist, liberal interventionist, and neorealist—emerged in early 1981 when the administration decided to "draw the line" in El Salvador against the guerrilla insurgency. Each position was rooted in the general fissures and divisions that had occurred in U.S. foreign policy during the course of the 1970s.

The confrontationalist approach, that of the Reagan administration, was endorsed by the entire New Right coalition. The liberal interventionist position, on the other hand, drew support from the Brzezinski faction of the Carter administration, and from the sector of the eastern establishment which remained committed to the old liberal policies of the Cold War years. Their position was similar to that articulated by the Kennedy administration in the 1960s which had combined reformism with counterinsurgency war in an effort to halt the advance of revolutionary forces in Latin America. Robert Pastor, who had worked with Brzezinski on Latin American affairs at the National Security Council in the Carter administration, became one of the main spokespeople for this position in the early 1980s.

The third position, the neorealist, was drawn in large part from other sectors of the eastern establishment and the Carter administration who had been profoundly disillusioned with the Vietnam war and who in the early 1970s had advocated a new approach to the third world. Andrew Young (the former ambassador to the United Nations), William Murat (an ambassador to El Salvador in the 1960s), Abraham Lowenthau (of the Woodrow Wilson Center for International Scholars), and Richard Feinberg (a member of the State Department policy planning staff under the Carter administration), were all figures who advocated a policy of accommodation with the revolutionary forces in Central America, and explicitly recognized these movements' legitimate claim to play a significant role in the region's governments.

The neorealist position represented a sharp break with the assumptions and trajectory of U.S. policy in the post World War II period. For the first time a group of foreign policy analysts, some of whom had served in government positions, argued that the United States could accommodate revolutionary movements without jeopardizing its national interests.

The Confrontationalists in Action

During its first year, the Reagan foreign policy team moved decisively to implement its confrontationalist strategy in Central America. A key objective of the administration was to end the "Vietnam syndrome," i.e., the opposition of the American people to the use of U.S. military power in third world conflicts. The administration recognized when it took office that it would be political suicide to dispatch U.S. troops to fight in Central America or in any other third world conflict. It would need time, time to begin projecting U.S. military power abroad to bolster U.S. regimes such as those in Central America and to "reeducate" the American people on the dangers of "international communism."

El Salvador became the first test case for applying this strategy. Soon after taking office, U.S. military advisers were dispatched to El Salvador, and the State Department released a White Paper which painted the Salvadoran civil war as inspired by Soviet and Cuban communists and fueled with arms from those countries. In this East-West conflict the United States had to draw the line against communist aggression. Purportedly to stop this flow of arms, the administration escalated the flow of military aid to the right-wing regimes in El Salvador and Honduras, and the groundwork was laid for projecting U.S. military power in the region through U.S. military maneuvers in the Caribbean Basin and the expansion of air and naval bases capable of handling U.S. war planes and ships.

Carter's human rights policy was quickly abandoned: the State Department under Reagan announced that instead of publicly criticizing "authoritarian" regimes for their human rights violations, it would lobby them behind closed doors to modify their repressive behavior. This shift to "quiet diplomacy" was partly justified on the grounds that authoritarian regimes of the right (however reprehensible their behavior) were preferable to "totalitarian" regimes of the left.

A key component of the administration's strategy was to move swiftly and decisively against the revolutionary forces, particularly in El Salvador where the threat of a new loss was the most immediate. The administration believed that it could win a relatively easy victory there through an infusion of U.S. military aid. "El Salvador will not be another Vietnam," the administration proclaimed, meaning that the guerrillas would be defeated without involving the American people in a costly and prolonged war.

The Reagan administration also began to move against the Sandinista government in Nicaragua. A program to economically destabilize the country was launched by cutting U.S. economic aid, and steps were taken to undermine the Nicaraguan government politically. The administration first collaborated with the opposition forces inside the country, and then in late 1981 the CIA began training and arming the remnants of the Somocista army in Honduras for armed forays into Nicaragua. The administration also embarked on an international campaign to isolate Nicaragua. Secretary of State Haig personally orchestrated this campaign by denouncing "Nicaragua's criminal actions against the Miskito Indians" (an indigenous group on the Atlantic

Coast), and lambasting Nicaragua before the Organization of American States as an "aggressor" nation in Central America.

Dissenting Opinions

Given the fissures that had emerged in the foreign policy elite, these actions inevitably ignited a major debate over U.S. policy in Central America. The liberal interventionists leveled the most vociferous attacks against Reagan and Haig's confrontationalist strategy. In general, the liberal interventionists were tied like the Reaganites to the cold war view that Marxist revolutionary movements had to be stopped; but they disagreed strongly with Reagan over tactics and how to effectively defend the hemisphere against communism. The liberal interventionists argued that the emphasis on military measures to solve the Central American crisis was ineffective and ultimately self-defeating. Robert White, the ambassador to El Salvador under Carter, who was fired soon after Reagan took office, wrote in the *New York Times* magazine that "military assistance plus covert action will not do it," and that "the administration's program for Central America is in deep trouble." He asserted that one could "describe the Administration's approach to Central America as a textbook case of boldness, ignorance, and ideological certitude combining to weaken the region's defenses against communist penetration."[4] And Robert Pastor wrote in *Foreign Affairs* that the Reagan administration, "by drawing lines against communist aggression and expanding military aid . . . had just about the opposite of its intended effect." In mid-1982 he argued that the administration strategy had failed, since "guerrilla strength in Central America is greater today than two years ago," and that "the governments of Cuba, Nicaragua, and Grenada were neither bluffed nor frightened into submission."[5]

While these critics argued against the particular strategy pursued by the Reagan administration in Central America, they were in accord with its fundamental objectives—to prevent the revolutionary forces from seizing power and to maintain U.S. economic and political ascendancy in the region. As Robert White, U.S. ambassador to El Salvador, succinctly stated: "President Reagan is right to concern himself with denying communism a new foothold in the Western Hemisphere." White went on to assert that U.S. intervention in the affairs of the region is justified: "The issue is not whether to involve ourselves in the affairs of our Central American neighbors, but the form and substance of that involvement."[6] The liberal interventionists argued that instead of focusing on military measures, the United States should place greater emphasis on supporting the political center in each country. By implementing reforms these groups would diminish the power of the local oligarchies and gain a base of support. A measured amount of U.S. military assistance to the "moderate" military sectors that respected human rights would enable these sectors to contain the guerrilla insurgents.

It was fitting that the liberal interventionists chose as their cause célèbre the issue of agrarian reform in El Salvador. Under Carter many of them had helped formulate the land reform program, which they viewed as essential to the strategy of building a political center in El Salvador to replace the oligarchy. They were appropriately alarmed by Reagan's backtracking on agrarian reform. Roy Prosterman, an AID consultant who helped draft the Salvadoran agrarian reform law, claimed that Reagan's failure to make a firm commitment to land reform "may forfeit the last, slender chance of a future for El Salvador that is not dictated in the short run by the violent right—and in the long run by the violent left."[7]

The Reaganites, of course, rejected the critique put forth by the liberal interventionists. They had attacked Carter during the 1980 presidential campaign for pursuing the same policies that the liberal interventionists were now promoting. The Reaganites asserted that the results of Carter's policies proved the fallacy of their approach: a "Sandinista-Marxist government" was in power in Nicaragua, and the regimes in Guatemala and El Salvador had been weakened by Carter's "naive human rights rhetoric."

To a certain extent, the arguments of the Reaganites were valid. Carter's (and the liberals') fundamental objectives were the same as those of all previous administrations—to contain radical revolutionary movements and to keep the region open to U.S. political and economic interests. The problem was that the tactics Carter used to pursue these objectives were not working in Central America. Carter tried to employ the human rights lever to get the regimes in Nicaragua, El Salvador, and Guatemala to modify some of their more repressive features, and to create a political opening that would allow the so-called democratic forces to emerge, but those efforts ended in abysmal failure, primarily because the dictatorial regimes (and the wealthy classes they served) would not tolerate reforms, and most of the so-called centrist groups were affiliated with the revolutionary movements.

Carter thus confronted the classic dilemma that other liberal administrations have faced in the postwar period—how to promote reforms and the political center without undercutting the effort to contain the revolutionary forces. In the case of Nicaragua, Carter simply could not come up with a viable strategy for removing Somoza from office and putting the opposition bourgeoisie in power. Even when Somoza defied the United States by refusing to enact any reforms that weakened his power, Carter did not pull out all the stops to bring down his regime. Ultimately the commitment to counter-revolution prevailed over the commitment to reform as the Carter administration maneuvered desperately in the final days of the regime to maintain Somoza's military apparatus (the National Guard) as a bulwark against the Sandinistas.

The threat of revolution in El Salvador also forced Carter to compromise his reform strategy. In his final weeks in office he extended military aid to the governing junta even though the new regime—which had initially called for reforms when it overthrew the right-wing government of General Roméro in October 1979—was increasingly falling under the control of right-wing forces. Here again, anticommunism won out. The Carter administration felt that if U.S. assistance was not extended, the regime might fall to the revolutionary forces.

Ultimately, the Carter administration failure in Central America was rooted in the more fundamental issues the United States faced in its relations with the third world. Pax Americana was drawing to an end. Third world revolutionary movements were gaining momentum and the United States simply lacked the economic and military capacity to control or contain the diverse political forces that were emerging in the third world.

The Neorealist Stance

The neorealists adopted a very different position in challenging the policies of the Reagan administration, one that questioned some of the tenets of U.S. postwar policy toward the third world. They rejected the view that the fundamental goal was to contain and destroy the leftist revolutionary forces. Andrew Young, in a speech at a conference in Atlanta on U.S. policy in Central America, declared that the rebellion in

Central America was justified. He said that the revolutionary movements are engaged in "defensive violence" and that U.S. blacks would have been compelled to follow the same road "had we not been offered a democratic alternative."[8]

And Abraham Lowenthau in an article titled "Let the Latins Have Their Turmoil in Peace," also argued strongly that the United States should accept leftist governments: "It may be [that] the best we can hope for in Central America is the establishment of independent, nationalist, even Marxist-Leninist regimes."[9] Lowenthau and others in the neorealist camp argued that the United States could even develop substantial ties with these regimes, particularly in the economic sphere. Lowenthau asserted that "all these nations should still be inserted firmly within the international capitalist economy. They will still be dependent on trade, finance, technology and investment from the United States, and they will be accessible to U.S. influence."[10]

Even though the neorealists advocated a dramatically new approach to the revolutionary upsurge in Central America, many of them had one objective which coincided with that of the liberal interventionists and the confrontationalists—to prevent the Soviet Union, Cuba, and the socialist bloc countries in general from expanding their influence in the Western Hemisphere. Contrary to the other schools, however, the neorealists argued that the pursuit of this objective required a new approach, one which would lead the United States to make some accommodation with these forces rather than prolonging the conflict and compelling the revolutionaries to regard the United States as their implacable enemy. This they argued would only drive the revolutionaries to look increasingly to the socialist bloc for ideological, political, and material support.

However, the anti-Soviet (and implicitly anticommunist) stance of some of the neorealists led them to adopt some positions on the Central American revolutionary movements that are actually close to those of the liberal interventionists. While recognizing the revolutionary movements as inevitable, these neorealists actually seek to impose limits on the movements once they are in power; internationally the new revolutionary governments should not be permitted to have extensive relations with the socialist bloc countries, and internally, the neorealists assert that the United States should search for ways to contain and control the more radical tendencies of the revolutionary movements.

The rapport between some neorealists and the more interventionist positions was reflected in a special report released in late 1983 by the

Atlantic Council, an association that contains many high level policy and business figures. In the report titled *Western Interests and U.S. Policy Options in the Caribbean Basin,* two members of the neorealist school, Richard Feinberg and Robert Leiken, join more interventionist figures such as Brent Scowcroft (former head of the National Security Council under President Ford) and James Greene (a business executive who undertook special diplomatic missions for President Nixon) in declaring that U.S. policy toward new revolutionary governments "should strive to keep them integrated into the western economic system and separate from the Soviet strategic network." While the report says that the United States should generally not undertake covert operations against revolutionary governments in the Caribbean Basin (because they are "counterproductive"), the report asserts that "Americans prefer liberal democracies," and it proceeds to advocate U.S. trade, aid, and cultural policies that are designed to support these types of governments rather than the revolutionary states.[11]

Thus, although Feinberg, Leikin, and other neorealists hold the general position that the United States will have to accept even "Marxist-Leninist governments in the Caribbean Basin," they, like the liberal interventionists, are distrustful of such governments and prefer to encourage and assist the "liberal democracies." Minimally, they endorse using U.S. aid and economic pressures to control the development of new revolutionary governments. The dilemma inherent in this position is that it is difficult to decide where the United States should draw the line if these measures are not successful in controlling the revolutionary governments. Should the United States employ more strident forms of intervention or should it simply let them pursue their own internal and international policies? The tendency, of course, would be not to admit failure and to increase U.S. pressures on the revolutionary governments.

The Obstacles to Reagan's Policy

The difficulties the Reagan administration encountered in Central America gave the liberal interventionists and the neorealists ample grounds to continue challenging Reagan's policies. By 1984 it was clear that the administration's confrontationalist strategy in Central America would not lead to victory, that it was running into major obstacles both within Central America and internationally. In the case of El Salvador, the administration was not able to deal any decisive blows against the Farabundo Martí Front for National Liberation (FMLN). While U.S. military assistance had strengthened El Salvador's armed forces, the military capacity of the revolutionary forces had also increased significantly. Clearly there was no cheap victory in sight and, in fact, administration officials in early 1982 had already begun talking about a war that would go on for "five or six years more," until the end of the 1980s.[12]

And on the human rights front, the "closed door diplomacy" of the administration had been no more effective than the public diplomacy of the Carter administration. Controlled elections were held in El Salvador in March 1982, but the Social Democratic forces allied with the FMLN did not participate and the elections were seen as a victory for the ultra-right forces. Agrarian reform virtually came to an end, and the murders and assassinations by the right-wing death squads continued unabated. By October 1982, U.S. Ambassador Hinton, no stranger to working with repressive governments (he was in charge of the AID program in Guatemala in the late 1960s when the repression took 8,000 lives) was so impatient with the situation in El Salvador that he proclaimed that the right-wing "mafia" was as big a threat to the country as were the guerrillas. Some in the Reagan administration rebuked Hinton for these remarks, but a year later Vice President Bush hand-delivered a letter from President Reagan to the Salvadoran government demanding an end to the death squads.[13]

A major blow to the administration's Central American strategy was a conflict which was totally unforeseen, the war over the Malvinas/ Falkland Islands. Prior to the war, the administration had believed that key Latin American right-wing regimes, such as the one in Argentina, would support and contribute to an OAS-backed "peace-keeping force" in Central America if the need arose. However, the U.S. decision to side with Great Britain against Argentina effectively destroyed U.S. plans to use the OAS. According to one high-ranking officer in the U.S. Southern Command, "that's the one thing President Reagan and Haig hung onto—the possibility of an international force," and "that's been undermined considerably" by the war.[14]

Aside from the loss of Argentine backing, the administration could not keep other governments in the Western Hemisphere committed to their position in Central America. Due to the Malvinas conflict as well as the marginalization of the Christian Democrats in the Salvadoran government, the Christian Democratic government of Venezuela began to forge a position independent of the United States and joined Mexico in calling for negotiations to end the conflicts in the region. (In January 1984 Acción Democrática, the Social Democratic party of Venezuela, came to power and adopted an even more independent position.) And Brazil, South America's leading military power, which provided the largest contingent of Latin troops during the OAS-backed intervention in the Dominican Republic in 1965, made it clear to Reagan during his trip there in December 1982 that it wanted nothing to do with the Reagan strategy of confrontation in Central America, especially in light of the fact that Brazil's burgeoning manufacturing industry began counting on increased industrial exports to third world countries such as Nicaragua.

But the major stumbling block for the Reagan strategy developed within the United States. Devoid of anything approaching a consensus over its policies, the Reagan administration found itself increasingly under attack on the domestic front. As happened in Vietnam, U.S. policy became the object of heated partisan debate. While the forces in the United States opposed to intervention were unable to stop the administration's military build-up in Central America, they were able to increase the political costs of the administration's policies through a series of congressional actions. In the case of El Salvador, aid was made contingent on presidential certification every six months that the Salvadoran government was making progress in key areas, such as agrarian reform and human rights. While Reagan repeatedly certified Salvadoran "progress," regardless of the actual conditions, the debate over certification somewhat weakened the administration's ability to step up the flow of economic and military support to the Salvadoran regime. In late 1983 Reagan vetoed legislation calling for certification, but the debate over human rights violations in El Salvador continued to be a major issue limiting U.S. military aid to El Salvador.

The administration's lack of a totally free hand was also revealed in the continuing debate over the role of U.S. military personnel in Central America. Severe restrictions were placed on U.S. military advisers in El Salvador by the War Powers Act (which came out of the Vietnam war) and by public fears of "another Vietnam." The U.S. advisers were not free to go into combat zones with Salvadoran troops. Opposition to U.S. advisers in Central America has also made the administration's position in Guatemala exceptionally difficult. In late 1982, the revelation that the U.S. had one military officer in Guatemala involved in training Guatemalan troops provoked a public outcry and a demand for an accounting of this situation by congressional committees concerned with Central American policies.

The Differing Political Projects

As the Reagan administration gained a greater understanding of some of the complexities of U.S. foreign policy (and an election year drew nearer), there were shifts in its approach to Central America which appeared to indicate it was moving closer to the liberal interventionist position. For example, the administration's early concern with securing relations with the so-called authoritarian regimes shifted as the White House, with some goading from the State Department, realized that to ward off domestic and international criticism the administration had to push these governments to make some real changes in their political systems. It soon became standard public relations policy for the Reagan administration to insist that it supported the "democratic center" between the right-wing and left-wing extremes, a position analogous to that of the liberal interventionists.

Following in the footsteps of the Carter administration, Reagan also endorsed elections as the way to create a democratic center. The administration supported the planned elections in Honduras in late 1981, and in El Salvador, the Duarte-led junta with U.S. help (including that of the CIA) held elections in March 1982. In the case of Guatemala, the administration made known its disgruntlement with the rigged elections of Lucas García in February 1981, and then after the coup by Ríos Montt, the State Department applied pressure which led the regime to proclaim that free elections would be held in 1985. And when Ríos Montt was ousted by General Mejía Victores in 1983 elections were moved up to mid-1984.

But in spite of these apparent similarities between the confrontationalists and the liberal interventionists, there are still critical differences, particularly over the political projects they support in Central America. The liberals support the Christian Democrats of El Salvador, for example, as the political party best suited to modernize the society and incorporate new sectors into the government. The Reagan administration, on the other hand, is less tied to this particular party: it is more willing to work with the business groups and the political parties that are right of center. These groups are viewed as being more in tune with the Reagan administration's belief in the "magic of the marketplace."

The importance of reforms is another issue in which the Reaganites part ways with the liberal interventionists. The liberals emphasize the centrality of reforms in creating a democratic center, while the Reagan administration views them as secondary, at times even as undesirable, since the reforms tend to alienate the very business and political forces that are viewed as the best guarantors of pro-U.S. stability.

This difference in political projects is also manifested in the case of Nicaragua. The Reagan administration, through its clandestine operations designed to destabilize the Nicaraguan government, has concentrated almost exclusively on supporting the Nicaraguan Democratic Front which is dominated by remnants of the Somoza regime and the old National Guard. The liberal interventionists in Congress, however, threw their support to the so-called moderate opposition led principally by Edén Pastora (Comandante Zéro) and Alfonso Robelo. These forces, which had opposed the Somoza regime, were viewed by the liberal interventionists as the most viable alternative to the Sandinista government.

Unable to win the support of the liberal interventionists and the Democratic party as a whole, Reagan in July 1983 made a bold move to reforge the old bipartisan consensus in U.S. foreign policy by forming the Kissinger Commission. Comprised of six Democrats and six Republicans, the commission's announced objectives were to review all aspects of U.S. Central American policy and to develop a long-range plan for the region that would preserve U.S. interests. From the start, however, the commission ran into problems, and instead of reforging a consensus over U.S. policy, it illustrated the deep-seated divisions that existed. Some of the more right-wing confrontationlists, such as Senator Jesse Helms, attacked Reagan's decision to appoint Kissinger as head of the commission, claiming that Kissinger could never be trusted because of his identification with the detente policies of the Nixon administration. Many liberal interventionists, on the other hand, maintained that the commission would do little more than endorse Reagan's policies of militarizing the region. Even one member of the commission, Robert Strauss, the former chairman of the Democratic Party who held high positions in the Carter administration, openly declared, "I rather strongly disagree with the administration's policies" in Central America.[15]

When the report was released in January 1984 it did not mitigate the divisions in U.S. policy. Democrats in Congress attacked key elements of the Kissinger Commission report, and even some conservative Republicans were appalled by the plan's high price tag—$8 billion over a five year period. The *New York Times* summed up the controversial impact of the commission with an article headlined "The Kissinger Report Could Sharpen Latin Policy Dispute."[16]

The Policy Morass

In sum, the fundamental domestic problem that the Reagan administration confronted in its Central American policies was that it could not restore the old bipartisan consensus. The extreme right wing worried that Reagan would sell out to the old Republican architects of detente and "appeasement," the liberal interventionists in the Democratic party insisted that Reagan's policies were too militaristic and not supportive enough of "reformist" forces, and the neorealists pointed out that the United States was only deepening the crisis by not trying to strike a deal with the revolutionary movements in the region. This opposition made Reagan's Central American policy the center of heated debate, and it meant that every move it made in the region was subjected to intense scrutiny. Military and economic assistance requests were discussed at length and usually curtailed by Congress, and Reagan's massive covert war against Nicaragua was systematically challenged by Democrats, making the "covert" war, in fact, an overt operation with the entire world watching as the Reagan administration tried to topple the Sandinista government with a mercenary army.

This level of domestic opposition placed the Reagan administration on notice that any direct military intervention by the United States in Central America would catalyze a new antiwar movement and ignite an internal political conflict reminiscent of the Vietnam war days. For the Pentagon brass, this situation was particularly disconcerting. The chief of staff of the army, General Meyers, went public with his concerns that the United States should not become involved in another land war as long as there was not a public consensus to support such a war. Alluding to how the lack of such a consensus led to defeat in Vietnam, Meyers said that the United States could not have "soldiers at the end of a string without having the support of the American people."[17]

Whither U.S. Policy in Central America?

However, a major problem for most of the opponents of Reagan's Central American policies was that they had no coherent and viable alternative policy to offer. The liberal interventionists in the Democratic party could criticize Reagan's policies for being ineffective and leading the United States closer to war, but as long as they accepted Reagan's central premise—that the United States had to stop the advance of the revolutionary movements—they were hard put to come up with a viable policy. Reagan recognized this critical weakness in the opposition when in his Central American policy address to a joint session of Congress, on April 27, 1983, he declared that in Central America the president and the Congress shared a "responsiblity" to defend U.S. "vital interests." His last words, "Who among us would wish to bear responsibility for failing to meet our shared obligation?" were a direct threat to the Democrats that they would be blamed if Central America were "lost."[18] Worried that they would indeed be blamed by Reagan, the Democratic members of Congress, when push came to shove on key legislation, would generally refrain from taking decisive action to stop Reagan's war policies.

The neorealist position, which should have been able to provide a clear alternative in this debate, was actually making little headway. The anti-Soviet stance of many neorealists had led them to adopt positions critical of the revolutionary movements. Furthermore, on the national level they had very little visibility and, in fact, few perceived them as distinguishable from the liberal interventionists.

In early 1984 a new anti-interventionist position was put forth by Policy Alternatives for the Caribbean and Central America (PACCA), a national organization founded by academics and several progressive think tanks. Its special report, *Changing Course: Blueprint for Peace in Central America and the Caribbean,* clearly stated that current U.S. policy can only lead to an expanded war and destruction in Central America, and that the revolutionary movements in many countries are the only viable alternative to the current regimes. The report did not argue, as do some neorealists, that the United States should be in the business of restraining the revolutionary movements once in power, and it declared that "the real crisis is the inability of the United States to respond appropriately to profound changes in Central America.[19]

This approach, if adopted, would clearly extricate the United States from the conflict in Central America and allow the region to find peace.

The basic question is: When, if ever, will this position or a similar one gain ascendancy in U.S. foreign policy? Will it occur only after the United States has unleashed a massive interventionary war in Central America and suffered a defeat similar to that in Vietnam? Or will reason prevail and intelligent policies be adopted that permit the Central American revolutionary forces to construct new societies without having to go through the devastating trauma of a Central American war?

The most likely scenario is that the United States will not extricate itself from Central America in an orderly fashion. Internal divisions over U.S. policy will continue and there will be no new foreign policy consensus. In the end the situation in Central America will resolve itself somewhat along the lines of Vietnam: the revolutionary forces will continue to make advances, and that combined with internal dissension in the United States will lead to the eventual collapse of the U.S.-backed regimes in El Salvador, Guatemala, and Honduras. But this end could be a long time coming, and U.S.-backed regimes will continue to extract a heavy toll in their countries as they desperately strive to hold off the revolutionary forces.

Notes

1. Seymour M. Hersch, *The Price of Power: Kissinger in Nixon's White House* (New York: Summit Books, 1982).
2. *Foreign Policy* I, no.1 (1970).
3. "Common Sense and the Common Danger," Committee on the Present Danger, November 11, 1976.
4. Robert E. White, "Central America: The Problem that Won't Go Away," *New York Times* magazine, July 18, 1982, p. 43.
5. Robert Pastor, "Sinking in the Caribbean Basin," *Foreign Affairs* 60, no.5 (Summer 1982): 1043.
6. By late 1983 there were signs that Robert White was changing his position and moving closer to the neorealist school. See "Perilous Latin Policy," Robert E. White, *New York Times*, May 2, 1983; and Robert E. White, "Central America," p. 22.
7. Roy L. Prosterman, "The Unmaking of a Land Reform," *The New Republic*, August 9, 1982, p. 21.
8. "Young Says Latin Violence is 'Defensive,' " *Washington Post*, December 12, 1982.

9. Abraham Lowenthau, "Let the Latins Have Their Turmoil in Peace," *Washington Post*, March 28, 1982.

10. Ibid.

11. Report of the Atlantic Council's Working Group on the Caribbean Basin, *Western Interests and U.S. Policy Options in the Caribbean Basin* (Washington, D.C., October 19, 1983).

12. "The Struggle for Backing on Strategy in Salvador," *New York Times*, March 14, 1982.

13. Bernard Weinraub, "U.S. Envoy Warns Salvador of Cut in Military Aid," *New York Times*, November 3, 1982.

14. Gerald F. Seib, "U.S. Military Training of Hemisphere Allies is Spurred in Panama," *Wall Street Journal*, August 3, 1983.

15. Robert Strauss on David Brinkley's This Week, July 24, 1983.

16. Hedrick Smith, "The Kissinger Report Could Sharpen Latin Policy Dispute," *New York Times*, January 15, 1984.

17. Richard Halloran, "U.S. Army Chief Opposes Sending Combat Forces to Aid El Salvador," *New York Times*, June 10, 1983.

18. Ronald Reagan, "Central America: Defending Our Vital Interests" (speech before the joint session of Congress, April 27, 1983).

19. Policy Alternatives for the Caribbean and Central America (PACCA), *Changing Course: Blueprint for Peace in Central America and the Caribbean* (Washington, D.C.: Institute for Policy Studies, 1984).

3. *The United States at War in Central America: Unable to Win, Unwilling to Lose*

Patricia Flynn

If we didn't nickle and dime it we could win this struggle. We could stop the Communist advance. Time is on their side. We can't fight a prolonged war, they can. If we feel we can live with Marxist-communist countries in the area that's fine. But I don't think we can.

—General Wallace Nutting, Commander of the U.S. Southern Command, Panama, May 2, 1983

Just as the North American people didn't ask anyone what kind of society they should build and what kind of government they should have, we ask that others repect our right to establish whatever government and society best meets our needs.

—Comandante Benedicto, Guatemalan guerrilla leader, March 1982

On July 19, 1979, the United States watched helplessly as thousands of Sandinista guerrillas marched victorious into Managua. The spectacle of Somoza's National Guard soldiers fleeing in the face of the advancing rebel army recalled the dissolution of another U.S.-supported army on the outskirts of Saigon four years earlier. But unlike the earlier defeat, this one signaled the beginning rather than the end of an era of deepening U.S. military involvement in a regional war.

The fall of Somoza, followed quickly by insurgent challenges to U.S.-backed regimes in Guatemala and El Salvador, provoked an immediate military response from Washington. The Carter administration had found it difficult to intervene militarily on behalf of Somoza on two grounds—the dictator was an international pariah and the memory of Vietnam meant strong domestic opposition to another U.S. military adventure in the third world. But a series of U.S. foreign policy setbacks, including the ouster of the Shah of Iran and the "loss" of Nicaragua, led to a concerted effort in Washington to reverse the "Vietnam syndrome." The creation of a Rapid Deployment Force in 1979, intended for intervention in third world crises, was only the most dramatic indicator that the U.S. military was preparing once again to assume the role of world policeman.[1] Central America became the test case for the new U.S. counterinsurgency of the 1980s.

Within a year after the Sandinista victory, the United States had devised a three-pronged military strategy to turn back revolution in Central America. First, the Pentagon mounted a massive rescue operation for the army of El Salvador by providing weapons, training, advice, and eventually combat support. Second, in an effort to undermine the Nicaraguan revolution, Washington launched an undeclared war against the Sandinista government in Managua, using a counter-revolutionary army created, funded, and directed by the CIA. Third, the Pentagon began a major military build-up in Honduras, part of an effort to fortify that country as a launching pad for intervention against revolutions in neighboring countries. Thanks to U.S. intervention, the whole region was soon at war.

Despite a growing determination within policymaking circles to impose a military solution in Central America, U.S. intervention was shaped by continuing fears of another Vietnam. Ironically, the Pentagon was most outspoken in warning that a war fought without political support at home could lead to another Vietnam-type disaster for the United States. While trying to avoid a direct commitment of U.S. forces—an option never discarded—Washington continued to escalate

U.S. involvement in a style designed to avoid provoking public protest. By relying on regional proxy forces and tactical maneuvers to bypass Congress, the executive was able to perpetuate the myth that the United States was not at war in Central America— because after all, U.S. boys were not doing the fighting. In reality, the United States was responsible for virtually every aspect of the Central American war except the fighting.

Four years after the Sandinista victory, the United States appeared headed inexorably toward direct intervention. As in Vietnam, its surrogate armies were proving themselves incapable of containing, much less rolling back, the revolution. And at each juncture the White House decision was the same: escalate the U.S. involvement in a wider and bloodier war.

Carter: Setting the Course for Intervention

The Sandinista victory sparked an intense debate in Washington over whether the United States should assume a more aggressive posture in Central America. U.S. military assistance to Central America had been cut back to a trickle during the Carter administration's human rights policy. El Salvador and Guatemala had received no official military aid since 1977, when their military governments moved first to reject U.S. aid before a human rights cut-off went into effect.[2] Even Somoza was subject to a cut-off of military aid in the final months of his regime. But concern over the prospect of a revolutionary regime consolidating itself in Managua, heightened by a mounting guerrilla threat in El Salvador, led to a major review of U.S. policy in the region.

The Pentagon and members of the National Security Council began to argue for a resumption of military assistance to anticommunist governments in the region—regardless of their human rights record—and a hard line toward Nicaragua. A more cautious approach initially held sway. But it wasn't long before the same concerns that later led to all-out militarization of U.S. policy under Ronald Reagan began to be expressed by Carter administration officials. Carter officials began to speak of the alleged threat to U.S. national security in the region and the danger of "falling dominoes."[3] In fact, the seeds for future military escalation were sown under Carter.

El Salvador: The United States Steps In

The pressing issue was El Salvador, the first domino in line to fall. Though the military junta that took power in October 1979 originally said it would combat revolution with reforms, the right-wing military officers who rapidly edged out the reformers had a different agenda: waging all-out war on the guerrillas and their supporters. By early 1980 the Carter administration had decided to support this fundamental shift in course by the government, though it continued to clothe its policy in reformist rhetoric. The choice flowed from the same assumptions that guided later U.S. policy: a guerrilla victory would be a blow to U.S. national security. The threat of revolution was real. In January 1980 the country's major guerrilla organizations, responding partly to increased government repression, had formed a political coordination body, the first steps toward the military unity that came later that year.

In February of 1980 the National Security Council gave initial approval to a $5 million military sales and training package for El Salvador, a small but important first step in what was to become major U.S. backing for the government's counterinsurgency war. Besides the transport, communications, and intelligence equipment included in the package, the Pentagon also dispatched three groups of U.S. military advisers in mobile training teams to instruct the Salvadoran army.[4]

Attempting to mask the real purpose of the aid, the administration called the military equipment "non-lethal," and said the purpose of resuming aid was to "help strengthen the army's key role in reforms." With government repression at an all-time high, U.S. diplomats said military advisers would help the Salvadorans wage "clean counterinsurgency."[5] Already Washington was sensitive to the problem that was to plague U.S. efforts at every step of escalation: how to present its backing of the war effort in a light that would not trigger public opposition. Congress went along, approving the aid package in March, the same month that Salvadoran archbishop Oscar Roméro was murdered by military-linked death squads.

By December 1980 the murder of four American churchwomen had embarrassed the White House into suspending the aid, pending investigation of their deaths. But within two months the Carter administration, responding to the largest ever offensive by the guerrillas' newly formed political-military coordination, the Farabundo Martí National Liberation Front (FMLN), had rescinded the suspension and authorized $5 million additional military aid. This move set a pattern that was to typify every stage of escalation in years to come. It was justified as an emergency, and came in response to a demonstrated increase in the military capacity of the guerrillas. Though the prematurely labeled "final offensive" launched in January proved overly ambitious for the relatively inexperienced and poorly armed guerrilla force, it did demonstrate that the FMLN was a serious military force that could inflict severe damage on the army. Attacks were well coordinated and the rebels managed to hold one provincial capital for eight days. Perhaps most important, at the end of the offensive the FMLN had consolidated its military control in several northern areas of Morazán and Chalatenango provinces, which were to remain undisputed guerrilla strongholds. The guerrillas didn't "win," but neither did the army.[6]

Citing the military threat from the guerrillas, Carter bypassed Congress and sent the $5 million in aid (for helicopters, artillery pieces, ammunition, and infantry weapons) from an executive contingency fund. An important threshold had been crossed. The fiction of "non-lethal" was dropped; this was now a serious counterinsurgency war. By the end of the month when Carter left office the number of military advisers had risen to twenty. The stage was set for the next round of escalation under incoming President Reagan.

Target Nicaragua

One of the arguments the Carter administration used to justify the emergency aid package was alleged evidence (never made public) that the Salvadoran guerrillas were receiving training, arms, and ammunition from Cuba and "communist nations." U.S. ambassador Robert White said he supported the aid because of a Salvadoran government report (later questioned by journalists and embassy officials) that a small group of guerrillas originating in Nicaragua had landed on a Salvadoran beach.[7] The Nicaraguan-Salvadoran link, which was to become a constant but never documented accusation justifying each stage of U.S. intervention, was the pretext for the first openly aggressive moves by the United States against Nicaragua. Citing Nicaragua's alleged support of the Salvadoran guerrillas, Carter ordered the suspension of U.S. economic aid to Nicaragua in January 1981. Secretly the administration also planted the seeds of the ensuing covert operation against Nicaragua. Carter ordered the expansion of U.S. intelligence

aganda campaign to convince public opinion that the Salvadoran guer-rillas were supplied by Nicaragua and the Soviet bloc (an unsubstan-tiated charge made in the administration's February 1981 "White Paper") coincided with the February 1981 decision of the National Se-curity Council to send additional military aid and advisers.[11] Without consulting Congress, the State Department announced that another $20 million in arms sales credits would go to El Salvador from the pres-ident's emergency contingency fund (for helicopters, vehicles, radar, surveillance equipment, and small arms). An additional $5 million was "reprogrammed" from funds that had been appropriated by Congress to another country. Just as significant was the decision to raise the number of U.S. military advisers to fifty-five, a step that implied a qualitative step-up in the U.S. role in the war.

The Nicaraguan-Salvadoran link once again came into play. Reagan's secretary of state, Alexander Haig, threatened to "go to the source" of the insurgency. In his view, this "source" was Cuba and its "proxy" in the region, Nicaragua. These menacing remarks were more than bluster. In March, Haig quietly ordered a review of what actions the United States could take against alleged arms flows from Nicaragua to the Salvadoran guerrillas. The administration requested that the De-partment of Defense present options for military action. The CIA was asked to consider a covert action plan.[12]

Ironically, it was the Pentagon, particularly high military officers, who recommended against direct U.S. military involvement. They ar-gued in a vein that characterized the military leaders' pragmatic cau-tion at every stage of U.S. escalation throughout the region. One objec-tion was that direct U.S. intervention in Central America would be too costly given lack of political support at home. Another was that it would jeopardize U.S. commitments elsewhere in the world.[13] This ar-gument reflected the Pentagon's early reluctance to grant Central America the same strategic importance as the Middle East and Europe. For the moment, the use of force by American military units was put on the back burner, but not abandoned.

Instead of conventional military tactics, Reagan opted for "uncon-ventional" warfare against the Sandinistas. This tactic dated back to post-World War II Europe when the U.S. Special Forces were created to carry out guerrilla actions against pro-Soviet governments in Europe. The first concrete step was a secret move by the Reagan ad-ministration in March 1981, revealed only to the Senate Intelligence Committee. Reagan reaffirmed the existing covert programs against

Nicaragua started under Carter, and also took an important step beyond by authorizing the start of a new covert *military* operation. The goal of this action was purportedly to stop the arms flow to El Salvador.[14]

Central Intelligence Agency director William Casey was quietly given the green light to significantly expand agency operations in Central America, and 150 agents were assigned to begin organizing the anti-Sandinista operation. CIA operatives began to make contacts with Somocista exiles in Miami, Florida, where, ever since the Sandinista triumph in 1979, paramilitary forces had been training for the avowed purpose of invading Nicaragua.[15] As a condition for U.S. aid, the CIA pressured the scattered anti-Sandinista groups, including former Somoza national guardsmen and the dissident Miskito Indian group, the Misura, to join under the banner of the Nicaraguan Democratic Front (FDN).[16] The largest covert operation since the Vietnam war was ready to be launched.

Letting the Salvadorans Do the Fighting

The same reluctance to applying direct U.S. military force shaped U.S. strategy in El Salvador. Although the administration carefully refused to rule out the use of U.S. troops, the preferred plan was to systematically apply U.S. advice, expertise, weapons, and training to help the Salvadoran army fight its own counterinsurgency war. Military officials were particularly worried about repeating what they viewed as the fatal error of Vietnam: committing U.S. forces in a war where political opposition prevented the military from using sufficient American force to win.

The administration's scope of action was also limited by a nervous Congress, who recalled a different lesson from Vietnam: what turned into a long and bloody war had begun with the dispatch of a small group of U.S. "advisers" and modest increases in military aid. Several moves to limit military aid and closely monitor any violations of the War Powers Act were followed in mid-1981 by approval of a law requiring presidential certification of progress in human rights and reforms as a condition for the release of military aid. In this ambience of mounting congressional opposition, Reagan felt compelled to promise that U.S. military "trainers" would not venture into combat zones, and promised to keep a fifty-five person limit on the number of advisers.

Officials were also optimistic during the first several years of the war that the guerrilla threat could be contained without direct intervention by U.S. forces. This optimism flowed mainly from an underestimation of the political and military strength of the FMLN. Pentagon officials noted that the guerrilla force was small (estimated at 2,500 in early 1981) and that it operated mainly in sparsely populated, only marginally important areas of the country. Furthermore, military advisers with experience in Vietnam felt the United States had a much easier battle on its hands. El Salvador, they said, was a classic "low-intensity" guerrilla war, fought by relatively unsophisticated guerrilla units. In Vietnam, on the other hand, the guerrillas had the support of heavily armed regular army units from North Vietnam and the advantage of the northern sanctuaries. The Vietnamese guerrillas also had a political advantage. They won significant popular support because many Vietnamese saw the war as an extension of the long nationalist struggle against French colonialism. By contrast, said U.S. officials, the Salvadoran guerrillas had little political support among the population.[17]

This overblown optimism about the prospects for success in El Salvador was tempered by a note of realism about the glaring deficiencies of the Salvadoran army. A highly classified Pentagon study of the Salvadoran military prepared in 1981 by Brigadier General Frederick F. Woerner (one of the army's foremost experts on counterinsurgency in Latin America, later to become second in command at the U.S. Southern Command in Panama) concluded that only a "dramatic restructuring" of the Salvadoran army could turn it into an effective counterinsurgency army.[18] In the words of one Pentagon official, El Salvador's army was essentially a nineteenth-century constabulary force when the United States stepped in.[19] As officials admitted at the time, the army would have collapsed in the face of the guerrilla threat if the United States had not stepped in with massive support. The pattern was set: the Salvadorans would do the fighting, but the United States would be in charge of everything from providing guns, helicopters, and training to deciding on the size of the army and what tactics it should follow.

The United States Takes Charge

The U.S. crash plan to modernize and restructure the army began immediately. A five-man U.S. advisory team moved into the Army

High Command headquarters to overhaul the command structure, streamline planning, and develop intelligence and communications techniques. U.S. Special Forces arrived in El Salvador to begin training the first of four 1,000-man "immediate reaction" (IR) battalions, the "Atlacatl." Two additional battalions were trained by U.S. Special Forces the following year: the "Belloso" in Fort Bragg and the "Atonal" in El Salvador. These elite battalions were meant to be the army's crack counterinsurgency troops—highly mobile units similar to the airborne rangers used in Vietnam. Trained in the techniques and tactics of guerrilla warfare (such as ambush, small unit patrolling, night attack, intelligence), they were expected to aggressively fight the guerrillas with guerrilla tactics. Creating these IR battalions was the core of the Pentagon's plan to completely overhaul the conventional warfare tactics used by the Salvadoran army. Typically the Salvadorans relied on massive frontal assaults (or sweeps) against guerrilla positions. These were less risky than the small unit tactics urged by U.S. advisers, but they were virtually ineffective against the highly mobile guerrilla units that easily escaped the army's cumbersome assault force.

The Pentagon also set out to rapidly expand the size of the army in order to reach the approximate ten-to-one ratio which counterinsurgency experts say is needed to fight a guerrilla war. Financed by U.S. aid, the army tripled in three years from 9,000 to 27,000 troops. (The United States did not count on the guerrillas' ability to expand at an even faster rate.) The army was also fully equipped with everything from U.S.-supplied M-16 rifles to UH-1 "Huey" helicopters, called by one rebel leader the "guts" of counterinsurgency warfare.[20]

Another Pentagon goal was to expand the army's tiny officer corps. In 1981 the first group of 500 officer candidates was sent to a crash training course at Fort Benning, Georgia. By late 1983, 900 Salvadoran officers (half the entire office corps) had been trained by the United States.[21] Despite the major step-up in U.S. involvement, the army made little headway against the FMLN during 1981 and 1982.[22] A series of government offensives against FMLN strongholds failed in most of their goals. The guerrillas evaded the army and were able to keep their supply and logistical networks intact. Even after the three rapid reaction battalions went into operation, the army still tended to rely on massive sweeps and invariably returned to the safety of their fortified garrisons at nightfall instead of pursuing the guerrillas. Despite U.S. urging to the contrary, the Salvadorans continued to operate as a "nine to five" army. The government sometimes called their sweeps a "success" when they retook towns previously held by the guerrillas, but the army troops inevitably withdrew and FMLN forces inevitably returned. The measure of success in this war of attrition was not holding territory, but rather the ability to wear down the enemy's forces. Indeed, it was the army which continually suffered the heaviest losses: 1,300 dead and wounded in the first six months of 1981 alone, according to the U.S. embassy.[23]

The FMLN, meanwhile, continually upgraded its military capability, using the zones of control it had established in the northern and eastern parts of the country as rearguard areas to train troops and to establish elaborate but highly mobile logistical support networks. They also began to solidify their political ties with the local population by setting up health clinics, schools, and even elected local government structures. In the summer of 1981 the FMLN launched its second major offensive of the war, inflicting heavy losses on the army and capturing large quantities of arms and ammunition.[24] Rebel forces also blew up the country's largest bridge, the Puente de Oro, which had linked the eastern half of the country to the capital city of San Salvador.

In the midst of the FMLN's summer offensive, U.S. ambassador Deane Hinton articulated the policy that continued to draw the United States deeper into the war: Washington would respond to any increase in guerrilla strength, he said, with a rise in U.S. aid.[25] Indeed, the administration's military aid requests for the coming year—$25 million in military sales, $1 million in training funds, and $40 million in security assistance— represented a 400 percent increase over the total military aid between 1959 and 1979. The FMLN carried out a spectacular raid against El Salvador's main air base at Ilopango in January 1982, damaging six U.S.-supplied helicopters and twenty warplanes. Washington responded with the biggest dose of U.S. aid yet—$55 million in emergency assistance from the presidential contingency fund— to help rebuild its air force. As one U.S. official boasted afterward, "We created the Salvadoran air force."[26]

A year after the Reagan administration had set out to win what had first looked to Washington like an easy victory in El Salvador, both sides described the military situation as a stalemate. But in fact, as U.S. General Wallace Nutting described it: "In that kind of war, if you are not winning you are losing."[27] The stage was set for another round of escalation.

Table 3.1
U.S. Military Aid to Central America*
Fiscal Years 1979-85
($ millions)

	Costa Rica	El Salvador	Guatemala	Honduras	Nicaragua
1979	—	.4	.2	2.2	.1
1980	—	6.7	—	4.0	—
1981	.3	35.4	—	8.9	—
1982	2.1	82.0	—	31.2	—
1983	2.6	81.3	—	37.3	—
1984	2.1	64.8	—	41.0	—
Total delivered 1979-84	7.1	270.2	.2	124.6	.1
1984 (proposed supplemental)	7.9	178.7	—	37.5	—
1985 (proposed)	10.0	132.5	10.3	62.5	—

Source: Figures compiled by the Coalition for a New Foreign and Military Policy, Washington, D.C.

*Includes Foreign Military Sales (loans), Military Assistance Program (grants) and International Military Education and Training Program.

Declaring War on Nicaragua

Against the background of the disturbing military stalemate in El Salvador and the Sandinistas' refusal to capitulate to U.S. demands in negotiations with the State Department in the fall of 1981, the White House ordered another review of U.S. policy in the region. A heated debate once again erupted, this time not over *whether* the United States should use military force but *how far* it should go.

Secretary of State Alexander Haig pushed for bold and decisive military action, including U.S. naval and air action against Nicaragua and Cuba. At the time, his proposal was rejected by others in the administration, including Pentagon officials, as too dangerous.[28] But in November the National Security Council (NSC) adopted a ten-point plan that nevertheless paved the way for deepening U.S. intervention. The plan included calls for increased intelligence and surveillance activities, a stepped-up U.S. military presence in the Caribbean, and "contingency planning" for the future use of conventional U.S. military force in case of "unacceptable" actions by Cuba.[29]

The centerpiece of the NSC decision was a plan to significantly escalate covert operations against Nicaragua. Besides reaffirming existing covert aid to "moderate political and economic forces" within Nicaragua, the NSC authorized a $19.5 million initial budget for the Central Intelligence Agency to begin training a 500-strong force to carry out paramilitary actions against Nicaragua. This group was to be joined by a 1,000-strong paramilitary force already being trained by Argentina, whose cooperation had been enlisted earlier that year by former CIA chief General Vernon Walters, a secret Reagan emissary. While not ruling out direct CIA involvement, the NSC stressed the importance of working through third countries, mainly Argentina and Honduras, and "third parties," primarily the anti-Sandinista exiles. With this NSC decision the undeclared war against the Nicaraguan revolution became a reality.

Covert War: A Smokescreen for Washington

The decision to pursue a "covert war" against the Sandinistas reflected the tension between the Reagan administration's determination to take strong military action and the political restraints on direct U.S. intervention. The third party paramilitary operation allowed Washington to preserve its "deniability"—a diplomatic smokescreen to shield it from criticisms and accountability both at home and abroad. And, as one high-level State Department official later explained, keeping the operation covert also provided a diplomatic loophole for Latin American governments who privately wanted to see the Sandinistas ousted but publicly would have had to condemn open U.S. intervention.[30]

Behind the covert action smokescreen, however, the United States came to play a crucial, if hidden, role in the war. Of three committees in charge of running the war, the one credited with being the "brains" of the operation (developing plans and issuing orders) was composed entirely of Americans—CIA officials and U.S. military officers representing the Southern Command. The overall command center was run out of the U.S. embassy in Tegucigalpa and reported to the ambassador, John Negroponte. Assigned to the post in the same month the covert war was approved, Negroponte was described as the "boss" and "spearhead" of the operation.[31] The Honduran army was delegated the task of operating the logistical support system set up to provide weapons and other supplies to the *contra* (as the counter-revolutionary army was called in Central America). While the Hondurans acted as go-betweens, the CIA provided the budget, helped broker arms purchases abroad, and supplied the sophisticated equipment needed for commando raids.[32]

But the United States was not just a broker. U.S. transport planes were seen on more than one occasion directly unloading arms and supplies in *contra* camps.[33] While training of *contra* soldiers was delegated to the fifty or so Argentinians secretly stationed in Honduras, some fifty U.S. military men trained *contra* commanders at a camp just outside of Tegucigalpa.[34] U.S. personnel assumed an even more prominent role when the souring of U.S.-Argentinian relations during the Malvinas/Falklands war caused Argentina to withdraw most of its advisers from Honduras in late 1982.

The United States also took charge of a massive intelligence-gathering operation to support the war. U.S. Air Force pilots and technicians based in Honduras conducted frequent reconnaissance flights along the border with Nicaragua. High-flying SR71 spy planes (successors to the U2) and AWACS planes (Airborne Warning and Control Systems) monitored movements in and out of the country. U.S. navy ships were stationed in the Pacific to monitor radio transmissions and movements. And the Honduran-Nicaraguan border bristled with sophisticated electronic sensors deployed by the CIA.[35]

By 1983 U.S. nurturing had turned the rag-tag band of poorly armed ex-guardsmen into a fully organized counter-revolutionary army equipped with automatic rifles, mortars, heavy caliber machine guns, trucks, and small aircraft. The FDN numbered an estimated 4,000; the 3,000 Indians of Misura (the *contra* organization on the Atlantic Coast) provided a less well trained and disciplined force. In the late spring of 1983 former Sandinista commander Edén Pastora, who rebuffed numerous U.S. efforts to unify with the FDN, opened his own anti-Sandinista front along the Costa Rican border. Pastora at first adamantly denied he was cooperating with the CIA, but he was reportedly receiving laundered CIA money through various Latin American sources.[36]

The Goal: Subverting the Revolution

From the beginning the purpose of the covert war was shrouded in a carefully managed ambiguity. This tactic was designed to keep the Sandinistas in a jittery state of alert as well as to de-fuse congressional opposition. Publicly, U.S. officials claimed that the objective of the covert operation was to curtail arms shipments by the Sandinistas to guerrillas in El Salvador. Frequent administration denials that the purpose was to overthrow the Managua government did little to convince a nervous Congress, which in 1982 had passed the "Boland amendment" prohibiting U.S. aid to groups trying to overthrow the Nicaraguan government. The reality of the covert war, however, simply did not jibe with official statements about its limited purpose. Time and again *contra* leaders said their aim was to overthrow the Managua government, not to interdict arms. As one contra commander put it, "If that's what the CIA told Congress, they forgot to tell us about it."[37]

In off-the-record briefings, U.S. officials were also more frank about the purpose of the paramilitary operation. They acknowledged it was a form of harassment designed to pressure for internal changes within Nicaragua—in effect, a tactic to subvert the revolution. In November of 1982, for example, State Department officials told Congress that arms interdiction was secondary, saying that the primary goal was to isolate and pressure the Sandinistas.[38]

But the planners of the covert operation clearly had an even more ambitious goal in mind: overthrowing the Sandinista government. Even Thomas Enders, one of the operation's backers sometimes credited with a softer line on negotiations with Nicaragua, spoke of the need to "get rid of the Sandinistas."[39] When Casey reported to congressional intelligence committees in 1981, he presented two versions of the operation's goals. The optimal goal of the plan was to overthrow the Sandinista government; the minimal goal, a program of arms interdiction. Casey's talk of the optimal plan created such consternation among some members of the congressional intelligence committee that he and other administration officials downgraded U.S. goals in all future briefings to Congress.[40] In fact, the administration's belief that the United States could not live with the Sandinistas only hardened as the revolution consolidated and radicalized, partly in response to U.S. destabilization efforts. But the biggest constraint against an attempt to overthrow the Sandinistas was the ineffectiveness of the *contra* army. It in-

creasingly proved itself incapable of being anything more than a
harassment to Nicaragua, albeit a costly one.

Preparing for a Military Solution

The administration's intentions vis-à-vis Nicaragua, as well as El
Salvador, were clearly laid out in a series of National Security Council
meetings in the spring and summer of 1982. The United States, said
one NSC document, has a "vital interest in not allowing the prolifera-
tion of Cuban model states." The conclusion: that the United States
"must work to *eliminate* Cuban/Soviet influence in the region."[41] In
keeping with this policy, the NSC decided to increase aid to El Salvador and to step up pressure on Nicaragua.

The discussion on Nicaragua focused not only on paramilitary operations. The option of conventional military action, earlier rejected as
too dangerous, moved from the back to the front burner. It appeared
that the administration was looking for what one Pentagon official
called a "threshold event" to justify stronger military measures against
the Sandinistas.[42] The acquisition of MIG airplanes from the Soviet
Union, noted an NSC discussion paper, "would provide opportunities
as well as challenges." The retaliatory options considered by the
NSC— upgrading the Honduran air force, dispatching a U.S. air
squadron to the region, blockading Nicaragua, invoking the Rio
Treaty, or destroying the MIGs—set the tone for increasingly aggressive U.S. moves in the region.[43]

The momentum was shifting decisively in favor of a military solution
in both Nicaragua and El Salvador. But with public opinion polls
showing a majority of the U.S. people opposed to sending troops to the
region, the Reagan administration still had to move cautiously. Besides
following the NSC's directive to launch a public relations campaign to
win public support for stronger military action, the administration
began to systematically prepare military options that would keep U.S.
troops in a background role. One of these was an option recommended
by the NSC: promoting "regional" military schemes that could serve as
a cover for a U.S. intervention.

CONDECA: The Regional Alliance Against "Subversion"

The obvious sponsor for any regional military intervention was the Central American Defense Council (or CONDECA), a regional defense pact originally formed at U.S. urging in 1964 to combat the threat of "communist subversion" in the region. Crippled by the 1969 war between El Salvador and Honduras, CONDECA finally collapsed when the new Sandinista government formally withdrew from the alliance.

In the wake of the Nicaraguan revolution, the United States put a high priority on reviving CONDECA. The importance of the alliance was as much political as military. Both U.S. and Central American officials admitted that even at its height CONDECA never had any real military clout (beyond, of course, what the United States provided it).[44] While regionally coordinated actions could certainly inflict damaging blows on the Sandinistas or the FMLN, they were no panacea for victory. Even more important, CONDECA could provide the United States with a legal pretext for introducing its own forces into the region under the provisions of the Rio Mutual Defense Treaty. It was the potential vehicle for what one U.S. military official called the "Central Americanization of any intervention."[45]

U.S. behind-the-scenes efforts to reactivate CONDECA began to pay off in early 1982 with the founding of the U.S.-promoted Central American Democratic Community (CADC), composed of El Salvador, Honduras, and Costa Rica. Although ostensibly a poltical grouping designed to isolate Nicaragua, the organization's charter specifically endorsed the notion of regional mutual defense under existing treaties, and agreed to promote "joint operations" against Cuba and the "revolutionary movements it foments."[46] The major stumbling block to a region-wide alliance was Guatemala. That country's military government, however sympathetic to the anticommunist aims of the alliance, initially refused to join. For one, Guatemala's military leaders were preoccupied with fighting their own counterinsurgency war. Relations with the United States had also been strained since U.S. military aid was cut back because of human rights violations. Guatemala's proud and nationalist military leaders, who had been historically more successful in their counterinsurgency war than the Salvadorans, were also resentful of massive U.S. aid to El Salvador.

The Reagan administration tried to mend relations with the regime of General Efraín Ríos Montt in early 1983 by proposing a resumption first of commercial military sales and then military assistance. Though

Congress refused to approve the aid, a new military government led by General Oscar Mejía Victores responded favorably to U.S. overtures. In October of 1983, the formal reconstitution of CONDECA was announced after a meeting between General Paul Gorman (the newly appointed head of the U.S. Southern Command) and the defense ministers of El Salvador, Honduras, and Guatemala (with Panama as an observer). Costa Rica still stood apart from the alliance, though the Reagan administration was eager to draw the country into its regional military strategy. In 1982 the United States began providing military aid to Costa Rica's police force.

The goal of the new CONDECA, according to the ministers, was to confront "Marxist-Leninist aggression" and to "employ the use of force in the defense of democracy." At a later meeting, CONDECA representatives discussed contingency plans for military action against Nicaragua and the FMLN guerrillas "with direct participation by the United States."[47] The alliance still stood on shaky grounds, however, due to Guatemala's continuing aloofness and the still unresolved border dispute between Honduras and El Salvador. The United States clearly provided the glue which kept the fragile alliance together. It was still an open question whether in a moment of crisis CONDECA would provide the vehicle for intervention sought by the United States.

The Militarization of Honduras

While efforts to solidify the regional alliance continued, Honduras remained the lynchpin of U.S. regional strategies. Joint military action with Honduras also offered the possibility of Rio Pact sanction. And under the leadership of General Gustavo Alvarez Martínez, a staunch anticommunist with an almost messianic view of his country's role in defending "democracy" in the Western Hemisphere, the Honduran armed forces appeared willing to enter battle against revolutionary forces in both Nicaragua and El Salvador. The Pentagon, however, had no illusions about the capability of the Honduran army, which was small, ill-equipped, and ill-trained. As in El Salvador, the first order of business was a massive program to modernize and overhaul the Honduran army. But even if that program were successful, any signficiant military action by Honduras in the region would require massive logistical backing from the United States. Promoting Honduras as a regional military proxy was one more path to deepening U.S. intervention.

The Pentagon's game plan for Honduras was to create a highly mobile counterinsurgency force that could be rapidly deployed to any of its borders. Given the relatively small size of the armed forces (12,000 troops and 5,000 security forces), the emphasis, said U.S. officials, was on *quality* rather than quantity.[48] Starting in 1981, Special Forces mobile training teams rotated in and out of the country, advising the General Staff and coaching Honduran soldiers on everything from radio communications to aircraft maintenance and small weapons use. Under the guise of joint military maneuvers, the Special Forces trained around one-third of the army in the next two years. U.S. military aid also skyrocketed, increasing tenfold between 1981 and 1983. Among other military hardware, U.S. aid provided Honduras with its first artillery pieces, night vision devices, communications equipment, and a fleet of high-speed patrol boats.[49]

Special emphasis was placed on upgrading the Honduran air force, a likely actor in any regional intervention. Already the most sophisticated in the region, the Honduran air force had a fleet of Super-Mystere jets acquired from Israel in the mid-1970s, and A-37 "dragonfly" bombers provided by the United States. Honduras' request for sophisticated F5E supersonic jet fighters, although endorsed by embassy military advisers, was put on hold by the White House. Despite their eagerness to sponsor what amounted to an arms race with Nicaragua, some administration officials argued for a delay in late 1983. They were leery that introducing F5Es would up the ante, giving Nicaragua an excuse to bring in MIGs.[50] Meanwhile, the United States provided Honduras with reconnaissance planes, trained Honduran pilots, and assigned U.S. advisers to help set up a pilot training school near Tegucigalpa.

Plans were also set in motion to sponsor a dramatic improvement in Honduras' military infrastructure for use both by Honduran and U.S. forces. The first indication came in the spring of 1982, when the Pentagon said it would request $21 million from Congress to improve "contingency" Honduran airfields at Palmerola, La Ceiba, and Goloson. Even before any funds were appropriated, U.S. army engineers used the pretext of a joint military exercise—the first scheduled with Honduras since 1965—to begin construction on another airfield at Puerto Lempira near the Nicaraguan border. During this July 1982 exercise, U.S. transport planes also positioned a 1,000-strong Honduran battalion at a new base near the border settlement of Mocoron, the staging grounds for the Misura *contra* forces. This move was part of a longer term plan to bolster the Honduran military presence along both the Nicaraguan and Salvadoran borders.

The exercise was an important precedent on two other grounds. It was the first in a series of so-called military maneuvers used by the Reagan administration as a pretext to expand the U.S. military presence in Honduras and to prepare for war. All of this was achieved without congressional approval since maneuvers receive funding from a Joint Chiefs of Staff discretionary budget. It was also part of an emerging pattern of military muscle-flexing designed to intimidate or possibly even provoke Nicaragua.

The Front Against Nicaragua

While the Reagan administration denied Sandinista charges that it sought a Honduran-Nicaraguan war as a pretext for U.S. intervention against the Sandinistas, U.S. policies were creating a highly explosive situation along the border. As the covert war progressed, Honduran forces played an increasingly active role against the Sandinistas. Besides acting as a conduit for supplies, the Hondurans also provided back-up artillery fire for the *contra* and frequently clashed directly with the Sandinistas.

On several occasions open war between the two countries appeared imminent. General Alvarez, who in 1982 had purged the army of leading opponents of a Honduran war with Nicaragua, was reportedly anxious to move against the Sandinistas. Ironically, it was the United States that restrained Alvarez on several occasions from launching a war, while nevertheless continuing to encourage a policy of confrontation. U.S. ambivalence stemmed partly from a realistic assessment of the Honduran army's capabilities. The Honduran army, said U.S. officials, would have a difficult time against the larger, highly motivated and battle-seasoned Sandinista forces, especially if they were defending their homeland. U.S. officials believed that Honduras needed more time and assistance to prepare for war. Some Honduran military officials agreed. "War with Nicaragua may be inevitable," said one young officer in early 1984, "but we're only 50 percent ready."[51] Whenever it came, a full-scale war with Nicaragua would involve the United States, and Washington was not ready to be involved in a regional war—yet.

The Front with El Salvador

The Salvadoran border also became a major focus of U.S. efforts to promote active Honduran involvement in regional counter-revolution. The strategic significance of the border region in the counterinsurgency war against the FMLN is obvious. From the rugged peaks on the Honduran side it is possible to look across to the mountain strongholds of the FMLN guerrillas in Morazán and Chalatenango provinces, which at some points are just a few miles away. In between lies a no-man's-land, the disputed pockets of territory known as the *bolsones*, where neither the Honduran nor Salvadoran army has exercised effective control since the 1969 war. U.S. officials have long contended that the *bolsones* offer FMLN guerrillas an important sanctuary.

In August of 1981 a *New York Times* reporter ran across Special Forces captain Michael Sheean in a remote mountain town on the Honduran side. He said the mission of his Special Forces team in Honduras, sanctioned by the National Security Council, was to support a military effort against the Salvadoran guerrillas.[52] In 1981 the mission of the Special Forces remained relatively modest: to assist Honduras in stepping up border patrols. While the public justification for helping Honduras to beef up its presence along the border was the interdiction of the alleged flow of arms to Salvadoran guerrillas, the goal was clearly to put pressure on the FMLN.

As the war in El Salvador heated up, the pressure was carried one step further. In mid-July 1982, as the Salvadoran army drove northward in a large offensive against guerrilla positions in Morazán province, 3,000 Honduran troops entered El Salvador in an attempt to form a pincer. Honduras mounted a similar operation in the border regions of Chalatenango and Morazán provinces in October. According to Salvadoran officers, Honduran forces participated directly in attacks on FMLN units.[53]

U.S. officials were clearly brokers of such cooperation. Undersecretary of Defense Fred Iklé held a joint meeting that same month with the defense ministers of El Salvador and Honduras. One week later General Nutting, who had earlier told the Hondurans that "the Pentagon was fully behind their collaboration with the Salvadorans," met again with the two defense chiefs, both of whom spoke openly of their collaboration.[54]

The long-term goal of such collaboration was clearly to trap Salvadoran guerrillas between the advancing Salvadoran army on one side and the Hondurans on the other. Such an operation, if successful, could deliver a crippling blow to the FMLN. But the obstacles to success were substantial. Even though the United States had engineered a peace treaty in 1980 formally ending the 1969 war, political tensions between the two countries continued to simmer, particularly over the *bolsones*. The old wound was further aggravated when El Salvador's 1983 constitution designated the country's borders as non-negotiable. Despite rocky relations, Honduran military officials, believing their own fate hinged on the outcome in El Salvador, were increasingly willing to cooperate as they watched the FMLN gather strength along the border.[55]

A key sticking point was military. Neither the Honduran nor Salvadoran armies appeared capable of a successful blocking operation. The two earlier attempts had failed miserably when the Salvadorans were unable to prevent FMLN forces from slipping through their lines. The Honduran army, moreover, did not posses the transport equipment, enough troops, or sufficient expertise to effectively seal the mountainous border. In 1983, U.S. special forces coached close to 3,000 Honduran soldiers in "interdiction" exercises. But no matter how much the United States primed the Honduran army, any significant border operation implied a major involvement by the United States.

The Internal Front: Preventative Counterinsurgency

Creating a base for regional intervention in Honduras also implied efforts to keep a lid on all political opposition to the military-dominated government in Honduras. The strategy adopted was "preventative counterinsurgency": nipping the opposition movement in the bud through a combination of selective repression and counterinsurgency. The targets included members and leaders of grass-roots organizations such as trade union and peasant organizations, and individuals suspected of having leftist sympathies, be they lawyers, students, or Salvadoran exiles. They also included members of the four small urban-based guerrilla organizations which appeared in 1980-81. The preventative campaign, in which official repression was mixed with death squad tactics, was reportedly directed by Alvarez, who had headed the internal security police (FUSEP) in 1981-82.[56] Though the toll of this selective repression was small compared to the scale of violence in El

Salvador, the disappearance of over one hundred people in Honduras in 1981-82 was an unprecedented occurrence in that country.

In addition to Argentine and Israeli advisers, the Honduran internal security forces also received assistance from the United States. The first group of U.S. military advisers to arrive in Honduras in early 1980 included specialists to train the Honduran army in urban counterinsurgency techniques. In 1981-82 U.S. training included advice to Honduran military intelligence officers in the "organization, support, planning, and coordination of urban and rural intelligence and counter-intelligence." Besides working with the COBRA, a SWAT-like urban counter-terrorist unit set up by FUSEP, U.S. advisers also helped train a highly secret, elite counterinsurgency battalion, the Special Operations Commandos (or COE).[57]

After a series of kidnappings and highjackings by guerrilla groups in 1981 and 1982, the preventative war was stepped up through searches of entire neighborhoods, raids on alleged guerrilla safehouses, and the passage of an antiterrorist act (April 1982) which restricted civil liberties and set maximum penalties for crimes against "state security." The Washington-based human rights group Americas Watch noted that the country was living in an "atmosphere of fear." The urban opposition was effectively silenced.

In mid-1983, however, another small guerrilla group appeared, this time in the jungles of Olancho province adjacent to the Nicaraguan border. U.S. forces participated in the brief counter-guerrilla operation by transporting the army's elite counterinsurgency unit to the site in U.S. army helicopters and by flying reconnaissance missions.[58] Although the extent of U.S. involvement was a carefully guarded secret, relatives of an American priest killed with the guerrillas also claimed to have evidence that U.S. military officials participated in interrogation and torture of captured guerrillas.[59] The Olancho guerrillas were quickly eliminated.

On the Threshold of Intervention

The likelihood that Honduras would become a base for intervention heightened as Washington watched events in Central America take a turn for the worse in late 1982. The immediate crisis point was El Salvador. Even more than Nicaragua, El Salvador increasingly threatened to be the spark which could ignite a Central American war.

The relative inactivity of the FMLN following the success of the March 1982 elections triggered a wave of optimism among U.S. officials and their Salvadoran allies. However, as one high-level State Department official ruefully commented in retrospect, the Salvadoran army failed to capitalize on the political momentum won with the election.[60] In a series of offensives in the second half of the year, the army showed all of its old weaknesses. It still fought a nine-to-five war and used conventional rather than counterinsurgency tactics, U.S. training and advice to the contrary.

The FMLN for its part displayed increasing military sophistication. Guerrilla forces, sometimes operating in units of up to 800 combatants, were able to meet the army's massive attacks with a solid line of defense—the first signs that the guerrillas were beginning to take on the characteristics of a regular army. The guerrillas were also sufficiently coordinated to be able to respond to an army offensive in Chalatenango by opening other fronts throughout the country.[61] The accumulating strength of the guerrilla forces was dramatically highlighted in October 1982, when the FMLN launched a four month offensive. This prolonged action tipped the tenuous military balance in its favor for the first time in the civil war. The FMLN's ability to coordinate operations on several simultaneous fronts reflected growing logistical sophistication and unprecedented cooperation between the four guerrilla organizations. As the October offensive progressed, the FMLN also accumulated an impressive arsenal of weapons captured from the army, including its first artillery.

Blows suffered by government forces were also severe. Casualties reached an all-time high, and by the summer of 1983 the Defense Ministry (known to underestimate army losses) reported that casualties had doubled over the previous year. An astounding 6,387 soldiers, almost one-third of the army, were reported killed or wounded.[62] The guerrillas' campaign of sabotage against economic installations also took a severe toll on the economy.

The FMLN's ability to seize scores of towns— including thirty-five in a two week period—was also remarkable. Their goal was not to hold territory but to inflict psychological and political blows that would chip away at the government's legitimacy. Their success was dramatic. In February 1983 the FMLN occupied the town of Berlín for two days. An important agricultural market center of 30,000 people, Berlín was the largest town they had ever held. The event galvanized the country. The army, unable to dislodge the guerrillas, responded with bombs, leaving at least sixty civilians dead and much of the town destroyed.

U.S. officials were especially disturbed at the performance of the U.S.-trained army, which persisted in its ineffective sweep operations against guerrilla strongholds in the north. Not only were the guerrilla positions quickly reestablished once the army withdrew, but the concentration of government troops in the north again allowed the FMLN to strengthen its presence in other parts of the country.

Added to the army's military incompetence were equally debilitating political tensions. Disputes between local commanders and the High Command burst into open conflict when the commander of Cabanas province, Colonel Sigfried Ochoa, staged an open rebellion against the U.S.-backed defense minister, Colonel Guillermo García. The rebellion was resolved only when a promise was made, with U.S. acquiescence, that García would be replaced. But the tensions continued to simmer. The army was, as one U.S. official put it, "paralyzed."[63]

Failure of the Contra *Offensive*

Prospects looked equally glum for the U.S.-backed *contra* army. In the winter and spring of 1983, the *contra*, responding to CIA directives, launched their first major offensive in northern Nicaragua.[64] Besides attacking rural settlements and harrassing the coffee harvest, the *contra* tried to set up military "task forces" deep within Nicaraguan territory. They also had a more ambitious goal in mind: permanently seizing the strip of land in northern Jinotega province that juts up into Honduras. This would be the first step toward declaring a provisional government. There was even talk at *contra* headquarters in Tegucigalpa of victory over the Sandinistas before the end of the year.[65]

By summer, however, the FDN's *contra* army had demonstrated itself incapable of being anything more than a harassment to the Sandinistas. Its major successes came from hit-and-run operations, which caused $70 million in losses to the Nicaraguan economy and forced thousands of Nicaraguan peasants to abandon their farms. Militarily and politically the invasion was a disaster. The *contra* failed to hold any territory and could not maintain their task forces inside the country. The thousands of *contra* forces who had infiltrated into Nicaragua were called back to their camps in Honduras "in such bad shape," said one FDN official, "that some of them straggled back to their bases literally without shoes."[66]

The Sandinistas were not intimidated, far less on the verge of collapse. Indeed, as a House Intelligence Committee report concluded in May of 1983, U.S. support of the *contras* was having the opposite political effect than intended. In the face of U.S. intervention and alliance with the universally detested Somoza exiles, popular support for the beseiged Sandinista government had only increased.[67]

Washington Faces the Crisis

The obvious failure of U.S.-backed military moves in the region set the stage for another major escalation of U.S. military involvement. At the White House, where the group of Cold War hard-liners close to Reagan (including Jeane Kirkpatrick, William Clark, and William Casey) had taken direct control over U.S. Central America policy, there was near panic over the deteriorating situation in El Salvador. The concern triggered another series of National Security Council reviews of U.S. policy in the region.

The mood in the White House was one of grim determination to do what officials cryptically referred to as "whatever is necessary" to promote U.S. goals in the region. "No one is looking for a broader conflict," said one official, "but the President isn't going to lose El Salvador. He isn't going to back down. He really means it when he says that the United States has a vital stake in what happens in Central America."[68] As in the past, the fear of losing in El Salvador spurred a renewed focus on reversing the revolutionary victory in Nicaragua. "You could conceive of the circumstance," said another official, "where not losing a country to communism means having to take one back."[69]

One point that virtually every high-level official in the administration agreed upon was that the U.S. military presence in the region was too small to achieve the objective of U.S. policy: turning back the revolution. But should the United States intervene? In the words of an interagency task force reporting to the National Security Council: "The situation in Central America is nearing a critical point. . . . It is still possible to accomplish U.S. objectives without the direct use of U.S.

troops (although the credible threat of such use is needed to deter overt Soviet/Cuban intervention), provided that the U.S. takes timely and effective action."[70]

As a result of these meetings, the NSC adopted a blueprint for yet deeper U.S. involvement. It called for the usual substantial increases in U.S. military aid to regional allies. But more importantly, it also involved a bold plan for a dramatic projection of U.S. military force into the region. One of the chief architects and implementers of the plan was General Gorman, just transferred from the Joint Chiefs of Staff office to replace General Nutting. The appointment of a four-star general to head the Southern Command was one of several signs that the Pentagon had upgraded the strategic importance of the Caribbean Basin in U.S. global priorities.[71]

The military build-up that followed was designed partly to intimidate the FMLN, the Sandinistas, and their alleged Soviet suppliers. In effect, it represented a last ditch attempt to gain time and avoid committing U.S. combat troops in Central America. But under the guise of "contingency planning," the administration was also systematically preparing for the regional war some offficials said they believed was inevitable.[72] It was a dangerous game of brinksmanship.

Honduras: War Preparations

The new policy became operational within weeks of the NSC meeting when the administration announced the start of the "Big Pine II" military maneuvers in Honduras, scheduled to last for an unprecedented period of six months. Reagan called it a "shield" for democracy, but Big Pine was a cover for the most spectacular display of U.S. military force Central America had yet witnessed. Two U.S. aircraft carrier battle groups, with 16,000 troops and seventy jet fighters each, were dispatched to Pacific coastal waters to feign a naval blockade against Nicaragua. U.S. naval assault ships unloaded 2,000 U.S. marines to practice an amphibious landing alongside Honduran soldiers on the Caribbean coast. And U.S. Special Forces parachuted into a remote jungle area north of the Nicaraguan border to stage a mock counterinsurgency campaign against imaginary guerrilla units infiltrated from the south. For six months, U.S. transport planes and helicopters flew in and out of Honduras, U.S. army truck convoys plied the roads, and over 5,000 U.S. troops were deployed to the country. Besides the show of force, Big Pine was a massive training exercise to prepare both Honduran and American troops for war.

Perhaps most important, the maneuvers were a vehicle to carry out two key elements of the NSC's blueprint: constructing military bases for U.S. use in wartime and "pre-positioning" U.S. forces and equipment.[73] By the time Big Pine II ended, U.S. army combat engineers had nearly completed a network of military installations designed to permit a rapid deployment of U.S. forces into Central America. These included:

—eight airfields lengthened and upgraded to handle U.S. C-130 transport planes, two of them long enough to accommodate the most sophisticated jet fighters;

—two powerful radar stations manned by U.S. marines, one near Tegucigalpa and the other on Tigre Island in the strategically located Gulf of Fonseca, a few miles from both El Salvador and Nicaragua;

—hundreds of wooden army barracks and administrative buildings;

—a U.S. combat hospital.

Pentagon plans to build storage facilities to pre-position ammunition in Honduras as well as a $150 million naval air base at Puerto Castillo on the Caribbean left no doubt that the Pentagon was getting ready for war.[74] By early 1984 the pre-positioning mapped out by the NSC was nearing completion. While still denying the United States had established a permanent military presence in Honduras, at the close of Big Pine II in February the Pentagon announced that joint military exercises would continue indefinitely. A U.S. army command center and 2,000 troops were left behind. The United States was poised for intervention, should the need or the opportunity arise.

Escalating the War: Nicaragua

The sense of urgency about the need for dramatic military action also spurred the Reagan administration to new initiatives in El Salvador and Nicaragua. These moves entailed a deeper U.S. involvement in the war on both fronts.

In an attempt to breathe new life into the faltering *contra* army, the administration planned a major expansion of its covert operation, including an increase in funds, personnel, and scope of the operation.[75]

The official budget request presented to Congress in the summer of 1983 was $50 million, but the classified budget was rumored to be as high as $80 million. Much of this money was to finance a near doubling of the *contra* army to 15,000 people. By this time the CIA had also assumed day-to-day control of the covert operation. Earlier efforts to shield U.S. personnel from direct contact with the *contra* were abandoned. U.S. intelligence agents began daily meetings with *contra* leaders and started actually pinpointing their targets and plotting attacks.[76] In early summer the CIA official in charge of the covert operation in Tegucigalpa ordered a basic shift in tactics: instead of hit-and-run attacks in rural areas, the *contra* were to begin targeting strategic installations throughout the country.[77] The plan immediately took its toll. In late 1983 the CIA helped plan a series of attacks. ARDE planes provided by the CIA bombed the Managua airport, and FDN commandos trained by the CIA hit the country's vital oil facilities at Corinto and Puerto Sandino. By March 1984 Nicaragua's main ports had been mined in an operation directly supervised by U.S. agents from boats offshore.[78] Nicaragua was forced onto a wartime footing. Bomb shelters were built in the capital, anti-aircraft guns were stationed on hilltops, and a military draft was initiated.

The familiar cycle repeated itself. In January 1984 the largest *contra* offensive yet against northern Nicaragua ended in failure when the Sandinistas sent an estimated 20,000 regular troops to reinforce militias and reservists along the border. The *contra* limped back to their camps in Honduras. Once again the Reagan administration came to the rescue, asking Congress for another $21 million emergency infusion of aid.

El Salvador: Americanizing the War

Rescuing the Salvadoran army from the brink of disaster was an even bigger dilemma, raising some of the same questions about counterinsurgency warfare that the United States had faced in Vietnam. Could the local army defeat a guerrilla insurgency against a repressive and corrupt government no matter how much U.S. aid was sent? Would the United States eventually have to send troops to prevent a guerrilla victory? And even with direct U.S. intervention, what would be the outcome?

Though General Nutting had told Congress in early 1983 that the

Salvadoran army could never achieve "total military victory" without a direct involvement of U.S. military personnel, no one argued in mid-year for such an involvement.[79] Some military officials in the administration spoke of sending 2,000 advisers, but the Pentagon came up with what they believed to be a more realistic proposal of 125.

With the Vietnam syndrome still very much alive and with a U.S. election year looming ahead, the Reagan administration opted instead for a plan that would avoid challenging the fifty-five advisers limit. One tactic involved stationing U.S. advisers in Honduras instead of El Salvador. In June the Pentagon announced plans to open a Regional Military Training Center (RMTC) at Puerto Castillo. Although nominally a Honduran base, it was built and largely staffed by U.S. personnel. Green Berets numbered 125 at the start, and six months later increased to 190. By the end of the year U.S. advisers had trained around 2,000 new Salvadoran troops at the RMTC. These included a fourth rapid-reaction battalion (the "Arce") and three smaller hunter battalions, as well as several Honduran battalions.

Within El Salvador the number of U.S. military personnel was also quietly increased. In mid-1983, twenty-three army medical specialists were dispatched to El Salvador to assist the army in revamping its medical combat support system. The Reagan administration claimed, however, that the mission was humanitarian rather than military. Members of the embassy military advisory group were also taken out of the adviser category, thus opening eleven new slots. By early 1984 the number of U.S. military personnel in El Salvador was estimated at ninety-seven, though the Administration still claimed it was within the fifty-five person limit.[80]

U.S. advisers were also drawn increasingly into direct involvement in the war, including combat support operations. At the army High Command, where a team of six U.S. advisers was assigned, Salvadoran officers in charge of giving orders to combat field commanders routinely deferred to their U.S. counterparts for decisions. "The people at our High Command deliberate and confer with the American advisers before taking any actions," said a Salvadoran colonel. By July 1983, U.S. advisers, who previously had been stationed in the capital, were also deployed to military garrisons throughout the country. Besides training new units, they gave advice on everything from intelligence to logistics and operations. They, as well as the Americans at the High Command, were also responsible for field operation plans. At Ilopango air base, the Americans worked side by side with Salvadoran commanders at the most elaborate war operations room in the country. The advisers helped set up the army's most sophisticated communications center atop Cacahuatique volcano. When the position was attacked by guerrillas in June 1983, they directed the army's unsuccessful defense.[81] Though still formally prohibited from going on combat operations (a prohibition which many advisers complained about bitterly) the Americans regularly operated in areas where fighting could break out at any moment. Indeed, there were several instances in 1983 in which U.S. advisers came under hostile fire. By early 1984 the Americans were regularly carrying heavy sidearms. Two years earlier, possessing such a weapon caused the expulsion of an adviser.

In mid-1983 it was revealed that four U.S. C-130 planes based at Howard Air Force base in Panama were carrying out regular reconnaissance flights over guerrilla-controlled areas in El Salvador, as part of an effort to provide tactical battlefield intelligence to the Salvadorans. This effort expanded in early 1984 when thirteen "Mohawk" reconnaissance planes based in Honduras began flying combat support missions over El Salvador, using direct radio communications to provide immediate intelligence to Salvadoran field commanders.[82] American advisers in El Salvador also reported they had occasionally been diverted into combat operations while on training missions with Salvadoran pilots.[83] Washington continued to maintain the fiction of noninvolvement, but there was no doubt that the United States was at war.

El Salvador's Last Chance: The National Plan

After more than two years of frustration over the failure of the Salvadoran army to respond to U.S. advice on how to conduct the war, the Pentagon decided the time had come to force the Salvadorans to accept its strategy. U.S. counterinsurgency experts from the Southern Command designed what came to be called the "National Plan"—according to some advisers, the army's "last chance" to turn the war around.[84]

After considerable resistance, the Salvadoran High Command agreed to launch the plan in June of 1983. It called for a massive military sweep to be followed by government-sponsored (and U.S.-funded) reconstruction programs. In theory, the plan would combine both military and economic measures to combat the guerrillas. This was the two-pronged strategy long advocated by counterinsurgency experts and already implemented in Vietnam fifteen years earlier. There it was known as the Civil Operations and Revolutionary Development Support program, or CORDS.

The immediate objective of the military offensive was to push the guerrillas out of the strategically important agricultural provinces of San Vicente and then Usulután, where the FMLN had grown dangerously strong. If the guerrillas could be contained in their traditional strongholds in Morazán and Chalatenango provinces, the way would eventually be open for a more ambitious direct assault on the guerrillas, perhaps in cooperation with the Honduran army. But most important, U.S. advisers saw the plan as a way for the army to seize the initiative from the guerrillas, tipping the military balance in favor of the government. Once an area had been secured, the government would move in with phase two of the program—a politically motivated campaign to gain the support of the local population and prevent a resurgence of guerrilla influence. Rebuilding the local economy, restoring such social services as schools and health clinics, and setting up civil defense patrols were all part of this second stage of "pacification."

But phase two of the San Vicente operation never got off the ground, nor did the National Plan live up to its name. Two months after U.S. and Salvadoran officials touted the 6,000-strong army offensive in San Vicente as a great success, the guerrillas had returned to the province in force. In fact, the FMLN had simply carried out a tactical retreat to neighboring provinces in advance of the announced army offensive. They used the next several months to regroup their forces. In Usulután, the next target province, the army's plan stalled from the beginning.[85]

The FMLN Seizes the Initiative

By September of 1983 the U.S. plan for turning the war around came to a halt as the FMLN launched its own offensive. The spectacular opening salvo—an attack on an army brigade headquarters in the country's third largest city of San Miguel—was a sign that the guerrilla war was entering a new stage. In the largest regular force operation yet mounted by the FMLN, an estimated 1,000 guerrillas were able to approach this provincial capital in heavy truck convoys along the open road. For the first time the guerrillas used heavy artillery, with impressive accuracy. They also carried out simultaneous attacks on several bridges and factories, making this the most complex logistical operation yet attempted by a guerrilla army. As one U.S. official commented, San Miguel showed that the FMLN's intelligence was better than the army's.[86]

The initiative shifted rapidly to the FMLN. Over the next three months, it seized over sixty towns and carried out actions in eleven of the country's fourteen provinces, including San Vicente and Usulután. An estimated one-quarter of the national territory was firmly under guerrilla control, and much of the country was contested. The most spectacular setback for the army came during two weeks in December and early January 1984, when the FMLN mounted successful attacks on some of the most well-fortified military targets in the country. Guerrilla forces occupied the U.S.-built communications stations atop Cacahuatique Volcano for the second time, destroyed the army's most modern military bases at El Paraíso (also built by the United States), and blew up the country's largest bridge at Cuscatlán, cutting a vital artery of communication with the eastern part of the country.

The Salvadoran army reeled from the blows. Casualties during one six-week period reached 800, and 400 soldiers were taken prisoner.[87] With morale at an all-time low, troops frequently chose to surrender rather than fight. As a result, the FMLN captured more weapons than at any time in the war. Even Pentagon officials admitted that half of all guerrilla weapons are captured from Salvadoran government troops.[88]

Ironically, just as U.S. advisers claimed that some army units were beginning to use the small-unit tactics they had long urged, the army entered the most serious backslide in its history. Just a few months after Undersecretary of Defense Fred Iklé gave assurances that the United States was seeking a military victory, his boss Casper Weinberger had to admit that the war was "not going well."[89]

Counterinsurgency in Crisis

U.S. counterinsurgency strategy was once again in crisis, but officials appeared oblivious to the lessons of the past and the realities of the present. Unable to win but unwilling to lose, the White House opted for another escalation of U.S. involvement. In early 1984, the Pentagon announced plans for the largest military aid package for El Salvador to date. It requested $400 million over the next year and a half, with $93 million to be granted on an emergency basis. The aid was to buy more trucks and artillery, to double the helicopter fleet, to provide new fighter bombers, and to expand the army by another 6,000 to 10,000 troops during 1984. The argument used to justify the request was a familiar one: with more U.S. training and equipment, more personnel and more time, the army could gain the upper hand.[90] The lessons of the four-year-long civil war, however, suggested otherwise. Despite over $750 million in military and security assistance and the best counterinsurgency advice the Pentagon could muster, the Salvadoran army was still no match for the rapidly expanding guerrilla force. Once dismissed by U.S. officials as insignificant, the guerrillas were now estimated by U.S. sources to have between 9,000 and 12,000 regular troops.[91] But contrary to the assumptions of U.S. policy, improving the ratio of government troops to guerrillas and the army's level of technical competence would not solve its fatal weaknesses, which were political rather than military. This was one of the lessons of Vietnam which military planners apparently failed to learn.

Low troop morale and the army's lack of aggressiveness reflected more than a military imbalance. They were also a sign that the soldiers, most of them poor teenagers forcibly recruited off the streets, were unwilling to fight for a system in which they had no stake. As a group of young soldiers told an American reporter in Chaletenango, "Why should we fight for the oligarchy when their sons are safe in Miami?"[92] The officer corps had fatal political weaknesses of its own. Despite U.S. efforts to "reform" the army, corrupt and incompetent officers remained in key command posts. They continued to fight a "nine-to-five war" and to siphon off both arms and food to the highest bidder, including the FMLN.[93]

Many officials reputedly linked to the rightist death squads, up to and including the minister of defense, Eugenio Vides Casanova, remained in power.[94] Under their leadership, "clean" counterinsurgency remained as illusive as ever. Though U.S. advisers paid lip service to human rights, it was no accident that the commanders they considered the most effective in fighting the counterinsurgency war were also those who were the least concerned about the niceties of human rights. Drying up the "sea" in which the guerrillas "swim," a dictum that counterinsurgency experts have borrowed from Mao Zedong, inevitably means targeting the civilian population. Not surprisingly, Salvadoran army and air force raids and sweeps continued to leave a trail of death and destruction among civilians. Far from winning "hearts and minds," government forces only convinced more and more Salvadorans that the army was part of the problem rather than part of the solution.

Indeed, the United States was faced with the same dilemma in Central America as it had been in Southeast Asia: its local allies were proving themselves incapable of winning on either the political or the military battlefronts. The alternatives, once again, were either to recognize failure or to escalate and widen the war. The words of Ronald Reagan left no doubt in what direction the United States was heading: "The national security of all the Americas," he said, "is at stake in Central America. If we cannot defend ourselves there, we cannot expect to prevail elsewhere. Our credibility would collapse, our alliances would crumble and the safety of our homeland would be put in jeopardy."[95] Nearly twenty years earlier almost identical words were used to justify massive U.S. intervention in Vietnam.

Notes

1. The Defense Guidance Plan adopted by the incoming Reagan administration noted that "we must revitalize and enhance our special operations forces to project U.S. power where the use of conventional forces would be premature, inappropriate or unfeasible." See unpublished paper by Daniel Volman, "The New Counterinsurgency: U.S. Military Strategy in Central America," (1981). See also Michael T. Klare, *Beyond the Vietnam Syndrome: U.S. Interventionism in the 1980s* (Washington, D.C.: Institute for Policy Studies, 1982).

2. Various means were used to get around this official suspenion of military aid and sales programs. Guatemala, for example, bought "civilian" helicopters valued at $10 million through the U.S. Commerce Department and then outfitted them with machine guns for use in counterinsurgency operations. See *Washington Post*, January 23, 1981. Israel also became a major supplier of arms to Guatemala and El Salvador after 1977.

3. Quoted in Arnon Hadar, *The United States and El Salvador: Political and Military Involvement* (Berkeley: U.S.-El Salvador Research and Information Center, 1981). On the policy debate within the Carter administration see William LeoGrande, "A Splendid Little War: Drawing the Line in El Salvador," in Stanford Central America Action Network, ed., *Revolution in Central America* (Boulder, Col.: Westview Press, 1983), p. 100.

4. *Washington Post*, February 4, 1980.

5. Quoted in Walter LeFeber, *Inevitable Revolutions* (New York: W.W. Norton, 1983), pp. 250-51.

6. For an account of the military situation during this period see Robert Armstrong and Janet Shenk, *El Salvador: The Face of Revolution* (Boston: South End Press, 1982), p. 183-88; and Richard Allen White and Jarke Almuli, *Counterinsurgency War in Central America: the United States Tries It Again* (Mexico City: Centro de Estudios del Tercer Mundo, 1983), ch. 5.

7. See account in Armstrong and Shenk, *El Salvador*, pp. 188- 89. White later questioned the evidence and withdrew his support for the aid.

8. *San Francisco Chronicle*, April 8, 1983.

9. Quoted in Steve Volk, "Honduras: On the Border of War," in *NACLA Report on the Americas*, November-December 1981, p. 27.

10. *Washington Post*, March 23, 1980.

11. The lack of evidence to support the conclusion that the Salvadoran guerrillas received Soviet bloc aid was thoroughly documented by the *Wall Street Journal*, June 8, 1981, and the *Washington Post*, June 9, 1981. The Reagan administration's continuing charges that Nicaragua was a major source of arms for the guerrillas were equally unsubstantiated. In fact, administration sources admitted on numerous occasions that there was "very little solid evidence" (see *Washington Post*, February 22, 1983) and that the Salvadorans had "little need" for outside arms (see *New York Times*, July 31, 1983).

12. *New York Times*, March 14, 1982.

13. High-level military officials continued to express reservations about a direct and massive commitment of U.S. forces in the region, largely on grounds that there was not domestic political support for such a move. See *Los Angeles Times*, July 27, 1983, *Wall Street Journal*, June 24, 1983, and *Washington Post*, May 22, 1983.

14. San Francisco Chronicle, April 8, 1983.

15. *San Francisco Examiner*, June 12, 1983.

16. *San Francisco Examiner*, June 13, 1983.

17. Interviews with Pentagon officials, Washington D.C., June 1983 and with U.S. military official in San Salvador, October 1983.

18. *New York Times*, April 22, 1983. General Woerner is known as one of the army's foremost experts on counterinsurgency in Latin America. In the mid-1960s he was in charge of the civic action component of the U.S.-supported counterinsurgency war in Guatemala.

19. Interview, Washington, D.C., June 1983.

20. *Listen Compañero: Conversations with Central American Revolutionary Leaders* (San Francisco: Solidarity Publications, 1983), p.24.

21. Mortimer Zuckerman, "The Battle Hymn of the Republic: Sojourn in El Salvador," *New Republic*, December 12, 1983.

22. See White, *Counterinsurgency War*, ch. 6.

23. Cynthia Arnson, *El Salvador: A Revolution Confronts the United States* (Washington, D.C.: Institute for Policy Studies, 1983), p.79.
24. See White, *Counterinsurgency War*, and Carlos Andino Martínez, "El Estamento Militar Salvadoreño Redefinido," *Estudios Centroamericanos*, May-June 1982.
25. *Washington Post*, August 21, 1981.
26. *New York Times*, October 2, 1983.
27. *Time*, September 7, 1981.
28. *New York Times*, November 5, 1981 and March 25, 1984; *Washington Post*, March 4, 1982 and March 6, 1983.
29. See *Washington Post*, February 2, 1982, March 4, 1982, March 6, 1982, March 10, 1982; *New York Times*, March 14, 1983; and *San Francisco Chronicle*, April 8, 1983.
30. Interview with State Department official, Washington, D.C., February 1983.
31. On the U.S. role in the covert operation see *New York Times*, April 3, 1983, *Newsweek*, November 8, 1982, and *Time*, April 4, 1983.
32. *Miami Herald*, December 8, 1982.
33. *San Francisco Examiner*, June 13, 1983.
34. *New York Times*, November 2, 1982 and April 3, 1983 and San Francisco Examiner, April 14, 1983.
35. *New York Times*, April 3, 1983 and *San Francisco Examiner*, April 14, 1983.
36. *Miami Herald*, December 19, 1982 and *New York Times*, November 8, 1983.
37. *Miami Herald*, December 18, 1982.
38. See *Washington Post*, January 1, 1983 and *Miami Herald*, June 12, 1983.
39. *Newsweek*, November 8, 1983.
40. See *San Francisco Examiner*, June 12, 1983; *New York Times*, August 5, 1983 and November 2, 1983. In November 1982 State Department officials indicated in congressional testimony that arms interdiction was secondary, saying that the primary goal was to isolate and pressure the Sandinistas. See *Washington Post*, January 1, 1983. In December Casey told Congress the *contras* were not strong enough to overthrow the government but could bring about internal changes. See *Miami Herald*, June 12, 1983.
41. *New York Times*, April 7, 1983 and *Washington Post*, April 17, 1983.
42. Interview with Pentagon official, Washington, D.C., June, 1983.
43. *Washington Post*, April 17, 1983.
44. Interviews with U.S. and Honduran military officials, Tegucigalpa, February, 1984.
45. *Washington Post*, January 13, 1984.
46. *White, Counterinsurgency War*, p. 252.
47. *Washington Post*, November 12, 1983.
48. Interviews with U.S. military officials, Tegucigalpa, February 1984.
49. See Cynthia Arnson and Flora Montealegre, "Background Information on

U.S. Military Personnel and U.S. Assistance to Central America," Institute for Policy Studies Update #7, November 1982; and NARMIC, *The Central American War: A Guide to the U.S. Military Build-Up*, April 1983.

50. Interviews with U.S. embassy officials, Tegucigalpa, February 1984.

51. Interviews with Honduran military and U.S. officials, Tegucigalpa, February 1984.

52. *New York Times*, August 19, 1981.

53. See White, *Counterinsurgency War*, p. 186.

54. *Latin America Regional Report*, March 20, 1981. See White, *Counterinsurgency War*, ch. 7.

55. Honduran and U.S. officials in Tegucigalpa said in late 1983 and early 1984 that the Honduran military believed the FMLN presented a more immediate threat to their country's security than Nicaragua.

56. Paramilitary death squads made their first appearance in Honduras in early 1981 just after Alvarez, who had received his military training in Argentina, became head of the FUSEP and invited Argentine advisers to the country. Disappearances of government opponents were carried out by heavily armed "civilians" believed to be off-duty military personnel—a style used in Argentina. Political prisoners were held in secret jails and often tortured. The accusations about General Alvarez' role in the repression were made by Colonel Leonidas Torres Arías, former chief of Honduran military intelligence. For a report on human rights violations in Honduras see Americas Watch, *Human Rights in Honduras: Signs of the Argentine Method* (New York: Americas Watch, December 1982). See also various issues of the bulletin issued by the Committee for the Defense of Human Rights, Tegucigalpa.

57. See Cynthia Arnson, "Background Information on El Salvador and U.S. Military Assistance to Central America," Institute for Policy Studies Update #6, March 1982; and Arnson, Update #7.

58. *Chicago Tribune*, September 22, 1983 and CBS News report, September 20, 1983.

59. Interview with the family of Father James Carney, Tegucigalpa, February 1984.

60. Interview with State Department official, Washington, D.C., June 1983.

61. See White, *Counterinsurgency War*, p. 122.

62. *U.S. News and World Report*, August 22, 1983. For a comprehensive analysis of the October offensive see Centro Universitario de Documentación e Información, "La Situación Militar: Balance y Perspectiva un Año Despues de las Elecciónes" (San Salvador: Universidad Centroamericana José Simeon Cañas, June 1983).

63. *Washington Post*, March 6, 1983.

64. *Miami Herald*, April 17, 1983.

65. *Washington Post*, July 2 and July 31, 1983.

66. *Washington Post*, September 29, 1983.

67. *New York Times*, July 15, 1983.
68. *Washington Post*, June 12, 1983.
69. Ibid.
70. *New York Times*, July 17, 1983.
71. *Washington Post*, January 3, 1984. In a shift from his earlier tendency to view U.S. security interests in Europe as overriding, Defense Secretary Casper Weinberger began to stress Central America's strategic importance. He noted that El Salvador is on the "mainland of the United States," and defending the mainland "ranks over and above all other priorities." *Washington Post*, June 15, 1983.
72. *Washington Post*, June 12, 1983.
73. *New York Times*, July 17, 1983.
74. The Defense Department submitted a request for $8.5 million to build ammunition storage facilities in its fiscal 1985 budget. According to congressional sources, the request for funds for the naval base was drawn up in late 1983 for inclusion in the fiscal 1985 budget, but later withdrawn by the secretary of defense's office due to fears that it would provoke a political storm in Congress.
75. *Miami Herald*, August 7, 1983.
76. *Miami Herald*, April 17, 1983.
77. *Washington Post*, September 29, 1983.
78. *Washington Post*, October 16, 1983 and *New York Times*, October 6, 1983.
79. *Miami Herald*, March 8, 1983.
80. *New York Times*, February 27, 1984.
81. *San Francisco Examiner*, June 1, 1983,
82. *New York Times*, May 24, 1983; *Los Angeles Times*, March 12, 1984.
83. *New York Times*, April 12, 1984.
84. On the U.S. role in the National Plan see *New York Times*, July 24, 1983; *Washington Post*, July 29, 1983; and *Newsweek*, March 21, 1983.
85. Interviews conducted in El Salvador, October 1983. See also *Washington Post*, February 2, 1984 and *New York Times*, August 4, 1983.
86. *New York Times*, September 6, 1983.
87. *San Francisco Examiner*, December 7, 1983.
88. *Washington Post*, March 28, 1984.
89. *New York Times*, September 19, 1983; and *Newsweek*, December 12, 1983.
90. *Los Angeles Times*, January 19, 1984.
91. *New York Times*, January 20, 1984.
92. Interview with Chris Hedges, El Salvador, February 1984. On forced recruitment see *New York Times*, January 27, 1984.
93. See *New York Times*, January 31, 1984. University researchers in San Salvador estimate that 30 percent of U.S. food aid supplied to the army winds up in the hands of the guerrillas.
94. *New York Times*, March 3, 1984.
95. *New York Times*, April 28, 1983.

4. Dollars for Dictators: U.S. Aid in Central America and the Caribbean

David Landes with Patricia Flynn

What we want is a long-range policy . . . the kind of development that will make these countries economically self-sufficient [and] give them a standard of living in which there isn't the fertile soil that is presently there for subversion.
—President Ronald Reagan, July 26, 1983

In a pattern reminiscent of the early days of the war in Southeast Asia U.S. economic assistance to Central America began to skyrocket in the early 1980s when revolution threatened to spread through the region like brushfire. Despite the controversy which raged over U.S. military aid to Central America, few voices rose to challenge the Reagan administration's frequent assertions that U.S. economic assistance was intended to alleviate social and economic inequality. With virtually no protest from Congress, U.S. economic assistance to the region increased almost eightfold between 1979 and 1983. As U.S. policy in the region met increasing criticism for its militaristic cast, Reagan administration officials countered that economic aid outweighed military by a three-to-one ratio. This, they claimed, was evidence of the U.S. commitment to peaceful rather than military solutions to the Central American crisis.

A critical examination of U.S. aid policies in the region, however, reveals another reality. Far from being an alternative to intervention, economic assistance, like military aid, is an integral part of U.S.-sponsored counter-revolution.

As during earlier political crises in Central America, the United States has used economic aid as a key instrument for promoting its foreign policy goals in the region. After the Sandinista revolution, U.S. aid dollars poured into the countries Washington views as strategic allies in its crusade against communism. Almost $2 billion in bilateral and multilateral economic aid went to El Salvador between 1979 and 1984 as part of a broader effort to bolster the government's counterinsurgency campaign and stave off economic collapse. Large increases in economic assistance to Costa Rica and Honduras were intended to stabilize the only two anticommunist governments in the region not threatened by revolutionary movements. At the same time the U.S. government halted economic assistance to Nicaragua, part of a plan to destabilize the only Central American country which has given priority to redressing social and economic inequalities.

Even Washington's plans for massive development assistance programs, the Caribbean Basin Initiative and the Kissinger Commission blueprint, were conceived as a strategy to contain revolution by removing its social and economic causes. But based as they were on the faulty notion that economic development based on private investment was a cure-all for the region's problems, these plans were bound to fail. Like similar efforts in the past, development schemes that avoided structural reforms would only aggravate the social inequalities that fueled revolution.

As this look at U.S. aid policies in the region over the past thirty years will show, U.S. economic assistance policies have successfully promoted U.S. economic interests and bolstered U.S. client regimes. But far from being a solution to the region's crisis, U.S. aid policies are part of the problem.

Guatemala: Showcase of Counter-Revolution

It was no coincidence that the pioneer U.S. economic assistance program in Central America came on the heels of what the U.S. government considered at the time to be the most serious challenge to its interests in Central America in decades. The year was 1954 and the country was Guatemala. The government of Jacobo Arbenz, a populist and staunch nationalist, had begun implementing a program that looked radical in the conservative context of the rest of Central America at the time. While Arbenz was a far cry from the procorporate, subservient leaders the United States had come to rely upon in Central America, his program was certainly not revolutionary. In fact, his goal was to modernize the Guatemalan economy along capitalist lines, particularly in the rural sector where land use was notoriously inefficient. The Arbenz government's controversial agrarian reform ordered the confiscation of unused agricultural lands, including those of the country's largest landowner, the U.S.-owned United Fruit Company.[1]

The U.S. government and its corporate backers quickly got up in arms. The staunchly procorporate Eisenhower administration labeled Arbenz a "puppet manipulated by the communists" (in a Cold War attack to be echoed nearly thirty years later by the Reagan administration). The Arbenz government was brought down by a conservative coup—planned, organized, and financed by the CIA. The United States then helped install the repressive military dictatorship of Colonel Castillo Armas which dutifully began to dismantle the Arbenz reforms. The counter-revolution was underway—financed and to a large extent shaped by the U.S. aid program.

What's Good for Business

The immediate goal of the Eisenhower administration was overtly political: to prop up its new client regime and prevent the collapse of the economy in the post-coup atmosphere of turmoil and uncertainty. Relative to the modest U.S. assistance program in place at the time ($60 million for all of Latin America), the effort in Guatemala was gigantic. The U.S. aid mission in Guatemala City increased from a staff of 10 in 1954 to 165 in 1959. And during that period an estimated $90 million was channeled to the military government.[2]

Beyond simply guaranteeing the survival of the United States' new client regime, U.S. economic assistance played a central role in helping to reverse the reforms of the Arbenz era. A major aim was to promote private business and to end nationalistic restrictions on foreign investors, particularly U.S. corporations. To guarantee these aims, a triad of U.S.-dominated institutions was put in charge of formulating an economic program for the Castillo Armas government. The U.S. International Cooperation Administration (the government agency in charge of U.S. aid programs at the time) worked together with the World Bank and Klein-Saks (a New York consulting firm company specializing in "private enterprise prescriptions for sick national economies") to set priorities. Key features were reversal of the agrarian reform, severe limits on trade unions and peasant organizations, and most important, special incentives and guarantees for foreign investors.

Once the government established its open-door policy toward foreign capital, the International Cooperation Administration paved the way for the entry of U.S. corporations. Besides contributing to a "stable investment climate," U.S. aid projects (often carried out in tandem with the international development banks) helped create the economic infrastructure such as ports, roads, and utilities necessary for the profitable operation of investors. Many of these construction projects were carried out by U.S. firms who operated under lucrative contracts with the U.S. government.

In a pattern that was to repeat itself time and again in the rest of Central America, the United States used its influence with other international lending agencies to ensure that their programs conformed to U.S. priorities rather than the development needs of the Guatemalan people. The World Bank, for example, was pressured to grant an $18 million loan for a highway whose main purpose was to open the remote Atlantic coast to development by private investors. Most rural

Guatemalans, meanwhile, continued to live in isolated communities where roads were few and far between.

Responding to the favorable climate provided by the new government, foreign investment began to pick up pace. But this was only a prelude to things to come.

The Trickle-Down Formula

U.S. policymakers hoped that Guatemala would become a showcase of capitalism in Latin America, a proven alternative to revolutionary change. But this entailed more than satisfying the interests of investors. Washington recognized that gross economic inequality had provided the impetus for Arbenz' populist reforms in the first place, and the same pressures threatened to produce radical solutions in other countries. If the Guatemalan model was to be successful in forestalling another Arbenz, this problem would have to be addressed. As one U.S. diplomat put it at the time, "The foreign policy of the United States is . . . on trial in Guatemala. Every nation in Latin America is watching to see how far the United States intends to go helping Guatemala—the first nation ever to return from Communism—in solving the acute economic and social problems it now faces."[3]

Washington's answer to reducing poverty while reinforcing capitalist business was known as the the "trickle-down theory." Its basic assumption was that the benefits of "development" fueled by private investment would "trickle down" automatically to the poor majority by creating new jobs and increasing incomes—thus removing the causes of revolution. Implicit was the notion that the aspirations of the poor could thereby be satisfied without basic structural changes.

First articulated by the probusiness ideologues of the Eisenhower administration, this recipe, with some variations and added ingredients, has been the prevailing formula for U.S. development efforts up to the present. It is, of course, the proverbial recipe for having one's cake and eating it too. Only it doesn't work: in Guatemala (and all of Central America), as Chinchilla and Hamilton document elsewhere in this volume, development fueled by private investment only made the poor worse off. The goal of satisfying the aspirations of the masses time and again fell by the wayside, and with it the hope for stabilizing the region for U.S. interests. The most dramatic example of this failure was the Alliance for Progress.

The Alliance for Progress

The advent of the Cuban revolution in 1959 spurred the United States to launch a massive economic assistance program throughout Central and South America. Recognizing the urgent need for action to head off the threat of revolution throughout the region, the Kennedy administration inaugurated the Alliance for Progress, to be implemented by the newly created Agency for International Development (AID). The alliance was introduced with a flourish of rhetoric about economic reforms and social programs to raise the standard of living of the poor. But the reforms were soon abandoned when local elites refused to go along. Instead of benefiting the poor, the tens of millions of U.S. aid dollars sent to Central America only further strengthened private enterprise capitalism.

From the beginning, the Alliance was closely linked to what President Kennedy called "our increased efforts to encourage the investment of private capital in the underdeveloped countries."[4] The program became the main vehicle for promoting the Central American Common Market (CACM). Contrary to early hopes that this regional industrialization scheme would strengthen local industries, the CACM was a boon for U.S. corporations which wanted to make Central America a target of their postwar investment drive abroad.[5] U.S. AID provided financing to key CACM institutions (such as the Permanent Secretariat and the Central American Bank for Economic Integration). It also gave the United States considerable leverage in setting economic priorities throughout the region. As investments poured into the country, Guatemala became the success story of the CACM and the long-awaited showcase of capitalism in the region. But it was a tarnished showcase, a reality which soon led to new problems for the United States.

U.S. Aid for Counterinsurgency

Given that the Alliance and its successor programs were conceived as part of a broader stategy of counter-revolution in the region, it is hardly surprising that economic aid went hand in hand with large doses of military aid designed to help local militaries quell popular unrest. In Guatemala, AID not only provided economic support to the military-dominated governments that carried on the tradition of the counter-revolution in the 1960s, but also took an active role in counterinsurgency activities.

The counterinsurgency campaign which got off the ground in 1966 under U.S. tutelage was a combined civilian and military effort similar in many ways to the "pacification" program being carried out in Vietnam at the same time. While the U.S. military supported the bloody military campaign against guerrilla insurgents and their peasant supporters in eastern Guatemala, AID was in charge of the civilian action component of the Guatemala pacification program.

Civic action programs—high visibility projects such as schools, health centers, roads, electrical projects—were a central element in the theories developed by U.S. counterinsurgency experts in the early 1960s on how to defeat rural insurgencies. The idea was first to separate the guerrillas from their peasant supporters by a massive military offensive, then to target the peasants with civic action programs designed "to win hearts and minds" away from the guerrillas. Although the development programs were presented in the most humanitarian of lights, there was never any doubt that they were integral to the counterinsurgency campaign. As the U.S. military adviser to the Guatemala civic action program stated at the time: "Civic action is a military weapon in counterinsurgency. I wish I could say that our main concern is in improving nutrition or in getting a better water system to the people. These are only by-products. The security of the country is our mission."[6]

AID started its "pilot" civic action program in Zacapa and Isabel, areas where the guerrillas were most active. Hot school lunches, new wells and access roads, and technical assistance to peasants were only some of the projects funded by AID as the army hunted down guerrillas in the area. Many of the personnel brought in by AID to run this and subsequent civic action programs had previous experience in Vietnam.[7] Further underscoring the close tie-in with the counterinsurgency campaign, the AID-proposed civic action program in Guatemala (as in other countries) was run by a U.S. "country team" which included representatives not only of AID but also of the CIA, the Department of Defense, and the U.S. Information Service. As we will see, a similar model was used almost twenty years later in the counterinsurgency campaign in El Salvador.

After the rural-based guerrilla movement was effectively silenced, AID continued its involvement in counterinsurgency through its police training program, run by the agency's Office for Public Safety (OPS) since 1961. As urban guerrilla activity in Guatemala increased in the wake of the defeats in the countryside, the size of the OPS program in Guatemala doubled between 1964-66 and 1967-69. The Office of Public Safety reported that it had trained over 30,000 Guatemalan police personnel by 1970.[8]

Nicaragua: Rewarding Somoza

While direct involvement in counterinsurgency reached its high point in Guatemala, U.S. economic assistance to the Somoza regime in Nicaragua also reflected the counter-revolutionary thrust of U.S. aid policies. From 1968 to 1978 Nicaragua received more U.S. economic aid dollars per capita than any other country in Central America.[9] U.S. generosity was partly intended as a reward for the Somoza family's unswerving loyalty as a regional ally. The Somozas cooperated in virtually every military intervention carried out by the United States in the region over the years—allowing Nicaraguan territory to be used as a launching pad for the Bay of Pigs and for the CIA-backed overthrow of Arbenz, and sending Nicaraguan troops to participate in the 1965 invasion of the Dominican Republic. Nicaragua also played a key role in the formation of CONDECA (the Central American Defense Council), a regional military alliance against "subversion" created at the behest of the United States.

The multi-million dollar investment AID made in Nicaragua, however, failed to provide internal stability for this crucial ally. In fact, the Somoza regime's blatant misuse of U.S. development assistance for the personal enrichment of the family and its close associates became a major destabilizing factor. As early as the 1950s the Somozas had used U.S. aid money to strengthen family-dominated financial institutions, which in turn became instruments to tighten their control over the economy.[10] As the Somoza dynasty's holdings grew to 30 percent of the agricultural land and some of the key industries, the family's economic rivals became political opponents. Somoza's blatant misuse of aid funds to augment his family fortune in the wake of the 1972 earthquake was the last straw for many businesspeople, who began to join the popular opposition to the dictatorship.

Not surprisingly the U.S.-backed development schemes sponsored by the Somoza government had done little to address the plight of the country's rural poor—the majority of the population, who became the main supporters of the Sandinista National Liberation Front. Instead of carrying out land reforms as part of the government's rural development programs, Somoza was expanding his own landholdings at the expense of poor peasants. Not surprisingly, support for the Sandinistas grew.

When it became apparent that the FSLN presented more than a passing threat, the United States responded by increasing its economic assistance to Somoza. In 1974 and 1975 Nicaragua received more U.S. aid than any other country in Latin America. Nicaragua became a dramatic illustration of a central dilemma in U.S. aid policy: channeling money to a narrowly based repressive government that disregarded the welfare of its people but safeguarded U.S. interests was ultimately counterproductive to U.S. purposes.

The growing threat from the FSLN in Nicaragua led AID into closer involvement with counterinsurgency. In one of its many efforts to openly support Somoza's attempt to defeat the insurgents, AID began funding a project called INVIERNO, the Institute for Peasant Welfare. Similar in intent to the civic action programs in Guatemala, IN-VIERNO's main purpose was to channel government resources to poor peasants in the coffee-producing regions where popular sympathy for the FSLN was high. It also provided a cover for a government intelligence network designed to cripple the FSLN. Through the institute informers were recruited to provide information about peasant collaboration with the Sandinistas. Together with a system of ID cards this information enabled government agents to compile an elaborate file system of people suspected of sympathy with the Sandinistas. The task of dealing with suspected collaborators fell to the dreaded National Guard, which was responsible for the death and disappearances of thousands during the years leading up to the revolution.

AID's New Look . . . and More of the Same

Apart from its tie-in with the antiguerrilla campaign, INVIERNO was one of the many rural development projects in Central America inspired by the "new directions" in U.S. aid programs during the 1970s. A host of catch words were used by AID bureaucrats to describe this new thrust. In political and social terms they talked about reaching the "poorest of the poor" (read: small peasants). This reflected a growing awareness among some development theorists that the majority of the population had not benefited from the development schemes promoted under the Central American Common Market. In economic terms they talked about "export-led development" and promotion of "nontraditional industries," such as tourism, new agricultural exports, and light assembly industries. These schemes were presented as solutions to worsening balance-of-payments deficits and severe unemployment. Although different from the development model promoted in the 1960s, this scheme contained the same fatal flaw: it stressed the central role of the "private sector" and side-stepped the need for structural reforms.

Not coincidentally, this "new direction" in aid also reflected the changing interests of U.S. investors who were seeking new opportunities for investment in the wake of the common market collapse. Agribusiness investment was viewed as one of the most promising areas of investment in Central America and became a priority for U.S. aid in the region.

One of AID's pet agricultural projects was the Latin American Agribusiness Development Corporation (LAAD), a Miami-based private finance corporation owned by fifteen large U.S. agribusiness and financial corporations. LAAD specializes in providing seed capital to private companies, such as food processors, involved in exporting nontraditional agricultural products. AID officials claimed that LAAD was a model for development: it offered markets and jobs to small farmers while promoting private investment. However, several AID-commissioned studies on the socioeconomic impact of one LAAD-funded enterprise in the Guatemalan highlands, ALCOSA, revealed that the project was "an unmitigated economic disaster" for many of the farmers involved.[11]

ALCOSA was described in LAAD's annual report as "a Guatemalan frozen food company" which supplies U.S. supermarkets with broccoli, cauliflower, and okra grown by Indian communities. In fact, ALCOSA was an affiliate of the U.S. food multinational Hanover Brands. As the AID study details, initially the company production contracts were with the more advantaged farmers—those who were "opportunistically entrepreneurial" and had sufficient financial resources to shift to the new crops. The sudden boom in the local economy touched off a speculative land market in which the smaller farmers lost their lands to those with more capital, becoming seasonal laborers. The net result of the ALCOSA operation was, as the study put it, "an increase in economic inequality."

Continuing to act like a good capitalist enterprise, ALCOSA began to turn increasingly for its vegetable supplies to smaller farmers who would settle for a lower price for their crops. But the results were no better for the small farmers, who became dependent on the company for their livelihood. In one community studied, the farmers developed a "bitter resentment" when they realized that the company manipulated quality control standards to cheat them of income. They were also being driven into debt by the high cost of fertilizers and other inputs required by company representatives. The worst blow came when AL-COSA suspended purchase of their crops at the peak of the harvest season and then decided to close its buying station there because of overproduction. The situation of the small farmers became desperate. They complained that "ALCOSA had urged them to grow cauliflower instead of corn and now there is nothing to eat. Their children had been forced to quit school and leave home to work as farm laborers or domestic servants."[12] The LAAD project was only one example of the results of the "new directions" touted by AID. Once again, U.S.-promoted development schemes failed to alleviate the plight of the poor majority. The unemployment problem in Central America was only aggravated, landlessness and poverty increased, and social unrest was on the rise (see Chapter 7).

Crisis Management

As the political, social, and economic crisis in the region exploded into the revolutionary upsurge of the late 1970s and 1980s, U.S. aid programs came to play an increasingly prominent role in the U.S. regional counter-revolutionary strategy. The resources of every foreign aid program administered by the U.S. government— ranging from AID development loans to "food for peace" to military aid and security assistance— were marshaled in the effort to bolster those Central American governments who stood for the status quo. The crisis orientation of the aid program was reflected in the declining importance of "development" assistance relative to "security assistance" in the form of the Economic Support Fund (ESF). From 1980 to 1982, ESF spending in Central America increased twenty-sevenfold, and by 1982 accounted for over two-thirds of all bilateral economic aid to the region (see Table 4.1). Widely recognized as the most political of U.S. aid programs (it is administered directly by the State Department rather than AID), ESF provides grants of foreign exchange to be spent by recipient governments without any strings attached.

Table 4.1
Total Bilateral Economic Aid, Central America
Fiscal Years 1978-84
($ millions)

	1978	1979	1980	1981	1982	1983	1984*
Development/AID	44.9	64.4	128.7	81.4	92.8	132.8	155.8
Economic Support Fund (ESF)	0.0	8.0	10.2	101.5	181.9	360.0	452.0
Food Aid: PL 480	7.8	20.0	32.8	54.1	69.6	93.1	102.1
Total	52.7	92.4	171.7	237.0	344.3	585.9	709.9

Distribution of U.S. Bilateral Economic Aid
(Percentage)

	1978	1979	1980	1981	1982	1983	1984*
Development/AID	85.2	69.7	74.9	34.3	27.0	22.7	21.9
Economic Support Fund/ESF	0.0	8.7	5.9	42.9	52.8	61.4	63.7
Food Aid: PL 480	14.8	21.6	19.2	22.8	20.2	15.9	14.4
Total	100.0	100.0	100.0	100.0	100.0	100.0	100.0

Source: Calculated from AID, *Congressional Presentation FY85, Annex III* (February 15, 1984); and Washington Office on Latin America.

*Estimate only; includes proposed supplemental aid.

The mushrooming U.S. economic commitment to El Salvador's military-dominated regime was key to U.S. efforts to prevent a guerrilla victory. The large amounts of aid poured into Costa Rica and Honduras (which by 1983 had become the second and third largest recipients of U.S. aid in the hemisphere) reflected Washington's determination to bolster these two U.S. allies as bulwarks against the revolutionary turmoil gripping the rest of the region (see Table 4.2).

Table 4.2
U.S. Bilateral Economic Aid: Central America
Fiscal years 1978-84
($ millions)

	1978	1979	1980	1981	1982	1983	1984*
Costa Rica							
Development/AID	6.9	16.4	13.6	11.5	11.5	27.2	23.1
Economic Support							
Fund (ESF)	—	—	—	—	20.0	157.0	130.0
Food Aid: PL 480	0.8	—	0.4	1.8	19.0	28.0	27.0
Total	7.7	16.4	14.0	13.3	50.5	212.2	180.1
El Salvador							
Development/AID	8.0	6.9	43.2	33.3	39.5	58.0	71.3
Economic Support							
Fund (ESF)	—	—	9.1	44.9	115.0	140.0	210.0
Food Aid: PL 480	—	2.9	5.5	35.3	34.9	46.7	51.5
Total	8.0	9.8	57.8	113.6	189.4	244.7	332.8
Guatemala							
Development/AID	4.5	17.4	7.8	9.1	8.2	12.5	21.6
Economic Support							
Fund (ESF)	—	—	—	—	10.1	10.0	0.0
Food Aid: PL 480	4.6	5.3	3.7	7.6	5.6	4.4	7.0
Total	9.1	22.7	11.5	16.7	23.9	26.9	28.6
Honduras							
Development/AID	13.0	22.0	45.8	25.7	31.2	35.1	39.8
Economic Support							
Fund (ESF)	—	—	—	—	36.8	53.0	112.0
Food Aid: PL 480	2.4	4.8	5.2	8.2	10.1	14.0	16.6
Total	15.4	26.8	51.0	33.9	78.1	102.1	168.4
Nicaragua							
Development/AID	12.5	1.7	18.3	1.8	0.0	0.0	0.0
Economic Support							
Fund (ESF)	—	8.0	1.1	56.6	0.0	0.0	0.0
Food Aid: PL 480	—	7.0	18.0	1.2	0.0	0.0	0.0
Total	12.5	16.7	37.4	59.6	0.0	0.0	0.0

Sources: AID, Congressional Presentation FY85, Annex III, (February 15, 1984), and Washington Office on Latin America, May 1982 and January 1984.

*Estimate only; includes proposed supplemental aid.

After a several-year hiatus in security assistance to Guatemala (re-sulting from the Carter administation's brief attempt to apply human rights criteria), economic problems, coupled with the threat from a re-surgent guerrilla movement there, spurred the Reagan administration to once again request substantial funding for the government. Guatemala subsequently received $10 million in ESF grants in 1982, and later that year the administration formally removed Guatemala from the State Department's list of "gross human rights violators," en-abling the United States to support multilateral bank loans to Guatemala. However, a new surge of government violence in late 1983 (including the murders of two linguists working for AID) undermined congressional support for State Department plans to substantially in-crease assistance to Guatemala in 1984.

The new Sandinista government in Nicaragua— which stood clearly against the system of elite privilege and subservience to U.S. business interests that typified the Somoza regime—was the exception in Cen-tral America. In the wake of Somoza's overthrow, the Sandinista gov-ernment became the target of a slowly building effort to topple the revo-lution. Aid became a principal element in that effort.

Subverting the Revolution

Although the end of the Somoza dictatorship met with mixed reac-tions in Washington, there was nearly universal concern about what course the Nicaraguan revolution would take. All sides of the estab-lished political spectrum agreed that it was imperative to prevent "another Cuba" in Nicaragua. And there was also wide agreement that U.S. economic aid would be a useful weapon in pursuing that objective. Nicaragua's dependence on U.S. aid (developed during the decades of Somoza rule), coupled with the desperate need of the war-torn economy for reconstruction funds, gave the United States considerable leverage. The only disagreement came on how this leverage should be used.

Immediately after the Sandinista victory an intense debate took place in Washington over this issue. The hard-liners, who started out in a weaker position within the Carter administration, pushed for a com-plete and immediate aid cut-off. They argued that the outcome of the Sandinista-led revolution was already decided: Nicaragua was irretrievably on the path already followed by Cuba and already represented a dangerous challenge to U.S. control in the region.

Others took a more pragmatic approach, advocating a large-scale aid program to maintain U.S. leverage and influence over the course of the revolution. The pragmatists also hoped that by steering aid to the private business sector the United States could bolster a more friendly and moderate political alternative to the Sandinistas and help prevent Nicaragua from moving into the socialist orbit.

The pragmatists temporarily won out when the Carter administration convinced Congress to pass a $75 million aid package for Nicaragua in its fiscal 1981 budget. A minimum of 60 percent of this amount was programmed to provide foreign exchange to private sector enterprises, a deliberate effort to slight the state-owned enterprises created when the Sandinistas confiscated all businesses owned by Somoza and his associates. As outspoken opponents of the egalitarian economic policies advocated by the Sandinistas and frowned upon by the U.S. government, the private sector was correctly viewed as a conservative brake on any radical change and the natural ally of U.S. interests. Indeed, by late 1980, private business organizations had become the spearhead of political opposition to the revolutionary government. The U.S. aid program became increasingly focused on support for these overtly anti-Sandinista groups.

The most important of these groups was the Higher Council of Private Enterprise (COSEP), an umbrella group of private sector business organizations, and the Nicaragua Development Foundation (FUNDE), a COSEP-affiliated cooperative association which the United States hoped would win support away from the rural cooperatives started by the revolutionary government. As Acting Assistant Secretary of State John Bushnell made clear in testimony before Congress in early 1981, continuing the U.S. aid program was part of a calculated attempt to influence Nicaragua's political future. "The private businessman, small farmers, free labor unions and many others who have held on for more than a year as a strong force against those who would establish a totalitarian state have earned our continued support," he said. He added that this support would continue "so long as the Marxist-led government accepts a pluralistic society and ends support from Nicaragua for the guerrillas in El Salvador and other countries."[13]

Destabilizing the Sandinistas

Bushnell's statement reflected the growing fear within U.S. ruling circles that the Nicaraguan revolution would have an impact beyond its own borders. The immediate concern was El Salvador, where the guerrillas were beginning to show remarkable strength. The threat of new revolutions, combined with the ideological predispositions of the incoming Reagan administration, pushed the U.S. government to move decisively against the Sandinistas. The Heritage Foundation, a rightwing think tank which supplied several of Reagan's key foreign policy advisers, had explicitly advocated a policy of destabilization against the Sandinista government in a pre-election report. This position was echoed in the Republican Party platform, which hinted at the ouster of the Sandinistas.[14]

In a campaign reminiscent of efforts to destabilize Salvador Allende's socialist government in Chile a decade earlier, the Reagan team began to apply U.S. economic muscle to strangle the Sandinistas.[15] As in Chile, the objective was to provoke an economic crisis that would fuel political opposition to the Sandinistas. The first move came in April 1981, when the administration cut off all bilateral government-to-government aid to Nicaragua, continuing a small program to bolster the increasingly militant conservatism of the private sector. The pretext used was Nicaraguan support for the Salvadoran guerrillas, although the administration failed then or at any later point to provide evidence of any such support. At the same time, a freeze was placed on all credits for subsidized food imports under Public Law 480 (known as the "Food for Peace Program").

As intended, the food aid cut-off exacted a severe toll on the Nicaraguan economy. Although the Sandinista government had launched a program to make the country self-sufficient in basic foodstuffs, the legacy of the Somoza era (when most of the country's richest farmlands produced for the more profitable export market) still weighed heavily. Despite increased agricultural productivity, the country still depended heavily on subsidized food imports, as it had under Somoza. Shortages of wheat-based products immediately followed the PL-480 cut-off.

In another step calculated to further squeeze the Nicaraguan economy, the Reagan administration also stopped Export-Import Bank trade financing and Overseas Private Investment Corporation (OPIC) investment guarantees that ensure investments by U.S. firms from nationalization. Without such backing, U.S. companies rarely undertake business ventures in the third world. As intended, these moves sent out a strong signal to U.S. companies that investments in Nicaragua would be a dangerous and risky business. The Sandinista government, though determined to strictly regulate foreign investment on terms beneficial to Nicaragua, was thus thwarted in its plans to attract badly needed foreign capital to participate in the new mixed economy. The administration's actions effectively cut off the flow of U.S. capital to the country.

The Multilateral Squeeze

More seriously, the Reagan administration has also used its muscle in the multilateral banks to block loans and credits to Nicaragua, another replay of the Chilean destabilization policy. According to a report in the *Wall Street Journal*, the administration had placed Nicaragua on a "hit list" of five leftist countries to which the United States would attempt to block loans from multilateral banks.[16] This policy has been most successful in the case of the Inter-American Development Bank (IDB) Fund for Special Operations, which grants long-term loans at well below market interest rates. The United States controls 35 percent of this fund's votes, giving it effective veto power since a loan from this fund requires a two-thirds majority.

In November 1981 the United States collaborated with its Southern Cone allies, Argentina and Chile, to force Nicaragua to withdraw its request for a $30 million loan from another IDB fund in which the United States does not itself have veto power. This loan would have rebuilt the country's fisheries industry, crippled when Somoza's business associates absconded with the fishing fleet after the revolution. A Treasury Department official stated at the time that "we had an overall political problem with the direction" of the Nicaraguan government.[17]

Even in the IDB, however, the United States has not always prevailed. In the fall of 1982 the IDB approved a $34 million loan to Nicaragua for a hydroelectric project despite the opposition of the United States. Argentina and Chile backed Nicaragua in this vote, doubtless part of the anti-U.S. backlash following the war between Argentina and Britain over the Malvinas/Falklands. And in September 1983 the fisheries loan was finally approved over the isolated opposition of the United States, when member countries refused to apply political criteria to an economically sound project.

Washington has also attempted to enlist the World Bank in its destabilization strategy, again with mixed results. In early 1982 Secretary of State Haig personally ordered the U.S. representative to the World Bank to vote against a loan to finance urban sewers and low-income neighborhood improvements in Nicaragua. With only 21 percent of the votes and objections from Mexico and some European donors that it was politicizing Bank lending, the United States was unable to prevail. The loan was approved.

Continuing its pressure, the United States began to bend the Bank's bureaucracy to U.S. policy. Although the United States had been arguing with the Bank that Nicaragua was following "unsound" economic policy, the World Bank staff apparently disagreed. An October 1981 staff report had earlier endorsed Nicaragua's economic reforms and described government policy there as "encouraging." With foreign aid and good management, said the report, "Nicaragua will indeed be able to reconstruct its economy as well as continue to enhance the social situation of its citizens."[18] However, by February of 1982, U.S. insistence that the Bank take a stand against Nicaragua began to have some effect within the Bank's higher management. A confidential internal memo recommended that the Bank put a squeeze on funds to Nicaragua until it made significant concessions to the private sector. The memo urged that additional aid be linked to Nicaragua's willingness to "follow our policy advice."[19] As a result, the Bank significantly cut back loans to Nicaragua.

Economic Warfare

Growing pressure on the Sandinista government to change its internal policies also came from other sources. In addition to the well-publicized CIA "covert war" against the Sandinistas which picked up steam in 1983, the United States opened yet another frontier in its economic war to unseat the government. In spring 1983 the Commerce Department announced a drastic reduction in Nicaragua's sugar export quota to the United States, an important form of indirect U.S. economic assistance to producing nations. Soon after, in June, the United States vetoed the final disbursement of a 1976 IDB loan to build roads serving a region of small coffee farms, citing Nicaragua's "inappropriate macroeconomic policies." Reagan officials stated that a resumption of aid would come at a high price. Specifically, they demanded that Managua end price subsidies and "revitalize the private sector"— changes that would have entailed a reversal of Managua's commitment to redistributive economic policies and a strong state sector.[20]

The economic blockade partially served its purpose. By 1983, the Nicaraguan economy was beginning to feel the pinch of reduced foreign exchange. Junta Coordinator Daniel Ortega estimated that U.S.-imposed economic sanctions ranging from the aid cut-off to the deep cut in the sugar quota had deprived the country of over $350 million in 1983.[21] Although the poor were eating better than before the revolution, the shortages and rationing further alienated the middle class and increased its political opposition to the government. The Sandinista leadership refused to buckle under U.S. pressure. With Nicaragua under attack not just economically but also militarily, the dominant popular mood in the country was defiance of U.S. attempts to intervene in spite of the hardship that entailed.

The Salvadoran Rescue Operation

The U.S. aid program in El Salvador has been the mirror image of that in Nicaragua. As aid to Nicaragua ground to a halt, U.S. assistance to El Salvador rose to an all-time high (making it the third largest country program worldwide, after Israel and Egypt). After the Farabundo Martí National Liberation Movement (FMLN) launched its first major military offensive against the government in 1980, it became clear that the embattled regime in San Salvador could not survive without massive U.S. assistance. Every aid program at the disposal of the United States was employed in the rescue operation. Even the most innocuous and apparently "humanitarian" assistance became part of the U.S.-sponsored counterinsurgency strategy.

Preventing the government's economic collapse was the first objective. The chaos and uncertainty caused by the civil war, combined with the already tenuous economic situation in the region, threw the Salvadoran economy into a state of crisis. Economic growth ground to a virtual halt as foreign investments "all but dried up" (according to the prestigious *Business Latin America*), and an estimated $1 billion in private capital fled to Miami and other safer havens in a space of three years. As exports dropped precipitously (from $1.2 billion in 1979 to $350 million in 1982), the country also faced a severe balance-of-payments crisis. One result was a 30 percent inflation rate and an estimated 50 percent unemployment rate in 1982, both of which took their political toll on the government.[22]

To confront this emergency, the United States began pumping large amounts of direct foreign exchange support into El Salvador in the form of Economic Support Funds. (Efforts were also made, as we will see, to marshal the resources of the international development banks for this purpose.) Total ESF grants jumped from $9 million in 1980, the first year of the program, to $45 million in 1981 and again to $140 million the following year (see Table 4.3). El Salvador's private sector, badly in need of foreign exchange to purchase raw materials and equipment to keep their businesses running profitably, were the major beneficiaries of the ESF program. Even the U.S. "development" assistance programs were designed to benefit the private sector. According to one analysis of the 1982 aid program, only 20 percent of total aid reached the poor people of El Salvador.[23] The ESF grants also took on a growing importance in underwriting the military side of the counterinsurgency campaign as the U.S. Congress became increasingly reluctant to provide the levels of military aid requested by the White House. While every form of economic assistance has supported the war effort by making more resources available for military purposes, this is particularly the case with ESF grants, which can be spent by the recipient government without any restrictions. As the *Congressional Quarterly* notes, the program's "primary purpose is to enable hard-pressed allies to increase their military spending."[24]

Aid to Counterinsurgency

AID's most direct involvement in the counterinsurgency war came with the U.S.-designed "pacification" program launched in mid-1983. Like the antiguerrilla campaign carried out earlier in Guatemala, the plan called for a military sweep to be followed by civic action programs designed to win the "hearts and minds" of the local population. Operation Well-Being, as the civic action phase was called, was also compared by U.S. officials to a similar program carried out in Vietnam, the Civil Operations and Revolutionary Development Support (or

CORDS, which spawned the infamous Phoenix program for assassinating Viet Cong cadres). As in Vietnam, AID provided most of the financing.

Table 4.3
Economic Assistance to El Salvador
Fiscal Years 1979-84
($ millions)

	1979	1980	1981	1982	1983	1984*
Bilateral Economic						
AID/Development	6.9	43.2	33.4	39.5	58.1	71.3
Peace Corps	1.6	0.5	—	—	0.0	0.0
Food Aid: PL 480	2.9	5.5	35.3	34.9	46.7	51.5
Economic Support Fund (ESF)	—	9.1	44.9	115.0	140.0	210.0
Total	11.4	58.3	113.6	189.4	244.8	332.8
Bilateral Financial Assistance						
Commodities Credit Corp. (CCC)	—	4.0	30.0	19.5	22.7	26.5
Export Import Bank	6.4	0.8	—	—	n.a.	n.a.
Housing Investment Guarantee	—	9.5	5.5	15.0	5.0	0.0
Overseas Priv. Invest. Corp. (OPIC)	8.5	—	—	—	n.a.	n.a.
Total	14.9	14.3	35.5	34.5	27.7	26.5
Multilateral Assistance						
World Bank	23.5	—	—	—	0.0	
Inter-American Dev. Bank	29.5	48.5	45.8	112.4	52.9	
International Monetary Fund	—	57.0	36.4	84.7	50.0	
Total	53.0	105.5	81.8	197.1	102.9	
Total Bilateral and Multilateral	79.3	178.1	231.3	421.0	375.4	329

Sources: Jim Morrell and John Eisenrath, "Arming El Salvador," Center for International Policy, (August 1982); Jim Morrell and Jesse Biddle, "Central America: The Financial War," Center for International Policy (March 1983); AID, Congressional Presentation FY85, Annex III (February 15, 1984); and AID, "U.S. Assistance to Central America FY 1978-1983" (mimeo), February 17, 1984.

*Includes proposed supplemental aid.

The director of the National Committee for the Restoration of Areas (CONARA), the Salvadoran government agency set up to run the civilian side of the program, candidly described its goals: "first, to give the Salvadoran government credibility with the population, and secondly, to give the Salvadoran government credibility with the U.S. Congress."[25] Funded primarily by AID, CONARA's efforts were focused mainly in San Vicente and Usulutan, two strategic provinces where the military hoped to root out guerrilla influence. However, the estimated $4 million provided by AID during the first six months of the program brought few tangible results for the local population. An estimated thirty schools were reopened (some of them in makeshift classrooms), thirty miles of roads were rebuilt, and a small number of primitive health clinics funded. In fact, the civic action programs were stalled by the army's failure to clear the guerrillas out of the target areas (see Chapter 3). But CONARA continued with some of the less visible but highly political aspects of its program—giving "reeducation" seminars to local communities and training local leaders in what some called "far right" political views.[26]

Even more controversial was AID's funding of the National Committee to Assist the Displaced Population (CONADES), a government relief agency that works with internal refugees. Many private voluntary organizations, including the Catholic archbishop's office, refused to work with the agency on the grounds that it used relief programs, particularly food aid, as a weapon against the guerrillas. Allowed by CONADES to distribute U.S. food aid, the army was able to cut off food supplies when guerrillas were suspected to be nearby, or to withhold food in order to force refugees to comply with government wishes. CONADES also ran a controversial program for monitoring displaced persons—described by some as a way to keep tabs on suspected guerrilla sympathizers, but defended by AID as a census to help program planning.[27]

Equally important to the war effort was AID's program to finance the rebuilding of the country's economic infrastructure, hit hard by the FMLN's highly successful campaign of economic sabotage. As the guerrillas understood well, economic sabotage had both a military and political impact. The destruction of bridges and power generators undercut the army's ability to prosecute its brutal war, and at the same time demonstrated the waning ability of the government to provide the population with security and basic services. U.S. efforts to remedy this situation by providing funds for seemingly innocuous infrastructure projects were, in fact, crucial to the army's ability to carry out military campaigns and maintain communications. They were also an important part of the effort to restore the population's confidence in the government.

Avoiding Congressional Scrutiny

As Congress grew increasingly restive with the lack of progress in the Salvadoran government's war against the FMLN—in spite of the hundreds of millions of dollars the United States had poured in—the Reagan administration began to tap the resources of less visible economic assistance programs to channel support to its beleaguered ally. The various programs providing credits for food and agricultural imports from the United States were called into service (as they had been during the Vietnam war). Both the Public Law 480 food aid program and the Commodities Credit Corporation (CCC) credits were handy channels of support, since their budgets were rarely scrutinized by Congress on political grounds. The two programs together provided $54 million in additional direct support to the Salvadoran government in 1982. The size of the CCC program in El Salvador increased more than sevenfold (from $4 million to $30 million) between 1980 and 1981, while PL-480 Title I funding leaped from $3 million to $26 million the same year. Title I funds have a double usefulness (see Table 4.3). Not only does it free up foreign exchange that would have gone to import food, the commodities received under the program are sold by the government locally, providing it with additional fiscal support.

One of the major advantages of the CCC program is its exemption from prior congressional approval. The CCC is an independent government financial institution administered by the Department of Agriculture. Thus, unlike the economic assistance and food aid programs which must submit planned country allocations for congressional approval, the CCC is required to report its spending to Congress only after the fact. The same is true of the Housing Investment Guarantee Program, whose expenditures in El Salvador tripled from $5 million to $15 million between 1982 and 1983. This program, which finances housing construction carried out by private companies, not only provides foreign exchange but also helps win political support for the government among the beneficiaries.

The Multilaterals: Act Two

U.S. bilateral aid, however, fell far short of the resources needed to sustain the Salvadoran economy. To help make up the shortfall, the Carter and Reagan administrations used their political clout to orchestrate huge increases in multilateral assistance to El Salvador from the World Bank, the Inter-American Development Bank, and the International Monetary Fund (IMF). Aid from these institutions to El Salvador doubled from $53 million in 1979 to $105 million in 1980, and total commitments doubled again in fiscal 1983 (see Table 4.3).

To gain this additional funding for its Central American allies, the United States pressured the multilateral banks to violate their own regulations and charters. In the wake of intense U.S. lobbying and over the objections of most of the European delegates, the International Monetary Fund approved a $36 million loan to El Salvador in mid-1981 despite the opposition of the fund's technical staff. This marked the first time that the IMF had approved a loan without the required staff endorsement, leading the IMF executive director to declare the loan a "serious precedent."[28] The following summer, two more IMF loans to El Salvador, totaling $84 million, were approved. This move by the IMF was crucial since the fund's endorsement is often regarded by the other multilateral banks as a precondition of their support.

U.S. control of the largest voting bloc in the Inter-American Development Bank has allowed the Carter and Reagan administrations to harness the bank to support the Salvadoran government. In late 1980 the Carter administration secured a $45 million loan to support the agrarian reform program, a key Carter political objective to marshal support to the ruling junta. Subsequent loans even more directly complemented the escalation of the counterinsurgency effort. First was a $31 million loan in late 1981 for construction of rural roads in areas where there is guerrilla activity. The clear intention was to improve the army's access. The IDB also has under consideration a loan to rebuild the strategically important bridge over the Lempa River, destroyed by insurgents in 1981. These loans are but the latest in a long series of efforts by the United States to use the IDB as means to help fund U.S. foreign policy goals, in violation of the bank's commitment to "nonpolitical" development funding.

As for the World Bank, the United States has succeeded in reopening the Bank's coffers to El Salvador, in spite of complaints from other Bank members that the loans are politically motivated and thus violate the Bank's charter. The World Bank had cut off all funding after the October 1979 coup, citing the great difficulty in sustaining economic development efforts in the face of an escalating civil war. Under U.S. pressure the Bank lifted this ban in 1983, when it prepared to approve two loans totaling $70 million. The loans—one to build a geothermal plant in the war zone and the second to provide balance-of-payments relief—are clearly politically motivated, in violation of the Bank's charter which requires that loans be considered on technical grounds alone.

The CBI and the Kissinger Commission: Old Wine in New Bottles

As the Reagan administration's hopes for a quick and easy solution to the regional crisis vanished and its policies met with mounting criticism in Congress, the White House began to develop programs which included components purportedly designed to promote long-term development in the region. In early 1982 the Reagan administration unveiled what it trumpeted as a "bold, new departure" for the region— the Caribbean Basin Initiative (CBI), a tripartite package of aid, trade concessions, and investment promotion. The $350 million CBI aid program paled in comparison to the $8 billion subsequently proposed by Reagan's Bipartisan Commission on Central America, headed by Henry Kissinger, in January 1984.

In both cases, the Reagan team referred to a new "Marshall Plan" for Central America, designed to promote development and provide a peaceful solution to the crisis. The rhetoric of development and peace, however, masked the administration's real intent: to win public support and congressional approval for its counterinsurgency policy. In the case of the CBI, the cold war thrust of the program was clear. Both the Sandinista government and the Maurice Bishop regime in Grenada were exluded on the grounds that they were in the grip of the totalitarian left. As some members of Congress justifiably complained, the CBI was merely a smokescreen to channel more funds to the war in El Salvador. The administration originally planned to send one-third of the total aid package to El Salvador, though Congress subsequently scaled down that country's share to a still substantial $75 million. All CBI funds, moreover, were Economic Support Fund security assistance, not development monies.

After funding El Salvador's war economy, the next largest chunk of CBI funds went to Costa Rica and Honduras. This followed the pattern set in 1979 when Washington began to rely on these two countries as poles of pro-United States stability in the midst of revolutionary upheaval. Aid to Honduras was actually the highest in the region in 1978-80, and substantial ESF grants to both countries began in 1981 (see Table 4.2). Washington correctly viewed stepped-up U.S. support as essential to prevent economic collapse. Both Costa Rica and Honduras were plagued by declining foreign exchange earnings, massive foreign debts, and rising inflation.

But far from guaranteeing stability, the rescue operation came at a high social and economic cost. In Honduras, for example, U.S. aid was tied to acceptance of U.S. demands to reduce corporate taxes (at a time when the government was on the verge of bankruptcy) and to phase out incentives to already weak domestic industries. U.S. economic assistance to both countries was also tied to compliance with the harsh austerity measures demanded by the IMF, including drastic cutbacks in social services, public sector employment, wage freezes, and the end of price supports for many necessities. The resulting decline in wages and skyrocketing unemployment only fueled the social unrest the United States hoped to forestall. Costa Rica was especially hard hit, with 70 percent of the population falling below the poverty line by 1982, compared to 25 percent in 1977.[29] Even Costa Rica's president accused the IMF plan of "destabilizing" the country after a wave of strikes and worker unrest.[30]

Even more than the CBI, the Kissinger Commission report became a vehicle to win political backing for U.S. attempts to impose a military solution in Central America. While stressing U.S. security interests and endorsing massive increases in military aid, the report also paid lip service to the need to combat revolution by removing its causes—"historic poverty, social injustice, frustrated expectations." The proposed solution was reminiscent of the Alliance for Progress: a massive five year development program to be largely financed by an $8 billion contribution from the United States. The commission's economic and military proposals were warmly embraced by Reagan, who was also quick to point out that "you can't have social reform while you're having your head shot off by guerrilla forces."[31]

Once again, Washington was promoting a program of counterinsurgency draped in the rhetoric of development as a way to avoid a fundamental redistribution of wealth and power. Indeed, the development proposals contained in the CBI and hinted at by the Kissinger report offered the same illusory remedies to Central America's social and economic problems the United States had supported for thirty years. They amounted to nothing more than a replay of the discredited trickle-down formula. Even the "new" element—promoting nontraditional industries such as LAAD-type ventures—harkened back to the failures of the 1970s. What Reagan so fondly called the "magic of the marketplace" had already proven an economic disaster for Central America—undermining the living standards of the majority of the population and helping create the conditions for revolution.

Notes

1. For more details on the Arbenz reforms see Richard H. Immerman, *The CIA in Guatemala: The Foreign Policy of Intervention* (Austin: University of Texas Press, 1982), ch. 3.
2. Suzanne Jonas and David Tobis, eds., *Guatemala* (New York: NACLA, 1974), p. 76-77.
3. Ibid., p. 76.
4. Steve Weissman, *The Trojan Horse* (San Francisco: Ramparts Press, 1974), p. 83.
5. See Chapter 7 this volume.
6. Jonas and Tobis, eds., *Guatemala*, p. 198.
7. Ibid., pp. 196-99.
8. Ibid., p. 199.
9. Calculated from AID, *U.S. Overseas Loans and Grants and Assistance from International Organizations: July 1, 1945-September 30, 1982* (Washington, D.C.: AID, 1983).
10. "Nicaragua in Crisis," *NACLA Report on the Americas,* November-December 1978, pp. 6-8.
11. This section relies to a large extent on David Kinley, "A Case Study Questions the Value of Reagan's Caribbean Basin Initiative," *Multinational Monitor* (May 1982).
12. Ibid., p. 19.
13. Inter-American Subcommittee, House of Representatives, March 23, 1981, p. 68.
14. See Cleto DiGiovanni, "U.S. Policy and the Marxist Threat to Central America," *The Heritage Foundation Backgrounder,* October 15, 1980, pp. 3-5.
15. For documentation of the destabilization of Chile see U.S. Senate, Staff Report of the Selection Committee to Study Governmental Operations with

Respect to U.S. Intelligence, *Covert Action in Chile* (Washington, D.C.: GPO, December 18, 1975).

16. Jonathan Kwitny, "U.S. Charged with Bias in IMF Votes," *Wall Street Journal*, May 18, 1983, p. 39.

17. James Morrell and William Jesse Biddle, "Central America: The Financial War," Center for International Policy, March 1983, p. 7.

18. Center for International Policy, "Aid Memo," May 11, 1982, p. 6.

19. World Bank, "Country Program Paper: Nicaragua," February 16, 1982 (mimeo), p. 13.

20. "U.S. Will Oppose Loans to Nicaragua," *Washington Post*, July 1, 1983.

21. "U.S. Bans Make Nicaragua Suffer," *San Francisco Examiner*, August 4, 1983, p. A12.

22. "Business Outlook: El Salvador," *Business Latin America*, December 1, 1982, pp. 380-81.

23. John Eisendrath and James Morrell, "Arming El Salvador," *International Policy Report*, Center for International Policy, August 1982, p. 6.

24. *Congressional Quarterly*, January 15, 1983, p. 92.

25. *Christian Science Monitor*, January 11, 1984.

26. Ibid.

27. *Christian Science Monitor*, January 12, 1984.

28. Morrell and Biddle, "Central America," p. 2.

29. *Asian Wall Street Journal*, December 7, 1983.

30. *Barricada*, International Edition: Managua, January 9, 1984, p. 11.

31. *San Francisco Examiner*, January 15, 1984.

5. Agrarian Reform as Revolution and Counter-Revolution: Nicaragua and El Salvador

Carmen Diana Deere

There is no one more conservative than a small farmer. [With agrarian reform], we're going to be breeding capitalists like rabbits.

—U.S. embassy official, El Salvador, 1980

If the [Nicaraguan] revolution has benefited a particular social sector, it is the peasantry. This explains why the vast majority of those who have taken up arms against the counter-revolutionary bands are peasants.

—Jaime Wheelock, minister of agriculture and agrarian reform, Nicaragua, 1983

The revolutionary upheaval in Central America once again has placed agrarian reform on the U.S. political agenda. Not since the Cuban revolution has agrarian reform assumed such importance for U.S. foreign policy and the maintenance of U.S. dominance in the hemisphere. The Sandinista victory in 1979 paved the way for Central America's first revolutionary agrarian reform. A year later the United States finally succeeded in forcing a reluctant military in El Salvador to introduce its own agrarian reform, hoping to de-fuse revolutionary demands and so "prevent another Nicaragua" in El Salvador.

The Nicaraguan and Salvadoran reforms represent quite different political projects. Both reforms have sought to win over the peasantry and rural workers. However, the Salvadoran reform has aimed to contain and pacify rural workers and peasants by giving them a stake in the existing system. Its explicit objective has been to broaden the ruling regime's base of support in order to avoid a victory of the revolutionary forces. By contrast, the Nicaraguan reform has intended to achieve a far-reaching distribution not only of land, but also of economic and political power on behalf of the majority of peasants and landless workers. Not surprisingly, the role of the United States in designing, financing, and implementing these two agrarian reforms has been quite different.

From the outset, the Salvadoran program was attacked by the oligarchy, who succeeded in blocking some aspects of it and delaying others. Even so, the Reagan administration has staunchly backed this program, while consistently trying to discredit and undermine the Sandinista reform as part of its strategy to destabilize the Nicaraguan revolution. Much to the chagrin of U.S. strategists in Washington, the U.S. policy has been unsuccessful in both countries. In El Salvador, U.S. efforts to implement an agrarian reform not only have been largely unsuccessful, but have exacerbated the revolutionary crisis. Peasant aspirations have been raised, while the U.S. embassy has been unable to assuage the opposition of the Salvadoran landed oligarchy to a reformist agrarian strategy. In Nicaragua, on the other hand, the agrarian reform continues to go forward, in spite of enormous obstacles, as more land is redistributed and more rural workers and peasants organized. This demonstrates that a genuine revolutionary reform is indeed a viable option for the region. The failure of the U.S. administration to achieve its objectives vis-à-vis the agrarian reform process in each country bespeaks the broader failure of U.S. policy to stem the revolutionary tide in the region.

Agrarian Reform as a Political Issue

The demand for land by peasants and landless workers has been a political issue in El Salvador and Nicaragua since at least the 1920s. In both countries, the development of the agro-export economy has come at the expense of the majority of the rural population. Peasants have been continually displaced and dispossessed of their landholdings. The lands suitable for export production, first for coffee and later sugarcane and cotton, have been increasingly concentrated in the hands of a few.[1] Peasant response to these changing conditions of production has by no means been passive. Dispossessed peasants formed the backbone of Sandino's army in the anti-imperialist struggle the General led in Nicaragua in the late 1920s and early 1930s. In El Salvador, landless rural workers provided the raw material for the rapid growth of the Regional Federation of Salvadoran Workers in the late 1920s. This organization of rural workers and peasants led to a rural insurrection in 1932, centered in the coffee regions, led by Marxist revolutionary Farabundo Martí. The uprising was quickly crushed by the military and oligarchy, and was followed by the massacre of an estimated 30,000 peasants.

The severe repression in rural areas in both countries discouraged attempts at rural organizing for the next thirty years. The oligarchies consolidated their hold and land reform was banished from the political lexicon. However, the land issue became even more pressing in the 1950s and 1960s. The expansion of cotton and sugarcane cultivation in this period resulted in waves of peasant evictions from the remaining communal lands. In addition, as the coffee producers introduced new technology and modernized their operations, many more peasants were forced off the haciendas, which were converted into modern capitalist enterprises.

In launching the Alliance for Progress in the early 1960s the United States recognized the need to address the pressing issues of inequality and underdevelopment if revolutionary social change was to be avoided in the Americas. U.S. support for agrarian reform was aimed both at containing the peasantry as a potential revolutionary force and at breaking the power of the Latin American landed elite. The traditional landowning class was viewed as a drag on economic development, especially industrialization, and its stranglehold on political power was recognized as a threat to the survival of the system. Moreover, it was argued, the redistribution of land to the peasantry would not only satisfy the peasantry's potential revolutionary demands, it would also spur growth by putting land into the hands of those who would work it most intensively, and through their higher incomes, lead to an enlargement of the internal market. A broader internal market, in turn, would stimulate investment and hence the overall process of growth. Agrarian reform was thus the ideal mechanism both to contain the peasantry and to establish the preconditions for successful capitalist development.

U.S. development assistance in the 1960s was contingent on the Latin American countries instituting agrarian reforms. But U.S. support for effective agrarian reforms, then as now, was subordinate to political considerations. Greater weight was placed on maintaining the status quo in the name of "national security" interests, albeit under repressive political conditions, than on land reform. In Nicaragua, the United States was content with Somoza's establishment of an ineffectual land reform and colonization institute (IAN), which concentrated on resettling people on the undeveloped frontier. In El Salvador, the intransigence of the oligarchy and the continuity of military rule kept agrarian reform off the official political agenda until the mid-1970s.

By the mid-1970s in both El Salvador and Nicaragua, landless rural workers constituted at least 40 percent of the economically active population in agriculture.[2] Moreover, capitalistic agro-export production had engendered a particularly perverse employment structure: few year-round workers but great numbers of temporary workers for the coffee, sugarcane, and cotton harvests, resulting in employment of the majority of landless workers for only four months out of the year. Not surprisingly, Nicaragua and El Salvador are characterized by extreme rural poverty and a highly unequal distribution of agrarian income.[3] Besides engaging in wage labor, peasants could attempt to rent marginal lands (i.e., those not suitable for export crop production) from large landowners or they could migrate to the agricultural frontier and squat on national lands. In both countries, the number of peasants renting land increased significantly after 1950. In El Salvador, renting has constituted the *primary* form through which peasants have access to land.[4] The vast majority of parcels which are rented are less than two hectares in size, compelling agricultural work to be combined with seasonal wage employment.

El Salvador has the highest person-land ratio and one of the highest rates of population growth (3 percent per year) in the Western Hemisphere. The only escape valve for growing population pressure on the land in recent years has been migration to Honduras.[5] By 1969 there were an estimated 350,000 Salvadorans in Honduras, many squatting on national lands. Ironically, the Honduran application of its own agrarian reform law led to the expulsion of the Salvadoran immigrants. Tensions between the two countries increased, finally exploding in a five-day war between the two countries in July 1969. The war exacerbated even further the conflict over land and its unequal distribution in El Salvador as tens of thousands of Salvadorans were forced to return home.

By the time of the 1972 elections, all of the moderate and left political parties were voicing the demand for agrarian reform. The return of the migrants had compounded an already difficult rural economic situation. Moreover, years of organizing work by church-affiliated groups was beginning to pay off. Although an official ban on rural unions existed in El Salvador throughout the 1960s, the incipient efforts by the church to organize peasants and rural workers led to the formation of the Christian Peasants Federation (FECCAS) in 1965. In that same year, the American Institute for Free Labor Development (AIFLD) began its activities in rural El Salvador, organizing training seminars for select peasants under government auspices. Three years later some AIFLD trainees set up the Salvadoran Communal Union (UCS) which carried out projects funded by AIFLD.[6] Despite different goals (FECCAS favored land redistribution and better wages over self-help projects) both groups carried the banner of agrarian reform and backed the moderate coalition which included the Christian Democrat, José Napoleon Duarte, as presidential candidate, and Guillermo Ungo, leader of the social democratic National Revolutionary Movement (MNR), in the 1972 elections. By all accounts, the moderate coalition won the popular vote only to have their victory denied by the military, who declared their own candidate, Colonel Arturo Molina, the winner.

Colonel Molina, as a representative of the "modernizing" tendency within the military, was astute enough to recognize the potential volatility of the land issue.[7] He proposed to set up a land reform institute, and to carry out a modest, pilot land reform, known as the agrarian transformation. However, the intransigence of the oligarchy prevented its execution. In the 1977 elections Molina was replaced by his minister of defense, General Carlos Humberto Roméro, a hard-liner.

At the grass-roots level, rural organizing met with heavy represssion during this period from the paramilitary group, the Democratic Nationalist Organization, or ORDEN. In 1975 FECCAS had joined the more militant farm workers' union (UTC), and the repression finally forced FECCAS-UTC underground where it joined one of the growing mass organizations in the country, the People's Revolutionary Bloc. The UCS remained as the only semi-legal organization working in the countryside.

In Nicaragua too, the decade of the 1960s was characterized by rural strife as increasing numbers of peasants were evicted from their lands in the region of expanding cotton cultivation. The peasantry attempted to fight back through spontaneous land invasions to which Somoza responded with increased repression. However, taking advantage of Nicaragua's favorable person-land ratio, a colonization program was instituted which relocated dispossessed peasants to the agricultural frontier.

By the early 1970s the church in Nicaragua had also become involved in rural organizing efforts. Agrarian committees were first organized on the coffee plantations, later spreading throughout the Pacific region of the country, pressuring for better working conditions. In 1978, under Sandinista leadership, these committees were fused into Nicaragua's first national rural organization, the ATC (Asociación de los Trabajadores del Campo).[8] The ATC quickly took up the demand for agrarian reform and played an active role in the armed struggle that finally defeated Somoza.

The Sandinista victory in Nicaragua in July 1979 began a new phase in the history of agrarian reforms in Central America. With the confiscation of all the property and landholdings of the Somoza family and their associates, the Sandinista agrarian reform was launched. The fact that within months the Salvadorans had announced their own agrarian reform was no coincidence. Determined that the Nicaraguan experience would not be repeated elsewhere in Central America, the U.S. government sought a way to stabilize the explosive situation in neighboring El Salvador. For the Carter administration, this meant a shakeup in the brittle and repressive rule of the oligarchy.

In October of 1979 a coup by reform-minded military officers and businessmen ousted General Roméro. The reformers set up a military-civilian junta which included such civilian progressives as Guillermo Ungo and Román Mayorga (rector of the Central American University). The junta immediately announced its intention to carry out a far-reaching agrarian reform. Their intentions were frustrated, however. While moderates and progressives were nominally in control of the government, effective state power continued to rest with the more conservative elements of the military. The military was, at this point, still strongly committed to the economic preservation of its long-time ally and patron, the oligarchy.

While the Carter administration recognized that agrarian reform was an essential element in the strategy to contain the growth of the revolutionary forces, it clearly felt the time was not ripe as long as the government included progressives with ties to the popular forces.[9] The last thing that would serve U.S. interests was a potentially radical reform that could mobilize the peasantry and rural workers under the banner of the left. If an agrarian reform were to be supported by the United States, it would have to be clearly defined and strictly implemented so that the left could not use the program to mobilize massive support to push for a more radical reform. The United States was unwilling to use its influence until circumstances were more favorable, which they soon became.

Frustrated by inability to alter the balance of real power in the country, and unwilling to be identified with continued state repression, the moderate-progressive junta members resigned in January 1980. Then in March, centrist Christian Democrats resigned from the second military-civilian junta, followed by the removal of most liberal officials with some connection to the popular forces.[10] With the appointment of Napoleon Duarte as head of the third military-civilian junta, the United States was finally ready to insist upon the implementation of an agrarian reform.

Meanwhile, the popular forces were growing in strength and their leadership was becoming increasingly unified.[11] No doubt this was important in explaining the success the United States finally had in convincing the Salvadoran military that at least a limited agrarian reform was absolutely necessary. The military agreed to carry out an agrarian reform when it was clear that the U.S. military assistance essential to its counterinsurgency war was contingent upon its enactment, and once it was assured it would have full control over the process. The Salvadoran agrarian reform was thus announced on March 6, 1980, followed by the proclamation of a state of siege and a step-up in repression throughout the countryside.

The Salvadoran Agrarian Reform

By 1980 it was clear that the only possible way to contain the growth of the organized popular forces in the countryside was to meet rural worker and peasant demands for fundamental change. If agrarian reform was to be taken away from the popular forces as an issue, and rural workers and peasants won over to the government side in the civil war, the agrarian reform had to be massive, creating an extremely large number of beneficiaries. For the reform to be successful, it also had to be carried out quickly, making the process irreversible, before right-wing opposition could crystallize.

The U.S. administration knew that the cost of the agrarian reform would be high, in both political and financial terms. The resistence of the Salvadoran landed elite had to be overcome, or at least assuaged, with full compensation and the ability to transfer their accumulated wealth overseas. USAID estimated that the agrarian reform would cost approximately $1 billion over a five-year period, 80 percent of this going to compensate the landholding class.[12] As it unfolded, however, the Salvadoran agrarian reform failed even on its own terms. The reform neither was broad enough to have any effect on the course of the war, nor was it implemented quickly enough to make the process irreversible. The agrarian reform, the key element in the U.S. designed counter-revolutionary strategy, simply exacerbated the intensity of class struggle in the Salvadoran countryside.

The United States as well as the Duarte administration underestimated both the tenacity of the Salvadoran oligarchy and the depth of its intertwining interests with those of the military, and the security forces which had maintained its class rule since 1932. This is one reason why the murders of peasants and rural workers in the countryside has continued unabated three years after the first announcement of the agrarian reform. The military and the oligarchy simply know no other means to contain and control the mass of the rural population.

Moreover, U.S. policy was highly contradictory. While embassy officials demanded that the agrarian reform be implemented, the increased military assistance and repeated pronouncements that the objective of the United States was the military defeat of the left only served to strengthen the power of the military over the reform-bent Christian Democrats in the junta, and the conviction of the right that the agrarian reform was, indeed, reversible. The March 1982 U.S.-orchestrated elections, won by a group of right-wing parties (though the Christian Democrats got the most votes of any single party), resulted in right-wing control of the Constituent Assembly. This signaled the demise of both the so-called centrist solution as well as the prospects for the implementation of a major agrarian reform in El Salvador.

The Agrarian Reform Laws

The Salvadoran agrarian reform announced in March 1980 was to consist of two phases. In the first phase, all properties consisting of over 500 hectares in size were expropriated; this was to be followed by a second phase, whereby all properties between 100 and 500 hectares would be affected. Cooperatives, to be made up of the workers residing on the estates, were to be formed under the direction of the Institute for Agrarian Transformation (ISTA). Landowners were to be compensated for their land, and the new cooperatives were to assume this debt, to be repaid over a thirty-year period. Landowners affected in either phase were allowed to keep from 100 to 180 hectares of their former estates as their right of reserve.

A month later Colonel Jaime Abdul Gutiérrez of the third military-civilian junta announced that Phase II of the agrarian reform would not be carried out. Vehement opposition of the strongest sector of the Salvadoran oligarchy, the coffee planters, led to its almost immediate abandonment. The bulk of the country's coffee production, the main export crop, takes place on farms of 100 to 500 hectares in size.[13] Phase II of the reform would have cut deep into the nerve center of the bourgeoisie's wealth. It speaks to their power that they were able to so quickly undermine the military's commitment to the U.S. administration and the Christian Democrats to carry out a far-reaching agrarian reform.

The two phases of the agrarian reform would have affected approximately 38 percent of El Salvador's farmland. Limiting the reform to only Phase I meant that only 15 percent of the nation's farmland would be affected and that the potential number of beneficiaries of the reform would be greatly reduced.[14] Once it was clear that Phase II would not be implemented, the U.S. administration sought some other mechanism to incorporate a larger number of the rural population in the process to meet the goals of the reform. The ill-fated Phase III, the "Land to the Tiller" program, was the result.

Under Decree 207, all tenants were allowed to purchase the plots which they currently rented or sharecropped as long as the total land area did not exceed seven hectares. Landowners affected under the decree were again to be compensated, and tenants were to purchase their parcels over a thirty-year period. During this period, sales of these parcels were prohibited; all further renting of land was also proscribed. Potentially the country's largest rural group, some 150,000 tenant farmer households, could have been benefited through the "Land to the Tiller" program.

The junta's proclamation of Phase III evoked an immediate hostile response from Salvadoran officials of all political persuasions, who claimed—and accurately so—that it was a U.S. imposition.[15] Roy Prosterman, an AIFLD consultant who designed the "Land to the Tiller" program in Vietnam, was the main architect. In 1980 he was brought to El Salvador under an AID grant supporting AIFLD-UCS activities.

Short-run political expediencies provide the only reason why Phase III of the reform was enacted. It was hoped that this group would provide the government with a base of support in the countryside. A U.S. official noted somewhat optimistically, "There is no one more conservative than a small farmer. We're going to be breeding capitalists like rabbits."[16] But the Land to the Tiller model was quite ill-suited to making Salvadoran peasants into viable small farmers.[17] Most (80 percent) land renting in El Salvador takes place on microfundia and usually on the worst lands, those most subject to erosion. Making tenants owners of these inferior plots only institutionalizes their precarious economic situation.

Implementation of the Reform

The expropriation of the 328 large farms affected under Phase I, and their organization into peasant cooperatives, was carried out rapidly and forcefully in the days following the announcement of the agrarian reform decree. The state of siege allowed the military to act with impunity, both in overcoming the resistance of recalcitrant landowners and in ridding the estates of potential beneficiaries sympathetic to the left.

The implementation of Phase III proved quite a different matter. The internal opposition was so strong that the military lost its will to carry it out, instead using their new legitimacy to further terrorize the suspect peasants.

The UCS denounced the paramilitary and military violence to which the peasantry had been subjected, adding that they had been excluded from any structured participation in the reform by a hostile bureaucracy. Phase III was announced in April 1980. By June, the executive councils of eight UCS departmental organizations had signed a protest stating their opposition to the agrarian reform due to the indiscriminate killing and assassination of peasant leaders.[18] Despite this protest, the violence continued to escalate extending to the semi-legal UCS itself. In the summer of 1980 an increasing number of UCS members began joining the popular organizations.[19] And by the fall of 1980 UCS/ISTA president, José Rudolfo Viera, appalled by the process of reform with repression, vigorously denounced the violence against his union and the peasantry.[20] Perhaps inevitably, he himself was a victim of the terror. On January 3, 1981, he was assassinated along with two AIFLD agrarian reform advisers from the United States. Those responsible have still not been charged. During 1981 the repression against the peasantry went unabated; at least ninety officials and activists of the UCS died along with a large number of potential peasant beneficiaries.[21]

The violent opposition that developed to Phase III is explained by the fact that it impinged not upon the larger landowners (theoretically encompassed in Phases I and II), but rather upon the numerically significant group of smaller commercial farmers and rich peasantry that own less than 100 hectares of land. This group previously had been given assurances of their exemption from the reform, and their inclusion had the unexpected result of turning many of them against both the reform process and the government, projecting them into the hands of the far right. They succeeded in delaying the implementation of the reform, as well as in undermining it, by taking matters into their own hands, often violently, with the support of the security forces.

The claim by its designers that Phase III would be virtually self-implementing was suspiciously naive if not manipulative. Declaring that tenants were now the owners of their rented plots by no means assured that tenants would remain in possession of their land or that they would not be obliged to continue paying rent. Effective possession required a land title, and the issuance of land titles depended on identification of beneficiaries by means of registration and verification. Eight months passed before the procedural regulations were even issued, and additional delays accompanied every step.[22]

Procedural delays gave landowners ample time to simply throw peasants off their rented parcels before the titles could be issued. According to a sample survey undertaken by the UCS with AIFLD assistance in April 1981, 18 percent of the respondents indicated that they had been evicted from their land parcels in the months since the reform was announced. Projected nationally, this meant that an estimated 25,000 tenant families of the projected 150,000 beneficiaries lost access to land before the spring plantings of 1981. According to the UCS thousands more have been evicted since then.[23]

Among the potential beneficiaries that were not evicted, the majority were forced to continue paying rent to landowners even after the program went into effect. Based on projections from their survey, the UCS estimated that approximately 75,000 peasant households were obliged to pay this illegal rent.[24]

Not until February 1981 were the first provisional land titles handed out. By the end of that year, some 20,842 provisional titles had been granted, largely due to the pressure of the UCS.[25] Less than 15 percent of the potential beneficiaries received titles. As the UCS warned in its December 1981 report to President Duarte, "we must be very clear in recognizing that the failure of the agrarian reform process is an immediate and imminent danger."[26]

But the Duarte regime was completely powerless, unable to either control the military or security forces or to implement the agrarian reform required by its U.S. ally. Although the fate of Phase III was clearly sealed with the murder of Viera and his advisers, the United States continued to stand behind the junta's declared commitment to a genuine reform process. The entire U.S. aid program was conditional upon the administration's certification to Congress in January 1982 that the Salvadoran government was making progress in implementing agrarian reform. The State Department dismissed the UCS charges, characterizing the agrarian reform as a "remarkable success story."[27]

President Reagan subsequently certified to the Congress that substantial progress was being made on the reforms in El Salvador, enabling the $25 million in military aid and $40 million in economic assistance budgeted for El Salvador in fiscal year 1982 to be disbursed. Immediately land titling in El Salvador dropped to a trickle, picking up again briefly only for the March 1982 elections.[28]

By then it was too late for the Duarte regime. The agrarian reform had certainly not been broad enough to create a base for the Christian Democrats in the countryside. The creation of the production cooperatives on the estates expropriated by Phase I benefited approximately 35,000 landless workers, but this fell far short of the targeted 60,000 beneficiaries. By the time of the March elections 27,215 provisional land titles had been issued under Phase III, but applications were already falling off sharply.[29] At best, less than 20 percent of Salvadoran landless households had been affected positively through the reforms.

Stacked up against the scale of the violence perpetrated against the peasantry—through assassinations, displacement and forced relocation, and intimidation—the agrarian reform certainly did not gain peasant or farmworker support for the government; more likely, it increased their support for the revolutionary process. Moreover, as we have noted, the expropriation of lands under 100 hectares has served to gain additional recruits for the right.

Since the March 1982 elections and the victory of the right-wing parties, the entire agrarian reform has been in jeopardy. One of the first acts of the right-dominated Constituent Assembly was to pass a resolution officially canceling the "postponed" Phase II of the agrarian reform and to "temporarily suspend" Phase III. While President Magaña immediately announced that the rights of peasants already designated as beneficiaries of the Land to the Tiller phase were protected, since the suspension of Phase III applied only to new rental contracts, the resolution was widely publicized, and precipitated a new wave of peasant land evictions and rural violence.[30]

While the Reagan administration played up Magaña's announcements, its reported pressures on the new Salvadoran government indicate that it was clearly aware that the entire agrarian reform program was threatened by collapse—and with it the administration's strategy.[31] Senator Charles Percy, head of the Senate Foreign Relations Committee, declared in June: "If the Salvador government is reneging on the land reform program not one cent of funds shall go to the government of El Salvador."[32]

The administration was apparently able to convince the military to take the threat seriously, and the first 251 definitive land titles under Phase III were handed out in June and July of 1982, allowing President Reagan to meet the certification requirement July 28. In July, however, provisional titling abruptly dropped off, and only 2,358 were handed out from July to the end of December.[33]

In January 1983 the president again certified that progress was being made on the agrarian reform. While Phase III had fallen far short of its initial goals, by that time some 35,936 peasants had filed for 57,236 hectares of land, approximately 4 percent of the cultivable land area of El Salvador.[34] At the same time, however, landlords had already evicted 4,792 peasants from the land they were in the process of buying, encouraged by the widespread confusion following the assembly resolution.[35]

On March 23, 1983, when the time allowed for applications was due to expire, the Constituent Assembly extended it for ten months. In July President Reagan duly certified to the Congress that despite some problems, progress was being made on land reform, and support from the military had halted the eviction problem. Reagan referred to an AID-funded study of the land reform program, not yet completed, which would confirm that the illegal evictions would not be nearly so high as during the same period last year.

The following week, the study report was released. Its findings, contrary to administration predictions, indicated that between 11 percent and 14 percent of peasant beneficiaries were evicted and that the evictions continued at nearly the same level as the previous year.[36]

As for Phase I, it too faces obstacles. Labor union officials have charged that the Constituent Assembly has filled the agencies in charge of implementing reform with hostile officials, and in January 1983 President Magaña admitted it was true of ISTA, in charge of managing Phase I. The result has been further delays: of the 328 cooperatives only 20 have received titles, even though 130 of the previous owners have been fully compensated.[37]

Land reform was dealt another legal blow in June 1983 when the Constituent Assembly completed a draft of the constitution containing the loopholes on Phase I which rightists had tried to legislate in March 1982. Although vaguely worded Articles 104 and 105 could be interpreted as paving the way for the destruction of Phase I by allowing former landowners to reclaim estates that had been legally subdivided and sold before and after the enactment of the reform, and by subjecting the maximum acreage allowed to one owner to a two-thirds majority vote of the assembly. Another provision in the articles seems to forbid further land redistribution.[38] The debate over the constitutional articles dealing with the land reform kept the Salvadoran Constituent Assembly deadlocked in the fall of 1983. And the debate was accompanied by a sharp rise in the killings by rightist death squads.[39] Thus, four years after the first agrarian reform legislation had been decreed, the right wing was still in a powerful position to prevent the United States from fully implementing its counter-revolutionary agrarian reform project.

The Nicaraguan Agrarian Reform

While touting the virtues of a shattered reform program in El Salvador, the U.S. administration has looked askance at the efforts of the Nicaraguan Sandinistas to carry out an agrarian reform designed to benefit the majority of the country's rural poor. Indeed, the purposes the Nicaraguan agrarian reform are designed to serve are the very ones that have caused the United States to launch a destabilization plan. The objective of the Sandinistas is to transform the social, political, and economic map of the country. The agrarian reform is the spearhead of the process of redistributing power and income to peasants and rural workers.

In contrast to Salvadoran land reform, Nicaragua's agrarian reform is far more than a land redistribution. It is intended to meet rural worker and peasant demands not just for land, but also for employment, higher incomes, and full participation in the process of agrarian transformation.

The First Two Years of the Reform

The fundamental restructuring of the Nicaraguan agrarian sector began in the 1979-81 period with the confiscation of the farms owned by Somoza and his associates. Attesting to the degree of concentration of land by Somoza and his allies, 23 percent of Nicaragua's cultivable land passed to the new "people's sector" through the confiscation decrees.[40] This consisted of some 2,000 farms encompassing approximately 800,000 hectares. The farms were reorganized into thirty-four state enterprises and are managed by the Nicaraguan Institute of Agrarian Reform (INRA) with worker participation.

The Sandinistas attempted to deal with the problem of landlessness both by incorporating the greatest number of workers possible into the reform sector, as well as through land rental regulations. An important factor in the Sandinista decision to create state farms on the confiscated land, rather than cooperatives based on private property, was the recognition that employment generation was to be a key challenge of the agrarian reform. Moreover, it was hoped that the creation of a social sector would prevent an imbalance between the benefits bestowed upon workers in the reformed sector and the situation of the mass of landless temporary workers and semi-proletarianized peasants. In the first year of the Sandinista agrarian reform, 45,000 landless workers were incorporated within the state sector. In addition, unused lands on the state farms were made available, rent free, to other landless workers to plant in basic grains. In these production cooperatives (CAS), or collective work agreements, as this arrangement is currently called, land as well as marketing and credit resources are collectively used. In the first year of the reform, some 451 of these production cooperatives were formed, not only generating employment, but stimulating the production of basic grains.

The Nicaraguan agrarian reform is unique in that because of the vast landholdings by the Somoza family itself, almost one-quarter of the nation's farmland could be confiscated with the full support of the agrarian bourgeoisie. But beyond this, the multiclass alliance upon which the defeat of Somoza had been based mitigated possibilities for carrying out redistribution of private lands during the first two years of the revolution. It was one thing to confiscate the land of Somoza, but quite another to affect private property in general. As a result, the Sandinistas relied on rental regulations to encourage the private sector to put unused lands into production.

The land-rental regulations required that all land rented to tenants in the previous two years, and all unused land, be made available to tenants and landless workers. The established rental rates, $14 per hectare for basic grains per season, represented a significant decrease in previous levels of land rent. A number of incentives were given for tenants to rent land collectively and form a production cooperative or CAS. Substantial sums of credit were made available by the National Development Bank, and a CAS received the lowest interest rate, 7 percent. In the first year of the agrarian reform, some 876 CASs were formed on private lands.

While the Sandinistas thus gave considerable support to collective forms of production on lands rented from either the private sector or the state, state support was also directed toward individual peasant farming. The primary vehicle upon which the Sandinistas relied to increase agricultural productivity and raise rural incomes among smallholders was the development of Credit and Service Cooperatives (CCS), in which individual smallholders share access to credit, technical assistance, and marketing arrangements. In the first year of the reform the amount of credit made available to small producers increased by approximately 400 percent over that extended the last year of Somoza's reign. The availability of cheap and timely credit was the primary impetus behind the formation of 1,185 CCSs among small and medium-sized property owners during 1980. All told, some 97,353 households received agricultural credit during the 1979-80 agricultural year, 76 percent as members of a CCS or CAS.

The rapid development of cooperatives in the first year of the Nicaraguan agrarian reform, some 2,512 in total, was due largely to the organizational efforts of the Rural Worker's Association (ATC). The ATC had primary responsibility not only for organizing the CAS and CCS, but also for organizing unions on state and private farms. The role that the ATC, and later the National Association of Farmers and Cattlemen (UNAG), have played in the Nicaraguan reform demonstrates the important role of rural worker and peasant organizations in ensuring the success of any agrarian reform. Both FSLN-affiliated, these mass organizations have worked hard to ensure that state policy be responsive to the demands of rural workers and peasants, and that workers and peasants in turn be active participants in defining the process of socioeconomic transformation.

Representatives from the ATC organize workers on state farms and share management responsibility in the consultative councils in charge of running the state farms. On private farms the ATC has struggled for employer compliance with legislation, especially concerning minimum wages and regulations concerning land rent ceilings; if landlords were unwilling to rent their unused lands to the peasantry at the established rates, the ATC has often been able to enforce compliance through land takeovers.

While many landowners complied with the regulations, making available unused lands at the lowered rental rates, this did not satisfy the land hunger of peasants and landless workers. The land takeovers continued, unsettling the agrarian bourgeoisie: during 1980-81 decapitalization of many of the private estates was increasingly widespread. Both of these factors—peasant demands and the problem of decapitalization—were important in spurring the development of a comprehensive agrarian reform law.

The 1981 Agrarian Reform Law

The Sandinista agrarian reform law was announced on July 19, 1981, and subsequently promulgated by the Nicaraguan co-legislative bodies, the Council of State and the Junta of National Reconstruction.[41] The new law provided for the expropriation of unused, underutilized, and rented land on farms greater than 350 hectares in the Pacific and central interior regions of the country and on farms greater than 700 hectares in the rest of the country. Also affected were lands leased by their owners under precapitalist forms of tenancy (sharecropping and *colono* arrangements) where total farm size either exceeded thirty-five hectares in the Pacific region, or seventy hectares in the rest of the country. Farms abandoned by their owners were subject to confiscation, whereas owners of land unused, underutilized, or not under direct management were to receive compensation in the form of agrarian reform bonds. Land was to be distributed free of charge to landless workers, sharecroppers, *colonos*, *arrendires*, smallholders with insufficient land, cooperatives, and state farms.

The intended effect of the new agrarian reform law was to protect efficient producers no matter what the size of their holding. The law attempted to eliminate once and for all precapitalist relations in the countryside, while preserving the flexibility of capitalist rental farming. All land worked in sharecropping or in labor-service arrangements (*colonos*) on farms greater than 35 or 70 hectares, depending on the region, was subject to expropriation, while rented land was only subject to expropriation on farms greater than 350 hectares. Thus, the law allows capitalist renting to continue on farms between 35 and 350 hectares. In the past, some 40 percent of cotton production by the bourgeoisie took place on rented lands.

The second stage of the Nicaraguan agrarian reform could affect some 1,200 additional farms and release up to 1 million hectares of land for redistribution.[42] With the implementation of this second stage, approximately one-half of Nicaragua's cultivable land could be affected through the agrarian reform process.

The new Nicaraguan law has a "land to the tiller" thrust similar to El Salvador's in that all tenants are to be made agrarian reform beneficiaries. But the differences between the two approaches are more noteworthy. First, Nicaraguan tenants will not necessarily receive the land on which they presently work since the law is not intended to punish small and medium-size producers who are engaged in land renting. Tenants can extricate themselves from rental arrangements by soliciting land from the pool of expropriated lands in the area; they will not be bound to marginal parcels of land. Thus, second, tenants and landless workers are guaranteed access to the amount of land necessary to provide an income equivalent to the minimum monthly agricultural salary.

Tenants may receive access to land either individually or collectively, in both cases receiving agrarian reform titles which guarantee dominion, possession, and the usufruct of land. Lands adjudicated under the agrarian reform cannot be sold, in order to avoid the process of peasant dispossession so prevalent during the 1950s. Land may be inherited, as long as it is not subdivided among the heirs, so as to avoid a process of minifundization in future years.

The Nicaraguan agrarian reform is more than a response to peasant and rural worker demands; these producers themselves have shaped the course of the agrarian reform. Indicative of this is the great degree of flexibility written into the agrarian reform law. Peasants and rural workers are not being compelled into predetermined forms of production. Rather, the degree of individual choice and local autonomy in the process makes this reform process unique in the Latin American agrarian reform experience.

Both the ATC and UNAG played a central role in the design of the new agrarian reform law and are playing a key role in its implementation. At the local level, they participate in commissions charged with identifying idle lands and organizing the peasants and rural workers that should be benefited. The UNAG has responsibility for organizing peasants and landless workers into the production cooperatives and the credit and service cooperatives. The ATC is organizing landless workers in Committees of Temporary Workers. They intend to acquire lands collectively for the production of basic grains during the off-season of export agriculture, in order to provide these workers with a year-round livelihood. The committees are also intended to provide the mechanism to ensure that the distribution of land does not dry up the seasonal labor market required for cotton, coffee, and sugarcane production, the basis of Nicaragua's agro-export economy.

The pace of implementation of the agrarian reform was initially relatively slow. This was due both to the need to organize rural workers and peasants before they can participate, and to the care the FSLN has taken to carry out the agrarian reform within the bounds of its alliance with the patriotic sectors of the agrarian bourgeoisie. As of July 1982, 242 properties had been expropriated, encompassing approximately 165,882 acres. Only about 40 percent of the land had been reassigned, 6,503 beneficiaries receiving titles either individually or as part of a production cooperative. The vice minister of agrarian reform explained that "it takes more time to identify good beneficiaries, especially if the emphasis is on cooperatives, than to identify bad hacienda owners.

We're working on it, but we don't want a single beneficiary to fail, so we won't be rushed—even by President Reagan." [43]

Nonetheless, the balance between those factors suggesting slow implementation and those factors favoring a more rapid implementation of the reform was finally tipped in favor of the latter by the military situation. Throughout 1982 Nicaragua had faced increasing counterrevolutionary attacks from U.S.-backed Somocista forces based in Honduras. The Sandinistas recognized that a more rapid implementation of the agrarian reform would strengthen the defense capabilities of the war zone as well as deepen peasant and rural worker commitment to defend the revolution.

During 1983 some 244,754 hectares of land were distributed to some 14,255 families. By the end of December 1983, the amount of land expropriated under the reform totaled 365,292 hectares and that transferred to beneficiaries, 338,193 hectares. [44] Thus, in its two phases the Nicaraguan agrarian reform has encompassed approximately 33 percent of the nation's farmland.

The Reaction of the U.S. Administration

The Reagan administration's policy toward Nicaragua is consistent with the strategy outlined in the Heritage Foundation background policy paper for the Reagan transition team, published in October 1980 (while Richard Allen, Reagan's ex-chairman of the National Security Council, was its president). This states that "although the Marxist government in Nicaragua might fall eventually of its own failures, the security of El Salvador requires the acceleration of the removal of the government in Managua." [45] Its specific policy recommendations toward this end included cutting off all aid to the Nicaraguan government to compound the economic difficulties, and "in a well-orchestrated program targeted against the Marxist Sandinista government, we should use our limited resources to support the free labor unions, the Church, the private sector, the independent political parties, the free press, and those who truly defend human rights." [46] These private organizations were seen as the vehicles for transforming economic difficulties in Nicaragua into political instability.

Increased U.S. support to Nicaraguan private sector organizations had begun in the final year of the Carter administration, when three-quarters of the U.S. grant assistance was targeted to the private sector.[47] However, the Carter administration appeared also to be pursuing a somewhat balanced loan policy, including government programs in agriculture, health, and education, aimed at meeting "basic human needs." In addition, a $1.4 million technical assistance grant had been provided for the agrarian reform.

Such programs for FY 1981 were scrapped early on in the Reagan administration. More aggressively, Reagan then cut off the remaining funds of the special congressional appropriations bill for Nicaragua (approximately $15 million) which was linked to administration certification that Nicaragua was not supporting "terrorist" activity in other countries (i.e., El Salvador). The cut-off also affected $9.6 million in PL-480 wheat credits which had no such clause. But the AID grant programs to the private sector already approved for FY 1981 continued disbursements.

Under the Carter administration, the preservation of Nicaragua's agrarian bourgeoisie was the necessary condition for the maintenance of a neutral, if not supportive, U.S. position vis-à-vis the Nicaraguan revolution. Perhaps reflective of this, discussion of a comprehensive agrarian reform affecting non-Somoza private property was largely tabled as long as the Carter administration remained in power.

While the enactment of the 1981 Agrarian Reform Law was primarily a response to internal demands, its timing also reflected the new pressures from the hostile Reagan administration. The maintenance of the private sector within the mixed economy was not so much at issue as its potential role as the cutting edge of the counter-revolution. The issues of political pluralism and the status of the mixed economy appear less important to the Reagan administration than the outright struggle for state power by whatever means.

The development of the counter-revolution, and bourgeoisie support for it, have made the terms of the class conflict much clearer, giving the Sandinistas a clearer, if less broad-based, mandate. The result has been a growing polarization, one which is based on a much sharper revolutionary consciousness among peasants and rural workers. In this context it has become more important to extend the agrarian reform, responding to rural worker and peasant demands through the enactment of a comprehensive agrarian reform law, than to assuage bourgeois fears over the course of the Sandinista revolution.

Conclusion: Agrarian Reform and U.S. Policy

Although the Reagan administration asserted in 1982 that the Salvadoran agrarian reform was "the most comprehensive program of land reform ever attempted in Latin America," the Nicaraguan agrarian reform far surpasses it.[48] Phase I of the Salvadoran agrarian reform encompassed only 14 percent of Salvadoran farm lands. Under Phase III, applications have been filed for an additional 3.9 percent of the agricultural land in use. If one compares this *only* with the lands that the Sandinista's confiscated from Somoza, which accounted for 23 percent of Nicaragua's farmland, it is evident that the U.S. government claim is erroneous.[49]

The Nicaraguan agrarian reform also far surpasses the Salvadoran reform in terms of its ability to promote the welfare of the rural inhabitants. As a political project, the Salvadoran reform did not contain the economic preconditions necessary to "breed capitalists like rabbits," much less to improve the standard of living of the majority of the rural population. The two agrarian reforms constitute contrasting political projects and, as a result, the two reform programs have markedly different impacts.

From this analysis it appears that continued U.S. support for the Salvadoran agrarian reform is counterproductive. The growth of the revolutionary process has not been contained, since the agrarian reform was neither broad enough nor implemented quickly enough. Increased U.S. military assistance and the outcome of the March 1982 elections created a highly contradictory situation, bolstering precisely those sectors of Salvadoran society bent on resisting the agrarian reform and any other processes of socioeconomic change. By closing the doors to non-violent change, the right has simply forced more people to support the revolutionary alternative.

Reagan administration policies toward Nicaragua have also had a result counter to that intended. The lack of U.S. support for the agrarian reform and the Nicaraguan process of national reconstruction in general, coupled with direct encouragement to the counter-revolution, has quickened the pace of the revolution.

What must be recognized is that the roots of the Central American revolution reflect centuries of economic exploitation and political repression at the hand of a small ruling elite, supported by the United States. Agrarian reform is just one of many fundamental changes which the people of Central America are today demanding. But if agrarian reform is to affect the basic conditions of poverty and underdevelopment, it must be carried out by a very different state than the United States has been willing to coexist with in the Americas. Only a state that has the support of Central America's rural workers and peasants, and is secure from U.S. intervention, can begin to set in motion an agrarian reform to foster the conditions of both economic and political democracy.

Notes

1. For Nicaragua's agrarian history see Jaime Wheelock, *Imperialismo y Dictadura: Crisis de Una Formación Social,* 5th ed. (Mexico City: Siglo XXI, 1980) and Orlando Nuñez, *El Somocismo: Desarrollo y Contradicciónes del Modelo Capitalista Agro-exportador en Nicaragua, 1950-1975* (Havana: Centro de Estudios sobre América, 1980). On El Salvador, see David Browning, *El Salvador: Landscape and Society* (Oxford: Clarendon Press, 1971).

2. For Nicaraguan data see C.D. Deere and Peter Marchetti, "The Worker-Peasant Alliance in the First Year of the Nicaraguan Agrarian Reform," *Latin American Perspectives,* 29 (Spring 1981), Table 1; for El Salvador, see Larry Simon and James Stephens, "El Salvador Land Reform, 1980-1981," *Impact Audit,* Boston, OXFAM America, 1981 (mimeo), p. 5.

3. It has been estimated that 60 percent of El Salvador's and 70 percent of Nicaragua's agricultural labor force earned annual incomes less than that required to meet minimum subsistence requirements; Simon and Stephens, "El Salvador Land Reform," pp. 7-8, Nuñez, *El Somocismo,* p. 43.

4. Simon and Stephens, "El Salvador Land Reform," p. 6.

5. An excellent analysis of the causes of population pressure on the land and of Salvadoran migration to Honduras is provided by William Durham, *Scarcity and Survival in Central America* (Stanford: Stanford University Press, 1979).

6. Philip Wheaton, "Agrarian Reform in El Salvador: A Program of Rural Pacification," Washington, D.C., EPICA Task Force, 1980 (mimeo), pp. 1-2.

7. Robert Armstrong and Janet Shenk, *El Salvador: The Face of Revolution* (Boston: South End Press, 1982), ch.3.

8. See Deere and Marchetti, "The Worker-Peasant Alliance," for an analysis of the origins of the ATC and its role in the struggle as well as subsequent agrarian reform.

9. Carolyn Forché and Philip Wheaton, "History and Motivations of U.S. Involvement in the Control of the Peasant Movement in El Salvador," Washington, D.C., EPICA, 1980 (mimeo), pp. 5-8.

10. See Harold Jung, "Class Struggles in El Salvador," *New Left Review* 122 (July-August 1980): 3-26, for an excellent analysis of this period.

11. For details on the unification process of the left, see Robert Armstrong, "El Salvador, A Revolution Brews," *NACLA Report on the Americas,* July-August, 1980.

12. Simon and Stephens, "El Salvador Land Reform," p. 64.

13. Ibid., p. 41.

14. According to the 1971 census, only 8,309 wage workers were employed full time on farms larger than 500 hectares. FAO, "Report on the 1970 World Census of Agriculture: El Salvador," Bulletin No. 25, 1979, p. 28.

15. Mac Chapin, "A Few Comments on Land Tenure and the Course of Agrarian Reform in El Salvador," June 1980 (mimeo), p. 20, notes that "AIFLD essentially wrote the 207 Legislation and handed it to the junta, bypassing the Minister of Agriculture."

16. Cited in Peter Shiras, "The False Promise—and Real Violence—of Land Reform," *Food Monitor,* January-February 1981, p. 16.

17. Simon and Stephens, "El Salvador Land Reform," pp. 52-56. The poor quality of the land which is usually rented is also well documented in Chapin, "Land Tenure," p. 13 and Durham, *Scarcity and Survival,* ch. 3.

18. Wheaton, "Agrarian Reform," p. 17.

19. Stewart Klepper, "The U.S. in El Salvador," *El Pulgarcíto* 6, no. 2 (May 1980): 8.

20. Renato Camorda, "Two U.S. Union Officials Gunned Down," *In These Times,* January 14-20, 1981.

21. Unión Comunal Salvadoréña (UCS), "El Salvador Land Reform," pp. 8-9.

22. UCS, "El Salvador Land Reform Update: The Land to the Tiller Program," December 10, 1981 (mimeo), p. 2.

23. Ibid., p. 8.

24. Ibid., p. 9.

25. Martin Diskin, "1982 Supplement," in *El Salvador Land Reform, 1980-1981, Impact Audit,* 2nd ed. (Boston: OXFAM America, 1982), table 4, based on State Department data.

26. UCS, "El Salvador Land Reform," p. 1.

27. Karen DeYoung, "Salvadoran Land Reform Imperiled, Report Says," *Washington Post,* January 25, 1982.

28. Diskin, "1982 Supplement," table 4.

29. Ibid.

30. *Latin America Weekly Report,* "Assembly Suspends Land Reform," WR-82-31, May 28 1982, p. 4.

31. Bernard Weinraub, "U.S. Pressing Salvador for Changes," *New York Times,* July 9, 1982.

32. Robert Costa, "El Salvador Land Reform Gutted," *The Guardian,* June 2, 1982.

33. John Strasma, Peter Gore, Jeffrey Nash, and Refugio Rochin, *Agrarian Reform in El Salvador* (Washington, D.C.: AID/Checchi and Co., 1983), table 74b.
34. Ibid.
35. Ibid.
36. Sam Dillon, "Salvadorans Lose Land Won in Agrarian Reform, U.S.-Funded Study Shows," *Washington Post*, May 28, 1983. The total number of evictions since the program was put in place varies depending on the definitions used to determine an evictee. The government limits it to those evicted who have already made a formal claim; this figure is 5,634, or 11 percent. The unions include those peasants eligible to claim who have not done so; this figure is 9,067 or 14.5 percent.
37. Lydia Chavez, "Politics and Costs Hinder Land Program," *New York Times*, January 22, 1983.
38. Edward Cody, "Party Says Land Reform Endangered," *Washington Post*, June 28, 1983; Juan Vasquez, "Land Reform: Key Salvadoran Assembly Issue," *Los Angeles Times*, September 19, 1983; and Lydia Chavez, "Farm Unions in Salvador Facing Battle to Preserve Land Program," *New York Times*, September 19, 1983.
39. Joanne Omang, "Land Reform Debate Heightens Tension in El Salvador," *Washington Post*, November 3, 1983.
40. Unless otherwise noted, the data on the Nicaraguan agrarian reform is drawn from Deere and Marchetti, "The Worker-Peasant Alliance."
41. FSLN, "Ley de Reforma Agraria," Managua, DEPEP, September 1981 (mimeo). The interpretation offered here draws on discussions with officials of Centro de Investigación e Estudios de la Reforma Agraria (CIERA) in Managua during July and September 1981, and August 1982.
42. "Wheelock detalla alcances de Reforma Agraria: Tierra segura a todo productor," *El Nuevo Diario*, July 22, 1981.
43. Joseph Collins, *What Difference Could a Revolution Make? Food and Farming in the New Nicaragua* (San Francisco: Institute for Food and Development Policy, 1982), p. 96.
44. Central American Historical Institute, *Update*, 3, no. 2, January 13, 1984, pp. 1-2.
45. The Heritage Foundation, "U.S. Policy and the Marxist Threat to Central America," *Backgrounder* #128, October 15, 1980 (mimeo), p. 2.
46. Ibid., p. 5.
47. U.S. AID, FY 1982, Congressional Presentation Document, pp. 120-23.
48. U.S. Department of State, Bureau of Public Affairs, "Democracy and Security in the Caribbean Basin," *Current Policy*, No. 364, February 1982, p. 4.
49. A detailed comparative analysis of each aspect of the two reforms is found in Carmen Diana Deere, "A Comparative Analysis of Agrarian Reform in El Salvador and Nicaragua," *Development and Change*, Winter 1982.

6. The U.S. Economic Stake in Central America and the Caribbean

Roger Burbach and Marc Herold

In the grand scheme of things, it would be ideal for the United States to export its dirty industrial base to the greater Caribbean basin where cheap labor abounds. The region is much more accessible and defensible than the Middle East or any other part of the world.

> *—Col. Bill Comee, U.S. Southern Command,*
> *Panama, February, 1984*

It isn't nutmeg that is at stake in the Caribbean and Central America. It is the U.S. national security.

> *—President Ronald Reagan, March 10, 1983*

We want to maintain a favorable climate for foreign investment in the Caribbean region, not merely to protect the existing U.S. investment there, but to encourage new investment opportunities in stable, democratic, free-market-oriented countries close to our shores.

> *—Vice President George Bush, December 5, 1982*

The threat to U.S. national security—this is the justification given for the large scale U.S. intervention in Central America. However, what U.S. political leaders generally fail to point out is that the United States has substantial corporate and economic interests in the region. These interests, which historically have been the motor force of U.S. expansion into the region, are crucial in explaining past and present U.S. interventions. During the days of Gunboat Diplomacy in the early twentieth century, the United States was usually quite open about its economic interests, sending in U.S. ships and marines to "protect American property" and to make sure that U.S. bankers collected their debts.

But since the 1940s U.S. leaders have tended to play down the importance of economic motives in explaining U.S. policy in the region, claiming that as a global power the United States has "global responsiblities" that require it to be particularly vigilant in opposing radical or Marxist movements in the Western Hemisphere. But throughout the postwar era, economic interests have continued to play a critical role in explaining U.S. actions in Central America and the Caribbean Basin. In the case of the CIA-orchestrated overthrow of Jacobo Arbenz in Guatemala in 1954, for example, U.S. business interests, particularly those linked to the United Fruit Company, were instrumental in lobbying for and helping arrange the ouster of Arbenz' elected government.[1]

Today, economic and corporate business interests are important in explaining why the United States has embarked on the most extensive intervention it has ever carrried out in Central America. Even President Reagan in laying out his national security argument points to some strategic economic considerations. In his address to the Joint Session of Congress in April 1983, he declared that one of the main reasons why the United States had to stop communism in the Caribbean Basin is that "two thirds of all our foreign trade and petroleum passes through the Panama Canal and the Caribbean." And Secretary of State Shultz, in a statement before the U.S. Senate, declared that "the health of the Caribbean economies also effects our economy. The area is now a $7 billion market for U.S. exports."[2]

The U.S. economic stake, in fact, goes far beyond the securing of U.S. trade routes and the maintenance of export markets. When one looks at the Caribbean Basin as a whole—just as Ronald Reagan and most U.S. leaders do—we see that U.S. corporate holdings in the region are substantial. Agriculture, manufacturing, mining, tourism, and commercial holdings account for $6.2 billion in productive invest-

191

ments, and another $16.9 billion is tied up in banking and financial operations in the Caribbean Basin. This constitutes about 9 percent of total U.S. investments abroad.[3] When compared to other third world regions, these figures put the Caribbean Basin in second place in economic importance to the United States, surpassed only by the rest of Latin America (i.e., South America and Mexico).

U.S. economic interests in the Caribbean Basin fall into six distinct categories: (1) agribusiness and plantation holdings, (2) manufacturing investments geared to the local markets, (3) investments in runaway shops, or export manufacturing, (4) mining and petroleum operations, (5) banking and finance-related activities, and (6) tourism and service industries.

To understand the full extent of these economic interests we shall take a concrete look at the U.S. stake in each of these areas throughout the Caribbean Basin. We can then see which business organizations are active in shaping U.S. policy toward the region. Finally we will grapple with the issue of just how U.S. economic interests are interlinked with national security interests in explaining the overall thrust of U.S. policy in the Caribbean Basin.

Agribusiness

Historically, the Caribbean Basin was one of the first major areas of expansion for U.S. capital. Indeed, in the early twentieth century the bulk of U.S. investments in the third world was found in the Caribbean Basin, primarily in sugar and banana plantations.* In Puerto Rico, the Dominican Republic, Cuba, Guatemala, Honduras, and Costa Rica, U.S. investors owned plantations that were run as economic enclaves. In addition to possessing large tracts of land, they controlled the local labor force, and they set up railroads, ports, and shipping facilities to move bananas or sugar to the U.S. market.

For over half a century the largest share of total U.S. investments was tied up in these enclaves. But by the 1950s economic growth in the Caribbean Basin, which opened up new investment opportunities,

---

*The United States also had some large investments in public utilities in the Caribbean.

combined with the rise of economic nationalism and the expropriation or voluntary selling-off of some plantations, reduced the relative importance of plantation holdings. Today these early agribusiness investments are surpassed by U.S. holdings in manufacturing and banking. But investments in plantation agriculture still represent a major stake for a handful of powerful U.S. corporations, namely Castle & Cooke, R.J. Reynolds (via its Del Monte subsidiary), Gulf & Western, United Brands, Hershey, and Haitian American Sugar. These corporations run large plantations in the Dominican Republic, Honduras, Guatemala, Costa Rica, Panama, and to a lesser extent in Belize and Haiti.

Each of the first four corporations mentioned above has diversified holdings in some of the countries where they operate. Some of these diversified investments are in new areas of agricultural production, such as pineapples, vegetables, coconuts, and palm oil production, while other investments are in food processing and manufacturing. In fact, the extensive investments of Castle & Cooke in Honduras and Gulf & Western in the Dominican Republic give these companies tremendous influence in the local economies. In Honduras, for example, in addition to Castle & Cooke's sizable plantation holdings which produce an array of fruits and vegetables for the export market, the company owns two breweries, a plastics plant, a cement plant, and a couple of margarine .and food processing plants. And in the Dominican Republic Gulf & Western runs tourist hotels and gambling casinos, is a major investor in the country's free trade zone in Santo Domingo, and produces chemicals, cement, and beef cattle.[4] Both these corporations are by far the largest single corporate enterprise in their respective countries.

During the 1960s a number of large U.S. food companies began using Central America as a base for fishing the rich waters of the Pacific and Caribbean. Shrimp and crustacean fishing ventures were established in Panama, Nicaragua, Costa Rica, the Cayman Islands, and El Salvador by such companies as Borden, Consolidated Foods, General Mills, International Proteins, and Ward Foods. As the technology of shrimp farming advanced during the 1970s, other often smaller U.S. companies, such as Maricultura S.A. and Shrimp Culture, established ventures in the region.[5]

In addition to the agribusiness investment stake in the region, the trade in certain agricultural commodities is also important to the U.S. economy as a whole. Today over 68 percent of the bananas, 33 percent of the sugar, and 19 percent of the coffee imported by the United States comes from the Caribbean Basin.⁶ These are certainly not strategic commodities since they are produced in other third world countries and in some cases in the United States itself. But the heavy trade in these selected commodities does illustrate how for years the United States has relied on the Caribbean Basin for large quantities of needed agricultural commodities.

Manufacturing

The diversification of the old plantation corporations has, in fact, placed them firmly in another investment camp which boomed steadily in the 1960s—local manufacturing geared to the internal markets, or import substitution industrialization. Starting in the 1950s U.S. multinationals began to realize that new profits could be made by catering to the needs of the upper classes and the incipient middle classes in the region. The formation of the Central American Common Market in 1961 gave a special impetus to these types of investment since bigger regional markets could be tapped. And the larger countries in the Caribbean (the Dominican Republic, Jamaica, Trinidad, and Haiti) also attracted multinational manufacturing capital, simply because they had the largest markets in the area.

A wide array of American products—ranging from Kellogg's corn flakes and Standard Brands Jello to Phelps Dodge copper tubing and American Standard toilet bowls—were produced in countries in the Caribbean Basin. While many of these plants did not require substantial amounts of capital— they were often assembling and packaging operations that relied heavily on imported parts or materials—the total number of investments throughout the region was quite substantial. By 1980 there were a minimum of 300 U.S. multinational investments in these types of enterprise. Well over half of the top 100 U.S. multinationals had one or more investments located in the Caribbean Basin.⁷

Runaway Shops

The other major area of U.S. manufacturing investment is in plants that assemble or manufacture products for export to the U.S. market.

Commonly referred to as "runaway shops," *"maquilas,"* or "export platforms," these enterprises search the globe for the cheapest exploitable labor resources and for the most favorable government concessions (i.e., tax incentives, government subsidized infrastructure projects, etc.). These runaway shops first began to proliferate in the 1960s, primarily in Southeast Asia (Singapore, Malaysia, etc.) and in northern Mexico.

But in the early 1970s, as labor costs rose in these regions, the *maquilas* began to move into other regions, including the Caribbean Basin. The Dominican Republic, Haiti, and El Salvador attracted the largest number of such investments, with each country granting special tariff and tax concessions and setting up special zones in which these plants could locate. Most other countries in the Basin have also attracted one or more of these low-wage enterprises. Examples of some of the products of these plants and the countries in which they operate are: stuffed toys (Haiti), pharmaceutical products (the Bahamas), "Aris Isotoner" high fashion gloves (El Salvador), computer parts assembly (St. Kitts and El Salvador), data processing (Haiti), women's undergarments (Jamaica, Antigua, and the Dominican Republic), watch assembly (Virgin Islands), baseballs (Haiti), and electronic component assembly (El Salvador, Trinidad, Haiti, Virgin Islands, etc.).

In many cases runaway shop investments in the Caribbean Basin are made by smaller, not widely known companies, particularly those based in the southern and western United States. Such companies as Transducer Systems, Harowe Controls, Lovable Company, and Bourns Inc. are involved in the region. For some of these firms, these Caribbean investments are their first venture abroad.[8]

Many U.S. firms are tapping the cheap labor resources of the Caribbean without even making any direct investments. "Subcontracting," whereby a foreign company contracts with a local agent or entrepreneur for a certain quantity of goods, is increasingly common. Under this arrangement, the U.S. company merely pays a set price for each article produced, and the local entrepreneur is in charge of organizing the labor force and seeing that the commodities are actually assembled or manufactured.

Recent technological advances even permit U.S. corporations to subcontract or directly employ secretarial workers in the third world. Dictated office reports or rough transcripts prepared in the United States are transferred to Caribbean countries using word processors and satellite communications systems. Sometimes they are typed and sent back to the United States on the same day. The English-speaking nations in the Caribbean, particularly Barbados and Jamaica, are the particular targets of this form of "office sharing." Companies as large as Citicorp and as relatively unknown as Satellite Data Corporation of New York are involved in this process, often paying wages less than half those paid for secretarial work in the United States.[9]

Largely because of its cheap labor force, extensive government repression, and denial of even minimal labor rights, Haiti is one of the most attractive countries for both the subcontractors and the *maquilas*. Referred to as the "Taiwan of the Caribbean," Haiti's recent economic development is closely linked to the production of light manufactured goods for markets in the United States. Over 80 percent of the modern industrial workforce is employed in one of 190 companies that assemble or produce manufactured goods for foreign markets. Already by 1978, the country's historic export leader, coffee, had been replaced by the export of textiles, electronic equipment, toys, and sporting goods.[10]

For the runaway shops, the Caribbean Basin has virtually unlimited potential for expansion. The passage of the Caribbean Basin Initiative, which abolishes most U.S. tariff barriers for countries in the region, is a major new incentive for the *maquilas* to set up operations there. U.S. firms can now treat the Caribbean Basin as a virtual extension of the U.S. economy. This new legislation, combined with rising labor costs in regions such as Asia and the geographic proximity of the Basin, make it increasingly likely that the Caribbean region could become the most important export platform for the United States market. Political and social factors, namely labor unrest and revolutionary upheaval, are the principal obstacles that could prevent U.S. corporations from turning the Caribbean Basin into the new sweatshop of the Americas.

Minerals and Petroleum

Although the United States is not heavily dependent on the Caribbean Basin for key minerals or petroleum supplies, the region nonetheless does have some important U.S. investments in mining and petroleum refining. The most important U.S. holdings in mining and smelting are in Jamaican bauxite. Large bauxite mining operations were opened up there in the 1950s by Reynolds Metals and Kaiser

Aluminum. Subsequently, Alcoa, Revere Copper, and Alcan also made sizeable investments in Jamaican bauxite mining and smelting, turning Jamaica into the largest bauxite and aluminum supplier for the United States.

Then in the mid 1970s the Jamaican government levied a bauxite export tax on the companies and compelled them to "Jamaicanize" their operations by selling 51 percent of their holdings to the government. As a result U.S. investments in Jamaica dropped from $302 million in 1976 to $229 million in 1979.[11] But the U.S. stake is still substantial, and under the new "free enterprise" government of Edward Seaga, there has been a resurgence of interest by foreign investors in Jamaica. Today Jamaica remains by far the largest single foreign supplier of bauxite for the United States.

Although outside of bauxite deposits, Central America and the Caribbean islands are not exceptionally rich in mineral resources, a spate of mining investments occurred in the late 1960s and early 1970s when the U.S. need for raw materials from abroad was seemingly insatiable. These investments were concentrated in nickel, copper, silver, and gold mining. The largest single investment ($195 million) was made jointly by Falconbridge and Armco in nickel mining in the Dominican Republic. INCO corporation set up another large nickel mining operation in Guatemala ($120 million) while Texasgulf and Canadian Javelin Ltd. both undertook exploratory copper mining operations in Panama. Gold and silver mines were also opened up in the Dominican Republic, Honduras, El Salvador, Guatemala, and Costa Rica during the 1970s.

However, the slow growth of the dominant capitalist economies in the late 1970s together with a surge of nationalism in the Caribbean Basin dealt a severe blow to these new investments. By 1982 the drop in international mineral prices led to the closure of the nickel mines in the Dominican Republic and Guatemala and the abandonment of the copper mining exploration efforts in Panama. Meanwhile, gold and silver mines owned by New York & Honduras Rosario (which merged with Atlantic Richfield) were expropriated in Nicaragua and the Dominican Republic in the late 1970s.

These setbacks for the U.S. mining industry in the Caribbean Basin were more than offset by the increase in U.S. petroleum investments. U.S holdings in petroleum jumped from approximately 1.4 billion in 1975 to 2.2 billion in 1981. Most of the petroleum investments in Central America are concentrated in marketing facilities and in small import substituting refineries. In Panama, a surge of investments occurred in bunkering and storage facilities, and in 1981, a $250 million project was begun to build a trans-Isthmus oil pipeline and the attendant oil storage facilities.

The Caribbean Basin as a whole is particularly important as an oil refining center for the U.S. market. In fact, the Caribbean is now one of the five major export refining centers of the world, with oil arriving from most of the important oil producers of the world—Venezuela, Mexico, Alaska, the Middle East, and Africa. The largest refining centers are in the U.S. Virgin Islands, the Netherlands Antilles, and Trinidad.[12] U.S. oil companies are also involved in refining on Martinique, Antigua, and Barbados. Among the firms that operate in these countries are Amoco, Texaco, Exxon, Occidental, and a couple of lesser known companies, Tesoro Petroleum, and Amerada Hess.[13]

In terms of actual petroleum production, the most important country in the Caribbean Basin for the past decade has been Trinidad and Tobago. It is sometimes compared to the Arab Emirate countries because its relatively small population (1.1 million) has a per capita income of close to $5,000, derived principally from petroleum.

Hoping to uncover more petroleum deposits in the Caribbean Basin in the 1970s and early 1980s, a number of U.S. companies undertook exploration efforts in the Dominican Republic, Jamaica, Antigua, Belize, Guatemala, the Bahamas, and offshore from Honduras and Barbados. Thus far the most important discoveries have been in Guatemala. There Basic Resources International S.A., an international consortium dominated by Rockefeller interests (later taken over by Western European capital), struck oil in the mid-1970s, and in 1978 it began construction on a 143-mile pipeline to link its inland oil fields with the Gulf of Mexico. At present the true extent of Guatemalan oil reserves is unknown, but they certainly are the largest in Central America and have already been pointed to as one key reason why the United States must maintain firm control of Guatemala and the rest of Central America.

Banking and Finance

The real boom in U.S. capital investments in the Caribbean Basin since the mid-1970s has been in banking and finance. Between 1976 and 1981 U.S. investments in this area jumped from $1.5 billion to $16.9 billion.[14] This dramatic increase is primarily due to the quest of the major U.S. banks for offshore banking operations abroad where they can evade taxes and regulations, and thereby increase their ability to move capital throughout the world. In the Caribbean Basin the primary centers of these banking investments are the Bahamas, Bermuda, the Netherlands Antilles, and Panama. The concentration of banking capital in these countries makes the Caribbean Basin one of the principal offshore centers for U.S. banks, rivaling and perhaps even surpassing Hong Kong, Singapore, and London in importance.

This surge in finance-related investments represents the "third wave" of U.S. investments in the Caribbean Basin, following the plantation and agribusiness investments at the beginning of the century and the manufacturing investments in the 1960s and 1970s. Banking and finance-related investments have in fact superseded all other U.S.investments in the region. In 1981, approximately 40 percent of U.S. holdings were in finance-related fields.

While these investments are of critical importance for U.S. finance capital, primarily because they give U.S. banks tremendous maneuverability in world financial markets, we should not overestimate their importance and impact on the Caribbean Basin. Clearly the bulk of this investment is "paper capital," which can be moved quickly from one region of the world to another. In fact, Panama's recent decision to levy a tax on banking operations there has caused some of them to move large amounts of capital out of the country, thereby reducing Panama's relative importance. Very little of the capital these banks hold is directly invested in productive activities within the Caribbean Basin. However, in some instances the presence of these banks does actually facilitate lending to local capitalists and governments. Here again Panama provides the example. As a recent *Wall Street Journal* article pointed out, thanks to the continued presence of a large number of international banks in Panama, the country has been able to weather the international liquidity and debt crisis better than any other country in Central America.[15] The fact that international bankers "know the scene" in Panama is certainly a factor in that country's continued access to credit.

Aside from these banking and finance activities, U.S. finance capital has also acquired high visibility in the Caribbean Basin through its extensive loans to the countries of the region. The total debt of these countries to international creditors stands at around $13 billion, of which at least $5 billion is owed directly to U.S. banks.[16] (The remaining debt is to the U.S. government and affiliated agencies, to international lending agencies such as the World Bank, and to other Western bankers.) These loans are concentrated in the Central American countries and in Jamaica, the Dominican Republic, and Trinidad and Tobago. While these debt levels do not approach those of Brazil and Mexico, they do give U.S. bankers a stake in maintaining "financial order" and stability in the region. Debt default by several of these countries could have serious international repercussions, particularly because of the "demonstration effect" (i.e., other countries would likely follow suit). Among the U.S. banks with the largest exposure in the region are Chase Manhattan, Bank of America, Citicorp, Wells Fargo, and First Boston.

The Tourist Industry

No single U.S. investment in the Caribbean has grown so steadily in the past three decades as that of the tourist industry. As the U.S. economy expanded and more and more Americans traveled abroad, starting in the late 1950s, the Caribbean became one of the major mass tourist centers of the world. An array of U.S. investors, ranging from big transnational firms to thousands of small enterprises, moved into the Caribbean Basin to develop and profit from this boom. Cuba was the first Caribbean island to draw large numbers of U.S. tourists, but with the revolution there in 1959, U.S. companies and American tourists moved on to others. The Bahamas, the Virgin Islands, the Cayman Islands, Antigua, Montserrat, St. Kitts, these and other countries in the Caribbean saw dramatic changes in their demographic profiles, their economies, and their entire social orders with the surge in tourism in the 1960s and 1970s. Traditional areas of the economy, particularly agriculture, were decimated, and today tourism is virtually the only basis of their economies.

The Bahama Islands have been in the forefront of the tourist boom. Today, 70 percent of the Gross National Product of the Bahamas is derived from tourism, with over 1.7 million tourists visiting the island annually. (The only other major industry on the islands are the offshore banking enterprises described previously.) While exact figures on U.S. investments in the Bahaman tourist industry are unknown, the total

U.S. investment in the islands is $1.5 billion and the largest share of that is found in tourist-related enterprises.[17]

While the impact of the tourist industry on the region is profound, it is virtually impossible to calculate the substantial profits that accrue to U.S. companies from the tourist industry in the Caribbean. Many of the businesses that benefit, such as travel agencies and advertising firms, do not have any direct presence in the Caribbean. Others, such as airlines and shipping firms, have no presence or investments other than the offices they need to service the tourists abroad.

And then there are the racketeering and gambling interests which have developed hand in hand with the tourism industry. It is no accident that one of the most important "growth" areas for the mafia is in the Caribbean. Meyer Lansky, for example, after seeing his widespread gambling and "entertainment" business shut down in the wake of the Cuban revolution, moved on to the Bahamas where he made millions and became one of the primary movers in opening up the islands to tourism.[18]

While we cannot possibly catalog and report on the myriad business interests involved in the Caribbean, we can point to some of the large corporations that have a major stake in Caribbean tourism. The most visible are the airline companies and the international hotel chains. Eastern Airlines, Pan American, TWA, American, Air Florida, and Delta—these are some of the major airline companies that move tourists in and out of the Caribbean. The hotel chains, which are often linked to the airlines, either through special tourist packages or even through common stock holding corporations, have the largest single direct investment stake in the region. Holiday Inn, Intercontinental Hotels, Hilton, Sheraton, Camino Real, and Western Hotels are the largest chains that operate in the region. And linked closely to both the airlines and the hotels are the car rental agencies such as Avis, Hertz, and Budget.[19]

The tourist industry places special political and social demands on the Caribbean countries. Most tourists that arrive from the metropolitan centers expect the beaches to be clean and the natives friendly, or even servile. The last thing they expect to deal with are nationalistic, assertive workers or "natives," who will upset their idyllic vacation dreams. This is why several of the Caribbean countries have launched "be nice" to tourists campaigns to make their countries appear more inviting to foreign tourists. Political or social upheaval are anathema to the tourist industry. The relatively benign experiment in "democratic socialism" undertaken by Michael Manley in Jamaica in the mid and late 1970s, for example, had a particularly devastating impact on the tourist industry. By the end of his term, tourism had dropped by over 50 percent. The government of Edward Seaga, with its free enterprise philosophy and its determination to create economic and social conditions that benefit the tourist industry, has been able to reverse this flow.

Impact on U.S. Policy

In sum, U.S. business interests throughout the Caribbean Basin are quite substantial. Virtually every major corporate sector in the United States, be it agribusiness, manufacturing, banking, mining, petroleum, or the service industries, has a significant stake in the Caribbean Basin.

Some very interesting characteristics emerge from this description of U.S. business interests in the Caribbean. One is that there are a large number of small firms and investors that have holdings in the Caribbean. Unlike the large multinationals, many of these firms have investments only in the Caribbean, and for them, the region is extremely important as they develop their investment strategies and future plans for international expansion. Another important characteristic is that among the big corporate interests in the Caribbean Basin, the Rockefellers clearly predominate. They are involved in tourism (through recreational holdings such as Rockeresorts, and through an interest in Eastern Airlines); in petroleum (through Exxon, and earlier through Basic Resources International); and in banking (through Chase Manhattan, which has offshore facilities in the Caribbean and has lent hundreds of millions to governments in the region). Ever since the early part of this century, the Rockefellers have been the predominant corporate group in the Caribbean Basin.[20]

These findings lead to the question of just what role U.S. business plays in shaping U.S. policymaking in the Caribbean Basin. Since U.S. business interests there are substantial, do we see that they are actively involved in supporting or advocating an aggressive, counter-revolutionary strategy in Central America? And is it possible that it is the U.S. economic stake which compels the Reagan administration to draw the line in El Salvador? If so, this raises the question of whether or not the assertion that U.S. national security interests are at stake is merely propaganda, designed to mobilize a reluctant U.S. public to support an interventionary policy that is mainly designed to protect U.S. business interests.

The Stance of the Corporate Community

There is no doubt that the corporate community as a whole wants to preserve the Caribbean Basin for capitalism in general, and in particular as an outlet for U.S. investments. Socialism, and the revolutionary upheaval which brings socialist regimes to power, are repugnant to the capitalists. Even if revolutionary change does not lead to socialism it is resisted by capitalists, because the attendant social and political upheaval disrupts the economy, throwing into question existing investments and making it difficult or impossible to plan new investments.

But even though these are the basic premises that guide the capitalists in their approach to the Caribbean Basin and the rest of the third world, the diverse business sector has a variety of views about what the U.S. government should do once it confronts a revolutionary situation. Some may favor direct U.S. intervention, while others may believe that such an intervention may be too costly, either in terms of its impact on the country involved, or because of the social, political, and economic costs that would accrue within the United States. In the case of Nicaragua, there was a sizeable sector of the U.S. business community, which at least in 1979-80 thought it could work out a modus vivendi with the Sandinista government.[21] Many of these business interests, of course, believed that they could coopt or persuade the Sandinistas to maintain a capitalist economy, thereby opening up the country for new investment opportunities. Even after Reagan supported the CIA in a clandestine war against the Sandinista government, some U.S. businesses tried to carry on "business as usual" with the regime. The Bank of America, in spite of pressures from the Reagan administration, tried to pull together a consortium of banks in early 1983 which sought $25 million in short-term credits for Nicaragua.[22]

Although these credits never came through because other U.S. banks held back, the Bank of America's efforts illustrate the general rule that U.S. business in the Caribbean Basin does not speak with a single voice. Some business representatives are adamant in their support of Reagan's tough stand in the Caribbean Basin, others are more inclined to look for a negotiated solution, one which would prevent a generalized conflict from erupting in the region. And even a few businesses would be willing to accept and work with revolutionary governments. In short, the different policy currents that exist among the foreign policy elites are also reflected within the corporate community. As Paul Joseph found out in his study of the corporate community during the Vietnam war, "political disagreements within the capitalist class substantially reproduce policy conflicts among the state managers."[23]

But this does not mean that there is no need to analyze the role of the corporate community in U.S. foreign policy. In fact, it is important to see just which corporate sectors are advocating an interventionist policy in the Caribbean Basin. In the case of the Caribbean and Latin America, a number of business organizations have been set up over the years to articulate the interests of the corporate community and to affect U.S. policy. As we see below, these organizations tend to be dominated by the very corporate interests which have the most at stake in the region.

The Corporate Lobbies

Several of the business organizations act in close concert with the interventionist policies of the Reagan administration. The Rockefeller family, and particularly the family's financial scion, David Rockefeller, has been especially active in linking the business community and the government together over Caribbean issues. One of David Rockefeller's most recent organizational endeavors in this arena is the U.S. Business Committee for Jamaica. Set up in 1981 in close collaboration with the Reagan administration, the committee's expressed goal is to facilitate the flow of U.S. capital into Jamaica to boost the government of Edward Seaga. The committee has also been deeply involved in coordinating U.S. policy toward Jamaica, particularly those aspects which deal with U.S. economic policy. Reagan has openly praised the committee and according to the *New York Times*, Rockefeller was instrumental in getting Reagan to purchase large quantities of Jamaican aluminum for the U.S. strategic stockpile.[24]

Another special project of David Rockefeller's is the Americas Society, which he also founded in 1981. This organization brings together under one umbrella several organizations which had been launched or funded by the Rockefellers over the years, including the Council of the Americas, the Center for Inter-American Relations, and the Pan American Society. The concern of the Americas Society with political issues was made clear from the beginning. Rockefeller stressed that the relationship between the United States and the other countries in the Americas is "not exclusively economic, but rather is based firmly in similar political aspirations." The first assistant secretary of state for Inter-American affairs under Reagan, Thomas Enders, endorsed the Americas Society, asserting that "the administration believes the private sector has a vital role to play in the hemisphere" and so "we are pleased that the Americas Society has been formed and we heartily endorse its objectives."[25]

Of the organizations that affiliated with the Americas Society, the Council of the Americas has been most consistently involved in shaping U.S. business and political relations with Latin America and the Caribbean. Founded in 1958, the council represents the leading U.S. corporate interests with a stake in the rest of the Americas. It has been active on a number of fronts: it sends business delegations abroad, encourages new investments, holds special forums or meetings between business and government leaders, and has directed its attention to the major problems confronting the United States in Latin America, ranging from the election of Salvador Allende in Chile in 1970 to the recent attempts to deal with the debt crises of the leading Latin American governments.

In the case of the Caribbean Basin, however, the Council of the Americas has deferred to another organization which it helped found in 1980—the Caribbean/Central American Action, or C/CAA. Today the C/CAA is unquestionably the key business organization dealing with the Caribbean Basin. Founded in response to the deepening political and economic crises in Central America and the Caribbean, the C/CAA received initial support from thirty-five corporations active in the region, ranging from Pan American and Eastern Airlines to Reynolds Metals Company and United Brands.[26] More than any other organization, the C/CAA reveals the growing collaboration of the government and business communities in the effort to halt the advance of the revolutionary forces. The C/CAA's founding committee included not only corporate sponsors, but also representatives of the National Security Council, the U.S. Congress, and the U.S. International Communications Agency. The C/CAA also received a grant from the Agency for International Development to help get started, and its first executive director, Peter Johnson, took a leave from the State Department to assume his new post.

The new organization in its early stages reflected both the growing ascendancy of western and southern U.S. business interests and the importance of medium-sized businesses in the Caribbean Basin. While Bill Moody of the Rockefeller Brothers Fund initially helped set up the organization, its key officers come from outside the eastern establishment. Robert West, Jr., head of Tesoro Petroleum Corporation based in Texas, has played a major role in founding the organization, serving as both its treasurer and president. West, in addition to managing his company's petroleum interests in Trinidad and Tobago, has also served as an official in the Texas Republican Party. The director of C/CAA until mid-1983 was Sam Segner, who is president of Internorth Inc., a Nebraska-based company which specializes in petroleum distribution. His interest in the Caribbean stems from his company's distribution of propane gas in Guatemala, Jamaica, and Puerto Rico.

While the C/CAA appointed Jimmy Carter as its first honorary chairman in 1980, after the elections that year it moved quickly to consolidate its relations with the Reagan administration. Reagan addressed the annual meeting of the C/CAA in 1981 and its executive director, Peter Johnson, was instrumental in encouraging the administration to launch a special economic assistance program for the Caribbean Basin which subsequently became known as the Caribbean Basin Initiative.[27]

Even more importantly, the C/CAA is directly involved in providing support for Reagan's policy objectives in Central America. In the case of El Salvador, the C/CAA is trying to strengthen that country's business community and to reactivate the economy. A special C/CAA advisory team, which received AID support, was dispatched to El Salvador in 1981. It in turn set up the Foundation for Social and Economic Development in El Salvador, which was designed to be "the technical and research base of the country's private sector," and to work with the government and other agencies on "economic problems and opportunities."[28]

The C/CAA's most ambitious operation in Central America is its "twinning program." Set up in April 1982 at a conference in Guatemala with AID support, the twinning program is aimed at strengthening the ties between chambers of commerce in the United States and similar business organizations throughout Central America. Under this program, the Chamber of Commerce in Minneapolis, for example, will "twin" with a chamber or business organization in Tegucigalpa, Honduras. The U.S. chamber will try to help its counterpart by sending small groups down to consult with local businesses and perhaps even by organizing some new joint investment projects.

The overtly political intentions of the twinning program were apparent at the first meeting when the chair asked which U.S. chambers would twin with the private business sector in Nicaragua (which is in general opposed to the Sandinista government). The C/CAA report on the meeting states that this was a "particularly moving moment" as nine U.S. chamber representatives stood and proclaimed their "solidarity" with the Nicaraguan representatives by twinning with them.[29]

The twinning program was coordinated closely with one particular set of business organizations in the region—those affiliated with the Association of American Chambers of Commerce in Latin America. Local chambers have been active for decades in every country on the Central American isthmus except Belize. These chambers, aside from having ties to the U.S. chambers of commerce, are important because they link together the local business interests and U.S. corporations with investments in the region. In Guatemala and El Salvador, for example, the chambers include virtually all the U.S. corporations with investments there and representatives of major sectors of the local bourgeoisies.

Corporate Interests and National Security

What do these activities by the C/CAA and other business organizations in the Caribbean Basin demonstrate? Clearly they show that the U.S. corporate community is very active in advancing its interests in the Caribbean Basin, and that in the present moment of crisis in the region significant corporate sectors are working closely with the U.S. government in an effort to maintain U.S. ascendancy in the region. In a certain sense the activities of the C/CAA can be characterized as "grass-roots organizing" between the bourgeoisies of the United States and the Caribbean Basin countries. They are strengthening their ties in an effort to preserve capitalism in the region and to ward off the advances of the revolutionary forces.

An analysis of the business organizations also reveals that there is a special alliance of business interests which is mobilizing support for Reagan's policies in the Caribbean Basin. Business interests in the

South and West, which comprise the hard core of Reagan's general support in the business community, are clearly taking an aggressive stance with him in the Caribbean Basin. But what is interesting to observe is that the Rockefellers, the old leaders of the eastern establishment, are collaborating closely with Reagan and his southern and western business allies. This is demonstrated in the case of the U.S. Business Committee for Jamaica and the C/CAA.

In mid-1983 the key business leaders active in organizing the business community around Caribbean Basin issues moved to forge a united front. On June 13 the Americas Society led by David Rockefeller and the C/CAA led by Robert West announced that they would effectively merge their organizations. David Rockefeller became the president of C/CAA and he was joined on that organization's board by several other members of the Americas Society. At the same time, the Americas Society board was expanded to include representatives of the C/CAA including Robert West. This interlocking of the two organizations' boards and activities brought together virtually all the corporate interests with a substantial stake in the Caribbean Basin, and it guaranteed that their advice and opinions would weigh in heavily in policy circles. As the C/CAA pointed out after the merger, the business community would now have "a greater combined impact," and be able to strengthen its role in "public policy advocacy."[30]

Unfortunately, the information available is not sufficient to reveal whether or not other sectors of the eastern establishment have lined up with the Rockefellers in consolidating their relationship with southern and western capitalists, and if they are supporting the policies of the Reagan administration. Certainly the fact that *Business Week*, a business publication that often reflects the views of the liberal eastern establishment, has come out with major articles criticizing Reagan's Central American policies indicates that important corporate sectors have serious reservations about U.S. policies in the Caribbean.[31] These sectors do support U.S. policies that specifically advance concrete U.S. business interests (like the Caribbean Basin Initiative) but they are wary of where the more militaristic measures will lead. As was noted earlier, the exact stance of corporate representatives on the issue of direct intervention will depend on their assessment of a variety of factors— whether they believe such an intervention could succeed, and what would be the political, economic, and social costs of intervention in this country.

This brings us to the final question—the relationship between U.S.

economic interests in the Caribbean Basin and the U.S. national security. Given the extensive U.S. investments in the region, and given its very close ties to the business community as a whole, is the Reagan administration merely striving to defend U.S. economic interests there? Is its assertion that the U.S. national security is at stake a subterfuge designed to mislead the U.S. public? Certainly neither the Reagan administration nor any other U.S. administration will ever declare to the American people that they are simply defending some narrow U.S. business interests abroad. As much as possible U.S. policies have to be cloaked in neutral if not altruistic or national security terms. However, this does not reduce the security issue to a mere subterfuge.

For U.S. political leaders and the entire capitalist class, the issues of national security and economics are, in fact, completely intertwined. If new revolutionary socialist governments come to power in Central America and the Caribbean, this threatens not only U.S. political and military control of the region, but also the ability of U.S. capitalists to extract economic resources and profits from the region.

In the Caribbean Basin, perhaps even more than in other regions of the third world, U.S. imperialism is an integrated system, a system in which economic, political, and military control are interlinked and inseparable. A challenge in any of these areas of control is inevitably viewed as a challenge to the entire system. This is why major sectors of the corporate community and the current state managers are collaborating in a desperate drive to maintain the entire system in the Caribbean Basin. They recognize that the rise of new socialist and anti-imperialist governments in the region will end the historic pattern of U.S. domination and compel the U.S. ruling class to find an entirely new basis for its relations with the Caribbean Basin countries.

Notes

1. Stephen Schlesinger and Stephen Kinzer, *Bitter Fruit: The Untold Story of the American Coup in Guatemala* (Garden City, New York: Doubleday, 1982) and Richard Immerman, *The CIA in Guatemala* (Austin: University of Texas Press, 1982), p. 119.
2. George Schultz, *Caribbean Basin Economic Recovery Act* (Washington, D.C.: United States Department of State, Bureau of Public Affairs, April 13, 1983).

3. Updated and revised figures from Marc W. Herold, "Worldwide Investment and Disinvestment by U.S. Multinationals: Implications for the Caribbean and Central America," paper presented at the Second Central American and Caribbean Seminar, Managua, Nicaragua, February 1983, table E.1. The Caribbean Basin is here defined as including the thirty-two countries and territories that are located in the Caribbean sea and the Central American isthmus. Neither Mexico nor any of the countries on the South American continent are included. Puerto Rico is left out because the large U.S. investment stake there, due to the special political and economic relation it has with the United States, would distort the economic picture of the region. Bermuda (where U.S. investors had $11.2 billion tied up) is also left out because the vast bulk of this is finance related (especially insurance). And Mexico even more than Puerto Rico has a special historic relationship with the United States which clearly separates it from the Caribbean and Central American countries. In any case, the inclusion of U.S. investments in Mexico and Puerto Rico would have only strengthened the argument that the U.S. economic stake is substantial and that this is an important factor explaining U.S. intervention in the region.

4. Roger Burbach and Patricia Flynn, *Agribusiness in the Americas* (New York: Monthly Review Press, 1980), Appendix.

5. Marc W. Herold, "Multinational Enterprise Data Base," Economics Program, University of New Hampshire, Durham, N.H.

6. U.S. Department of Commerce, Bureau of the Census, "U.S. General Imports, Schedule A: Commodity Groupings by World Area," 1980 and 1981.

7. Herold, "Multinational Enterprise Data Base."

8. See for example *Forbes*, February 1, 1982, pp. 45-46. A detailed listing of over 150 recent U.S. investments in the Caribbean and Central America can be found in the appendix to Herold, "Worldwide Investment."

9. Andrew Pollack, "Latest Technology May Spawn the Electronic Sweatshop," *New York Times*, October 3, 1982 and Kevin P. Power, "Now We Can Move Offshore Work to Enhance Output," *Wall Street Journal*, June 9, 1983.

10. *Manchester Guardian* and *Le Monde* International Edition, June 21, 1981.

11. Calculated from U.S. Dept. of Commerce, *Survey of Current Business*, various issues.

12. *NACLA Report on the Americas*, October 1976.

13. *Miami Herald*, April 25, 1981. See also *C/CAA Caribbean Data Book* (Washington, D.C., 1983).

14. Herold, "Worldwide Investment," Table E.1.

15. *Wall Street Journal*, November 1982.

16. Federal Financial Institutions Examination Council, "Country Exposure Lending Survey," Washington, D.C., June 1982.

17. *Financial Times*, January 27, 1981.
18. Louis Turner and John Ash, *The Golden Hordes* (New York: St. Martin's, 1977).
19. *C/CAA Caribbean Data Book*.
20. See for example, Oscar Pino-Santos, *El asalto a Cuba por la oligarquia financiera yanqui* (Havana: Casa de las Americas, 1973), Marc W. Herold, "Finanzkapital in El Salvador, 1900-1980," *Economic Forum* 14, no. 1 (Summer 1983), "The Rockefeller Empire: Latin America," NACLA Newsletter 3, no. 2 (April-May 1969), and V. Perlo, *The Empire of High Finance* (New York: International Publishers, 1957), p. 160.
21. John F.H. Purcell, "The Perceptions and Interests of United States Business in Relation to the Political Crisis in Central America," in Richard Feinberg, ed., *Central America: International Dimensions of the Crisis* (New York: Holmes & Meier, 1982), p.107.
22. *Euromoney*, April 1983.
23. Paul Joseph, *Cracks in the Empire* (Boston: South End Press, 1981), p.189.
24. Jeff Gerth, "Reagan's Jamaican Push Helps U.S. Industry," *New York Times*, April 28, 1982.
25. Tom Barry et. al., *Dollars and Dictators*, (Albuquerque, N. M.: The Resource Center, 1982), pp. 42-43.
26. *C/CAA in Action*, A Bimonthly newsletter of Caribbean/Central American Action, July 1980.
27. Interview with Peter Johnson, Summer 1982.
28. *C/CAA in Action* (September-October 1982).
29. *C/CAA in Action* (March-April 1982).
30. Ibid.
31. "Central America: Why the Crisis Will Deepen," and Editorial: "Rethink Central American Policies," *Business Week*, May 23, 1983.

7. Prelude to Revolution: U.S. Investment in Central America

Norma Stoltz Chinchilla and Nora Hamilton

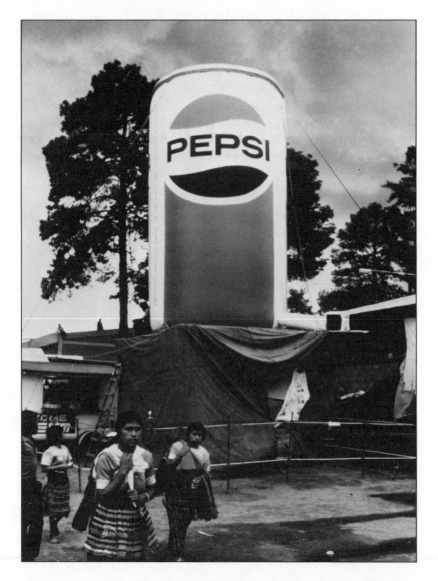

A great regional market is opening up in Central America and alert American companies and businesses around the world are eyeing its tremendous potential and diverse investment opportunities.

—Robert E. Service, economic officer of the U.S. embassy in Nicaragua

There is considerable evidence that Central America is gradually entering a more mature period with respect to the political side of life. . . . It has recently been said that businessmen in Central America will no longer put up with the wild political gyrations which have been the tradition of the area. There is no question that the economic and business element is beginning to exert more and more of a stabilizing influence on the political and social life of Central America.

—Colgate-Palmolive, cited in Industrial Development, *July 1964*

It was over a century ago when railroad contractor Minor Keith began to ship bananas from Puerto Límon, Costa Rica, to the U.S. port of New Orleans, initiating a process which would result in the consolidation of U.S. economic and political hegemony in Central America. By the early decades of this century bananas had become the major export crop of Costa Rica, Honduras, and Guatemala, and U.S. banana companies, most notably United Fruit and Standard Fruit, controlled every phase of their production and marketing.[1] At the same time, the companies wielded unparalleled political power in the so-called banana republics—bribing government officials, backing candidates favorable to their interests with vast sums of money, and as a last resort, counting on the backing of U.S. military power.

Today, the economic and political structures of the region are much more complex, the result of an interaction between emerging groups and forces within Central America and new forms of foreign capital penetration. The creation of a regional common market in 1960, plus generous incentives offered by host governments, drew foreign investment and loans to Central American industry and related ventures. By 1970, foreign capital was expanding beyond traditional export agriculture, taking advantage of export expansion and diversification programs which in many cases it had helped to initiate. Economic penetration into such areas as manufacturing has tied every aspect of the Central American economies into the dynamics of foreign, especially U.S., capital. In at least some countries the result has been substantial change in the economic structure, including the creation of a modern industrial infrastructure—roads and highways, ports and dams, electric power plants, modern communications systems, and airstrips.

But within the affected countries it has also aggravated political and economic contradictions which are now irresolvable within the existing framework. A particular kind of foreign investment—unregulated, unplanned, and based almost entirely on foreign inputs—and the resulting alliance with internal groups and classes fiercely wedded to the economic and political status quo, have been factors in the deep and generalized economic crisis in the region as well as the emergence in several countries of broad-based revolutionary movements. Just how foreign investment contributed to the creation of a crisis so profound that it can only be resolved through a revolutionary movement that challenges its unrestricted operation is the subject of this chapter.

215

Traditional U.S. Investments in Central America

Prior to World War II, U.S. investments in Central America had been almost exclusively in mining, construction, transportation, and export agriculture (especially bananas). U.S. banana companies operated in enclaves, set apart from the rest of the economy: often company executives lived with their families in compounds that were small replicas of U.S. suburbs with green lawns, white picket fences, and the latest U.S. movies flown in for their entertainment. These companies had a monopoly or vitual monopoly over the sectors of production in which they invested: for example, United Fruit owned a controlling interest in the railroads on which it shipped its bananas, the telephone and telegraph system which facilitated its communications between Central America and the United States, the electricity company which supplied it with power, and the shipping lines on which its crates were carried in refrigerated holds.

During the 1930s the Somozas in Nicaragua and a succession of military governments in Guatemala, El Salvador, and Honduras solidified their political control, generally in the interests of U.S. investors and the Central American landowning oligarchies based on coffee, cotton, and livestock. Successive land takeovers by the large landowners, supported by the government, resulted in the decimation of the indigenous communities (except in Guatemala, where they continued to cultivate their private plots and in some cases communal lands in the highlands) and the transformation of smallholders into tenant farmers, landless rural workers, or a semiproletariat farming on marginal plots with seasonal work on coffee, sugar, and cotton plantations.

By the late 1940s, however, this structure was being challenged by industrial groups—often themselves descendants of the landowning families— who recognized that markets for industrial goods could not develop where the majority of the population lived at subsistence levels. At the same time, labor unions and progressive and nationalist elements among the middle class—professionals, students, and even sectors of the government and military—began to protest U.S. hegemony and military dictatorships, and to call for political democracy, economic modernization, and in some cases basic reforms. This movement was most cohesive in Guatemala, where the governments of Juan José Arévalo and Jacobo Arbenz sought to establish conditions for nationalist capitalist development, culminating in an agrarian reform which affected the interests of the U.S. banana companies and the traditional oligarchy. The Arbenz government was overthrown in 1954 in a CIA-sponsored coup, and that of coup leader Castillo Armas, more friendly to the unfettered operation of U.S. business, was installed in its place.[2]

Partly as a result of the reform movement in Guatemala, liberal U.S. policymakers began to recognize that political and economic stability in Central America could not long be sustained in a region where a small minority of foreign investors and landowning interests, backed by unrestrained repression, exploited the majority of the population. This perception was reinforced by the Cuban revolution in 1959. The result was the Alliance for Progress, with its complementary elements of aid and counterinsurgency. Guatemala became the prototype for an extension of foreign investment by U.S. corporations into infrastructure projects and new industries, encouraged by U.S. officials and a succession of military governments in Guatemala. While the Alliance for Progress promoted a new form of U.S. government penetration in Central America and the rest of Latin America, the Central American Common Market established conditions for the expanded penetration of U.S. capital through the spread of the Guatemalan model to the rest of Central America.

The Central American Common Market: Mechanism for U.S. Capital Penetration

The idea of a Central American Common Market originated in the early 1950s through the collaboration of economists from the U.N. Economic Commission for Latin America (ECLA) and young technicians from the Central American countries who shared a concern about the periodic crises resulting from dependence on a few agricultural exports—coffee, bananas, cotton—subject to wide price fluctuations on the world market. ECLA had developed an industrialization program for the larger Latin American countries such as Argentina, Brazil, and Mexico based on the domestic manufacture of former imports, primarily consumer goods. With the elimination of trade barriers and the linking of the consumer markets of the five countries (Guatemala, El Salvador, Honduras, Nicaragua, and Costa Rica), an import-substitution model was also feasible in Central America.

The most aggressive industrialists emerging in Central America after

World War II were those of El Salvador. In many cases members or descendants of the coffee oligarchy themselves, they recognized that the opposition of the oligarchy (and the military which controlled the state in its interests) to agrarian reform and other redistributive measures would prevent development of an industrial market in El Salvador. They tried to resolve this dilemma by seeking markets elsewhere, specifically by penetrating the markets of neighboring countries; successive military regimes thus supported industrialization through bilateral trade treaties, including such measures as tax and tariff exemptions. Despite some opposition by industrial groups in the other Central American countries who feared Salvadoran competition (due, for example, to lower wages in El Salvador), the Salvadoran government by 1953 was able to contract limited bilateral treaties with each of the other four countries. By 1956 Guatemala had also signed treaties with all the other Central American countries except Nicaragua.[3]

Thus both ECLA and the Central American industrialists, particularly from the more populous and relatively developed countries of Guatemala and El Salvador, desired to eliminate tariffs and create a common market, but for somewhat different ends. ECLA and the economists wanted a balanced program of industrial growth, while the industrialists were concerned mainly with the expansion of existing industries. The ECLA plan advocated restrictions on free trade, and required government planning, since the unrestricted operation of the capitalist free market would widen the gap between the more economically developed countries and the smaller, weaker ones. The elimination of tariff barriers would be gradual, and certain types of industry having a natural monopoly in the entire region would be designated integration industries and protected from competition for ten years. These were to be divided evenly among the five countries and exempted from taxes on imports of raw and intermediate materials.

ECLA's concerns were to some extent shared by the smaller Central American countries (especially the Costa Rican private sector and the Honduran government), but for the most part industrialists favored a more rapid integration process and opposed "socialistic" government intervention in the free market. The views of the latter were closer to those in the United States who believed the promotion of private investment (domestic and foreign) and the free operation of market forces would bring about social and economic development through the "trickle down" effect.

Although the basic organizational structure for the common market was established in the 1950s, including the Permanent Secretariat of the General Treaty of Central American Economic Integration (SIECA), and several technical studies were conducted by ECLA, progress toward the integration of the Central American markets was slow. This was due in part to the gradual approach recommended by ECLA, in part to limited funds available to expand investment in the relevant countries, and in part to a lack of cooperation among member governments reluctant to relinquish any element of national power to regional agencies, a problem which persisted through the following two decades.

By the end of the 1950s there was a general consensus that the common market concept was faltering and that industrialization could not go forward without external financing. At the same time, U.S. policymakers were rethinking their Central American strategy and U.S. corporations were being drawn to a broadened Central American market. In a series of meetings with government officials from the Central American countries, U.S. officials promised substantial financial assistance—provided that regulations governing the common market were modified. Restrictions on foreign investment and free trade should be eliminated; the gradual process of tariff elimination between the five countries should be accelerated with tariffs eliminated immediately; and monopoly privileges and the integration industries concept, which interfered with the free flow of investment and with competition, should be discarded.

Promises of substantial economic assistance quickly convinced the governments of Guatemala, El Salvador, and Honduras to accept most of the U.S. conditions, and a tripartite treaty which accelerated the pace of the integration program, calling for internal free trade for most products, was signed under the auspices of a U.S. mission including representatives from the Export Import Bank and the precursor agency of the Agency for International Development (AID). In December 1960 the General Treaty on Central American Economic Cooperation was signed by the economics ministers of four countries (excluding Costa Rica) and was ratified by Guatemala, El Salvador, and Nicaragua in the following year. Honduras ratified the treaty in 1962 and Costa Rica in 1963.

By 1963 the United States had provided $20 million in aid to the common market countries—double the $10 million provided by ECLA between 1951 and 1963. Between 1961 and 1969 the United States provided over $1 billion—70 percent of all external assistance. Through its economic control of the key integration agencies, especially SIECA and the Central American Bank for Economic Integration (BCIE), the United States had succeeded in divesting the common market of the controls posed by the principles of balanced growth and government planning. The new Central American Common Market was a region to which U.S. corporations had unrestricted access.[4]

Patterns of Foreign Investment

Once the common market plan had been remodeled to meet the interests of U.S. capital and leading business groups of the larger Central American countries, foreign capital began to flow into the region in the form of direct investments by transnational corporations, and loans from governments, private banks, and international lending agencies. In the next two decades it penetrated—and transformed—every sector of the Central American economies. Manufacturing plants, often subsidiaries of U.S. companies and operating with U.S. inputs and technology, broadened the market for such amenities of modern life as Colgate toothpaste, Firestone tires, and Coca Cola. Loans from the U.S. government, international agencies, and private banks expanded the resources of domestic private and government banks available to private investors. U.S. agribusiness firms promoted the development of new cash crops destined for U.S. supermarkets and created new markets for imported seeds, fertilizer, and insecticide among large and small farmers. Communications systems and hydroelectric plants, necessary for industrial expansion, were built with foreign technology and under contract with U.S., European, and Japanese firms. New hotels, casinos, and other services financed by U.S. "Sunbelt" investors provided luxurious enclaves for foreign tourists and wealthy Central Americans.

Foreign Investment: The Corporate Invasion

The most visible form of capital penetration was direct foreign investment. The formation of the common market transformed a previously untapped and insignificant market into a new frontier for foreign capital. In addition, U.S. corporations were attracted by tax exemptions and other incentives offered by Central American governments anxious to lure foreign capital. Ads placed in major U.S. newspapers by Central American governments and business groups extolled their particular countries as havens for foreign investment. Guatemala could claim the largest purchasing center, while Honduras pointed out its "history of respect for private property . . . without a single case of expropriation." This was a specific advantage over its larger, more prosperous neighbor which during the nationalist Arbenz administration (1950-54) had briefly deviated from the norms of hospitality due to foreign investors by expropriating unused lands owned by the United Fruit Company for redistribution. The Nicaraguan government passed new legislation eliminating any controls on profit repatriation and other forms of capital remittance, and did not even require foreign investors to register. As stated by the president of Nicaragua's central bank, "We don't impose restrictions on foreign capital by keeping records of it."[5]

The common market changed the direction of foreign investment at the same time that it broadened its scope. In contrast to past foreign investment, most of the new direct investment in the 1960s and 1970s was in manufacturing, specifically manufacturing for exports among the common market countries. This shift in investment orientation was particularly striking in the fruit companies—traditionally responsible for export enclave investment—which now began to diversify into manufacturing. By the mid-1970s United Brands (the former United Fruit) had twenty-five establishments in Central America—six in Costa Rica, five in Guatemala, thirteen in Honduras, and one in Nicaragua. While some of these subsidiaries were directly or indirectly related to banana production (including the Tela Railroad Company and a steamship company as well as packing and refrigeration companies in Honduras), United Brands also had holdings in food production (palm oil, margarine, etc.), electronic data processing systems, plastics, and communications. Castle & Cooke, which purchased Standard Fruit (now Standard Brands) in the 1960s, acquired twenty-five firms, eighteen of them in Honduras, in such areas as steel, beer, cement, soap, plastics, communications, banking, and real estate.

Most investment capital came from manufacturing companies, which entered Central America and established subsidiaries specifically to take advantage of the common market. Such companies as Foremost, Phelps Dodge, Westinghouse, Alcoa, Kimberly Clark, Atlas Chemical, Borden, and Consolidated Foods set up subsidiaries or in some cases bought out existing companies. While the bulk of new investment was in food processing and chemicals, which accounted for 84 percent of U.S. manufacturing investment in 1966 and 64 percent in

1976, there was also investment in other manufactures, such as textiles, paper products, auto assembly, and electronics. Like the banana companies, several of the food companies diversified into unrelated products, reflecting the growth of U.S. conglomerates in the 1960s. Beatrice Foods, for example, had subsidiaries which produced leather, chemicals, and plastics in Nicaragua and textiles in Guatemala.[6]

Between 1959 and 1969 total foreign investment in Central America almost doubled, from $388.2 million to $755.3 million, while that in manufacturing increased fifteenfold from $14.6 million to $228.8 million. In relative terms, the share of manufacturing in total foreign investment increased from 3.8 percent to 30.8 percent during this period, comprising 60 percent of all new foreign investment. Although European and Japanese investment increased steadily between 1960 and 1980, that of the U.S. continued to dominate in both absolute and relative terms, reaching over $1 billion in 1980.

Estimates of the contribution of foreign investment to total manufacturing investment in Central America during this period tend to understate the importance of foreign capital. According to World Bank estimates, direct foreign investment accounted for 15 to 17.5 percent of all fixed industrial assets between 1962 and 1969; total foreign resources, including foreign loans as well as new direct investments and reinvestment by foreign subsidiaries, accounted for an estimated 28 percent of total investment resources.[7] But much of the other 72 percent that was considered to be Central American, including credit from local banks and the Central American Bank for Economic Integration, depreciation, and local investment, also came from foreign sources; most of the BCIE funds and many of those from local banks came from foreign loans.

One of the main types of foreign investment in this period was joint ventures with local capital. These provided a mutually beneficial arrangement in which domestic businesses gained access to foreign capital and technology while foreign investors benefited from local access and the hedge against possible expropriation. In 1970 it was estimated that approximately half of the foreign firms in Central America had local capital participation. Later statistics for El Salvador indicate that joint ventures comprised three-fourths of new investments between 1960 and 1978.[8] Foreign corporations have maintained majority control in most firms, however, and in some cases have bought out local companies or driven them out of the market.

These links with foreign capital have strengthened certain sectors of the local bourgeoisie, in some cases contributing to the emergence of new groups within the capitalist class. During the process of industrialization conflicts occurred between the traditional oligarchy and industrial "modernizers" in each of the Central American countries. These were more pronounced in Costa Rica and Guatemala than in El Salvador, where the industrialists were often from the same families as the coffee oligarchy and investment funds for industrialization had come from coffee earnings in the immediate post-World War II period. The DeSola family, for example, one of the largest coffee exporting landowners in El Salvador, was linked with Unilever in setting up margarine, soap, and detergent factories.[9] In contrast, the major beneficiaries of foreign investment in the Nicaraguan private sector were a relatively new group originating in the postwar cotton boom and organized around the Banco Nicaraguense, or Banic (formed in 1953). The Banic group developed close links with U.S. AID and U.S. corporations, including Consolidated Foods, Booth Fisheries, Pepsi Cola, United Fruit, General Mills, and ABC Television.[10] Foreign capital was also important, although less so, in the expansion into industry of more traditional groups such as the Granada livestock interests which formed part of the Banamerica group. This group was centered in the Banco de America (no relation to the Bank of America), which received funds from the First National Bank of Boston and was 33 percent owned by Wells Fargo.

Political office also provided numerous opportunities to take advantage of foreign capital penetration and the common market to enter the capitalist class. The classic case in Central America has been that of the Somozas. They used the foreign capital windfall accompanying the common market to expand their holdings, already substantial in rice and cotton plantations, sugar refineries, a steel mill, a cement factory, and a national airline, to industries geared to the common market. The Somozas were able to out-compete the private sector through such simple expedients as demanding payoffs from other companies and not taxing their own firms. In Guatemala, El Salvador, and Honduras, which are directly or indirectly under military control, individual officers as well as the armed forces as an institution have benefited from foreign investment, a process which is most advanced in Guatemala.

Foreign investment was a major factor in the growth of manufacturing, which in turn fueled the economic growth of the 1960s, averaging 7.7 percent annually for the region as a whole. Trade among the Central American countries increased 700 percent during the decade, as local companies and foreign subsidiaries produced and exported to other Central American countries products that had formerly been imported from the industrial countries.

But the growth of import substitution industries did not lead to the economic development that its advocates had predicted. The problems inherent in the absence of adequate controls on the operation of the market became evident in the distorted industrial structures which emerged in Central America. Foreign corporations operating with minimum restrictions had little incentive to produce efficiently in the host countries by using local materials or to produce consumer necessities for the local market. In many cases, production by foreign subsidiaries consisted simply of last-minute processing or last-stage assembly of imported components. In El Salvador, for example, Alcoa made aluminum shapes from imported industrial intrusion ingots, Lenox manufactured plastic dishware from imported plastic powders and resins, and Crown Zellerbach produced corrugated cardboard boxes from imported paper.[11] More extreme examples can be found in the chemical industry, where the domestic manufacturing component consisted of little more than pouring imported chemical mixtures into imported containers. In such cases, import substitution industries simply replaced imported consumer items with imported components, at little saving of foreign exchange, and sometimes even increasing import costs.[12]

Another source of inefficiency was the absence of restrictions on investment by foreign corporations seeking a share of the small Central American market. There are certain industries, such as oil refining, tire manufacturing, and auto assembly, in which a single firm of optimal size can provide for the entire market. Yet as of 1969 there were six oil refineries (with three additional ones planned), two tire subsidiaries, and six auto assembly plants. Similar inefficiencies occurred in other industries, in which two or three optimally sized firms would meet the needs of the region but five more were in operation. This meant that most of these firms operated well below capacity, resulting in high operating costs as well as heavy advertising costs to compete for limited markets and otherwise wasting resources, including foreign exchange earnings.

Foreign investment is also widely believed to have reinforced imbalances within the region by concentrating on the more populous and economically developed countries to the detriment of the smaller and weaker ones. New foreign investment in manufacturing went disproportionately to Guatemala, which received twice as much manufacturing investment in the 1960s as any other country ($90.3 million in 1969), while Honduras had considerably less ($20 million). Whether or not foreign investment was responsible, regional imbalances had indeed been aggravated in the 1960s, as was revealed in regional trade. As indicated above, trade between the five countries had grown substantially (from $32.7 million in 1960 to $263.2 million in 1969), for the most part in manufactured products (especially clothing and textiles), which accounted for 83 percent of the total in 1969.[13] However, within the common market the larger countries, Guatemala and El Salvador, were net exporters while the smaller countries, especially Honduras, became net importers. In the period 1966-68, Honduras had a negative balance of trade within the common market of $16,738,000, Nicaragua of $20,383,000, and Costa Rica of $5,977,000 (annual averages).[14]

By 1968, technicians and government officials in the three smaller countries had begun to demand readjustments in the common market to compensate for problems they were confronting. The inability to tax imports from other Central American countries combined with tariff exemptions on imports for industrial use cut into government revenues. Increased costs of industrial inputs (particularly for last-stage assembly industries), combined in some cases with declines in earnings from traditional exports, led to negative trade balances. In the case of Costa Rica, fiscal problems were aggravated by increased expenditures for economic development and social programs in health, education, and welfare.[15]

The "Soccer War"

Tensions had been building up between Honduras and El Salvador, exacerbated by such perceived inequities in the operation of the common market. Imports of manufactured goods from El Salvador were having a negative impact on the incipient industrialization program of Honduras. At the same time, there was an escalation of long term conflicts, including border disputes and the migration to Honduras of Salvadoran rural workers who had been forced off their land. Many of the Salvadoran immigrants had established farms in Honduras or found jobs as urban or rural workers, and Honduran nationals began to see them as a threat, competing with Hondurans for jobs and land. In the late 1960s President Lopez of Honduras, under pressure to implement the 1963 agrarian reform passed under his predecessor, and unwilling to redistribute the vast holdings of the traditional oligarchy and the banana companies, his bases of support, decided to respond by forcing the Salvadorans off the land. The return of Salvadoran migrants confronted the Salvadoran government with the costs of repatriating them and the Salvadoran oligarchy with the prospect of growing political instability and opposition from the new expanded rural population lacking land or jobs.

While industrialists in both countries opposed hostilities, the two governments, lacking legitimacy and facing growing opposition in their own countries, took advantage of the situation to stir up the nationalist sentiments of their respective populations. Border incidents increased in 1969 and finally the nationalist passions aroused by the competition of the two countries in the world cup soccer semi-final, ignited the situation into a war.

The "soccer war" was quickly brought to an end by the intervention of the Organization of American States (OAS), but resulted in the breaking of relations between El Salvador and Honduras and the withdrawal of Honduras from the common market. Subsequently a four-member market (of El Salvador and the three neutral countries) was ratified, and bilateral treaties were signed by Honduras with Guatemala, Nicaragua, and Costa Rica.

This crisis was a further factor in the reassessment of the common market by the governments of the respective countries, officials of SIECA and ECLA, U.S. government and international lending agencies, and academicians, which had begun in the late 1960s and continued into the 1970s. Apart from the problems of imbalance stressed by the smaller countries, there was a general sense that the possibilities for expansion of manufacturing on the basis of import substitution had been exhausted given the limitations of the market.[16] The import substitution model itself was coming under attack elsewhere due to its failure to generate continued growth in such countries as Argentina, Brazil, and Chile. Other problems, including the failure of traditional exports to generate enough earnings to finance the growth of imports and, in some countries, problems of unemployment and underemployment (especially in El Salvador, aggravated by the return of 65,000 Salvadorans from Honduras at the time of the soccer war) were additional factors in reassessment.[17]

New Directions: The Export Drive

The net result of this reassessment was the decision by common market governments to promote nontraditional exports, which it was argued would lessen the dependence of the Central American economies on traditional exports, offset increased costs of imports, and provide additional employment. U.S. corporations were once again quick to take advantage of opportunities provided by Central American governments seeking to promote new export-oriented industries. Along with other foreign corporations they had, of course, long been involved in financing and marketing export products even when these were produced by nationals. The role of the banana companies in the shipment, financing, and marketing of bananas has been noted. Cotton exports in Nicaragua were controlled by twenty exporting firms, most of them owned by or associated with foreign companies, and those in El Salvador were financed by Citibank. Most Salvadoran coffee was purchased by Nestlé and other agribusiness firms.

The rapid growth of hamburger joints and fast-food restaurants in the United States in the 1960s and 1970s created a growing market for cheap beef exports from Central America. Beef production in Central America was also encouraged by substantial loans from the World Bank, AID, and the Inter-American Development Bank (IDB). Between 1961 and 1975 Costa Rica received $75 million for agricultural projects from these agencies and private banks, much of it used for beef production. During the 1970s U.S. agribusiness interests increased their presence in Central America through investments in livestock production, processing, fertilizers, herbicides, and marketing. The Latin American Agribusiness Development Corporation (LAAD), formed by the Bank of America in 1970 and composed chiefly of U.S. banks and agribusiness firms (including Borden, Inc., Castle & Cooke, Caterpillar Tractor Company, Goodyear Tire and Rubber Company, the Bank America International Financial Corporation, and Chase Manhattan Overseas Banking Corporation), invested $7.5 million in livestock, 62 percent of this in Guatemala, Costa Rica, Honduras, and Nicaragua. United Brands also diversified into processed meat in Central America and elsewhere; in 1978 its meat sales were double its banana sales.

The combined attentions of U.S. agribusiness firms and lending agencies have had a predictable effect on beef production and exports. Beef exports from Central America increased from 13.7 thousand tons in 1960 to 66 thousand in 1970 and over 114 thousand in 1979, 90 percent of this to the U.S. market. Today, Costa Rica, Honduras, and Nicaragua export over half their beef products. But while the Central Americans are producing more beef, they are eating considerably less. Between 1960 and the mid-1970s, beef consumption dropped 41 percent in Costa Rica, 38 percent in El Salvador, and 13 percent in Guatemala and Nicaragua.

Another effect of the growth of the livestock industry has been the shifting of lands formerly used for other purposes to ranching. In some cases cattle ranchers have taken over the holdings of small producers, throwing them off the land and cutting into subsistence production. The conversion of agricultural estates to livestock production has also tended to increase unemployment, since the number of workers needed for ranches is considerably less than required for agriculture. Finally, ranching has encroached on forest land; one-third of the forest land in Costa Rica has been converted to pasture and 250 square miles of forest land in Nicaragua is lost each year, much of it to grazing.[18]

In addition to beef, U.S. agribusiness firms have been attracted to the production of fruits and vegetables for export, largely to U.S. supermarkets. As in the case of livestock, one effect has been the conversion of land formerly used for subsistence production to production for export, and of a formerly self-sufficient agricultural sector to one open to, and dependent upon, market forces. Since Central American produce has had difficulty in penetrating U.S. markets due to quality controls and import restrictions in the United States, these changes have introduced a high degree of uncertainty among small producers who have no assurance that they will be able to sell what they produce. Some small export producers have not even earned sufficient income to buy the food they formerly grew themselves, much less to pay off debts to agribusiness firms for seeds, fertilizer, and other inputs.[19]

The 1970s also saw a resurgence of foreign investment in two export sectors traditionally associated with foreign corporations: mining and petroleum. The two largest foreign holdings in Guatemala are *Exploraciones Mineros de Izabal* (EXMIBAL), a nickel-producing firm 80 percent owned by International Nickel of Canada (itself controlled by U.S. capital) and 20 percent by Hanna Mining of Cleveland, and Basic Resources, an international consortium based in Europe investing in oil production. Both investments originated in the wake of the 1954 overthrow of Arbenz, when the U.S. and Guatemalan governments again collaborated to transform Guatemala into a haven for foreign business.

Hanna Mining Company benefited from a decree passed by the post-1954 government facilitating large-scale mining and obtained several mining concessions. In 1960 the International Nickel Company, the largest nickel producer in the capitalist countries, joined Hanna to form EXMIBAL, which helped the Guatemalan government draft a new mining code in 1965. EXMIBAL's intervention in mining legislation, from which it obviously benefited, as well as subsequent manuevers such as having itself declared a "transformation industry" to avoid paying mining taxes, antagonized nationalist sectors of the population, including academicians, professionals, labor and political leaders. In 1969 the Faculty of Economics and Law of the National University held a public review of the EXMIBAL concession, concluding with the recommendation that a new mining code be drawn up and EXMIBAL's status as a transformation industry be withdrawn. Despite an extensive public relations campaign undertaken by EXMIBAL, public outrage was such that the government was forced to review EXMIBAL's status in the early 1970s. However, the government reviewing team was heavily stacked in favor of EXMIBAL, whose critics were then silenced by paramilitary groups and right-wing death squads. In February 1971 a new agreement was signed between the Guatemalan government and EXMIBAL which cut into some of the former concessions enjoyed by the company but did not begin to address the issues raised in the Economics Faculty review.[20]

The operations of EXMIBAL and Basic Resources in the northern regions of Guatemala have had a devastating effect on the indigenous communities of these regions. In 1978 a pipeline from the oil refineries to the Atlantic coast of Santo Tomás was approved by the Guatemalan government, and a highway from Lake Izabal, site of the EXMIBAL operations, through the Transversal strip was under construction. Both projects raised the value of land in the affected areas, including a 100,000-acre estate of then president Gen. Romero Lucas García, and government officials and businessmen quickly established claims to land in the region, using legal means or threats to remove the traditional inhabitants, Kekchi and Pokoman Indians. When a contingent of peasants from the village of Chabon in Alta Verapaz province went to the municipal center of Panzos to obtain a hearing on their land claims in the region, government troops fired on them, killing 100 men, women, and children.

Confrontations between the companies and government on the one hand and the indigenous population on the other have continued, and many of the Indians have joined the revolutionary groups of Guatemala.[21] Strikes and sabotage against EXMIBAL led to losses and in 1981 the decision was taken to close down its operations.

While investments in mining and petroleum are more important in quantitative terms, the fastest growing area of foreign investment in Central America has been the *maquiladores*, labor-intensive industries or phases of industries which are moved into countries with low labor costs to produce commodities or parts for export. During the 1960s and early 1970s the Mexican border region became a haven for runaway shops looking for cheap labor. In 1973 there were some 448 *maquiladores* in Mexico, chiefly in electronics and the garment industry. But by this time Mexican workers had begun to organize, and companies began to look to Central America and the Caribbean for a cheaper and more docile labor force.[22]

They found what they were looking for in Haiti and El Salvador. The Salvadoran government was anxious to attract new industries to reduce its high level of unemployment and underemployment (estimated at 45 percent in the mid-1970s), aggravated by the return of Salvadoran migrants from Honduras at the time of the 1969 war. The existence of a large labor reserve army, of course, made El Salvador attractive to foreign investors. They were given added incentives in the form of a free trade zone in San Bartolo (near the capital city of San Salvador) where credit, infrastructure, and even factories were supplied by the government, taxes were eliminated for a ten-year period, and strikes were outlawed. Several electronics and garment firms moved to El Salvador, including those seeking to escape labor problems elsewhere, such as Texas Instruments, which closed its factory in Curaçao (Netherlands Antilles) when the workers went on strike for a week in 1972.[23] The *maquiladores* played a large role in the increase in foreign investment in El Salvador, from $66.6 million to $104.6 million between 1970 and 1975, but the number of jobs created was too small to have much impact on El Salvador's high level of unemployment.[24]

During the 1970s most Central American governments began to develop tourism as another means to earn foreign exchange, thus attracting foreign speculators, especially from the U.S. Sunbelt, anxious to make a quick profit through investments in luxury hotels, casinos, and other tourist attractions.

Along with U.S. capital and technology came specialists in U.S. business techniques. The International Executive Service Corps (IESC) is a U.S.-based outfit which provides administrative, management, and technical personnel with experience in U.S. companies to firms abroad. One of its major centers of operation in the 1960s was El Salvador (second only to Iran in number of IESC projects). By 1967 IESC boasted that over 50 percent of industry's share in GNP was accounted for by companies in which IESC had programs. While IESC does not provide capital, its specialists have considerable power, sometimes exercised in subtle ways. One example is IESC specialist James Hawley McCutchen in Poma Hermanos, a family holding company with subsidiaries in such areas as auto distributorships, aluminum manufacturing, and housing development. McCutchen sits in on board meetings where he has no vote but, as one director puts it, "When the time for decision arrives, we have all learned to study the expression on his face, and vote accordingly."[25]

The economic role of foreign corporations does not end with capital, technology, management, and input. Foreign investment often opens a market for trade, as subsidiaries of foreign corporations as well as national industries import machinery, parts, and other inputs from corporate headquarters in the United States and other industrial countries. Governments contract with foreign corporations to supply equipment for infrastructure projects. Loans from agribusiness firms are often tied to the purchase of agricultural equipment, fertilizer, insecticides, and other agricultural inputs from the creditor firm, and loans and grants from government agencies (such as AID) may be tied to imports from the donor country.[26]

Sometimes, as indicated above, all the components of a given product are imported with only last minute assembly or processing taking place in Central America. Between 1963 and 1969, imports of industrial equipment and machinery reached an estimated $501.5 million, more than half the total investment in fixed industrial assets. U.S. exports to the common market countries grew from $408 million in 1971 to $1.57 billion in 1978, more than its total fixed investment in the region. In 1980 U.S. exports to Guatemala alone reached $548 million. Major categories were food, fertilizers, pesticides, synthetic resins, paper and paperboard, electric power and telecommunications equipment, and construction and mining machinery. The United States now provides more than 56 percent of the manufactured imports to Central America although it accounts for only about one-third of total imports.[27]

Finance: The Invisible Link

Contrary to the ideology of free enterprise and free trade promoted by U.S. corporations and the U.S. government, state intervention is, in fact, essential for capitalist industrialization. In Central America as elsewhere, governments have provided the resources for investment in necessary infrastructure—roads, ports, airports, hydroelectric plants, and communications systems. They have also provided cheap credit to private investors; and, of course, have continued to play a role, often repressive, in the control of labor and the maintenance of political stability. In the case of free-trade zones such as San Bartolo in El Salvador, the government even provided the factories to house new industries.

At the same time, the Central American governments were hard pressed to meet their financial obligations. On the one hand, government revenues were adversely affected by the virtual elimination of tariffs within the common market and the various tax and tariff exemptions provided to new, especially foreign, industries. Between 1960 and 1971 in El Salvador, for example, the value of tax exemptions from outside the region increased from $2.5 million to $13 million and taxes received from imports from outside the region dropped from $27.9 million to $21.7 million, despite the increase in total imports. On the other hand, efforts by Central American governments, under pressure from the United States and international lending agencies, to institute new taxes at different periods during the 1960s and 1970s were 2adamantly resisted by landowners and industrialists.[28] When pressures from the World Bank and the IMF led to efforts by the Mendez Montenegro government in Guatemala to institute income tax reforms in 1968, the proposed legislation was denounced as evidence of an international communist conspiracy.[29] In some cases, attempted tax reforms appear to have been a factor in the overthrow of governments which tried to institute them, as in the military coups which ousted the Ydigoras government in Guatemala and the Villeda Morales government in Honduras in 1963.[30]

Foreign loans offered a welcome, though temporary and ultimately disastrous, way out of this dilemma. During the 1960s loans from U.S. government agencies and other foreign governments, international lending institutions such as the World Bank and the Inter-American Development Bank, and foreign private banks constituted more than half of the net capital flows (i.e., new investment and reinvested earnings minus disinvestment, and new loans minus amortization and interest payments) into the region.[31] In the 1970s foreign borrowing increased substantially in all five countries. By the end of the decade the Central American countries had entered a vicious cycle of indebtedness, obtaining new loans largely to pay escalating debts.

Table 7.1
Net Foreign Capital Inflows into Central America
Totals 1966-70

	Guatemala	El Salvador	Honduras	Nicaragua	Costa Rica	Central America
Total	255.1	120.0	147.0	213.2	189.5	894.8
Private	165.3	82.7	81.3	152.6	183.4	665.3
DFI[1]	108.0	37.7	48.5	70.1	96.4	360.7
Loans[2]	57.3	45.0	32.8	82.5	87.0	304.6
Official	59.8	37.3	65.7	60.6	6.1	229.5
Loans[2]	49.3	21.8	47.0	43.4	−13.6	147.9
Grants	10.5	15.5	18.7	17.2	19.7	81.6
Total loans	106.6	66.8	79.8	125.9	73.4	452.5
Total loans and grants	117.1	82.1	98.5	143.1	93.1	534.1
Loans and grants as % of total capital inflow	46%	68%	67%	67%	49%	60%

Source: SIECA, anexo 9, cuadro 1.

1. Reinvested profits, investments, minus disinvestments
2. Net value (Loans minus interest payments and amortizations)

As noted above, it was the promise of U.S. financial aid which convinced the Central American governments to accept the U.S. version of the common market plan. Subsequently, loans from U.S. agencies and international institutions dominated by the U.S. government ensured the modification of the common market plan according to the doctrine of the free market. AID provided 62.5 percent of the initial capital of the Central American Bank for Economic Integration. By June 1981 the BCIE had received $981 million in loans: $195 million from AID,

$190 million from the IDB, $172 million from individual U.S. banks, and $424 million from an international consortia of banks.[32] The BCIE in turn, along with AID and the IBD, has been a major source of funds for private and government financial institutions in the Central American countries. Between its establishment in 1961 and 1978 the BCIE provided over $1 billion in loans, chiefly for roads, hydroelectric projects, airports, and tourist facilities.[33] It has also helped to finance the operations of such corporations as Colgate Palmolive, U.S. Steel, United Brands, Castle & Cooke, Hercules, and Phelps Dodge.[34]

Loans to the BCIE and direct loans to Central American governments facilitated the control of financial resources in Central America by foreign, especially U.S., interests, but foreign financial intervention did not end there. Domestic banks constituted another important conduit of foreign financial influence. Both the Banco Nicaraguense and the Banco de America of Nicaragua, financial centers of the two major economic groups outside the Somoza family—the Banic and Banamerica groups, respectively—depended on foreign capital. Chase Manhattan was a major source of finances for Banic while Banamerica was 33 percent owned by Wells Fargo and also received funds from the First National Bank of Boston.

These financial links strengthened the alliance between U.S. capital and the Nicaraguan bourgeoisie. The Banco Caley Dagnall, linked to the most important coffee group in Nicaragua, was 70 percent foreign owned prior to the revolution. In Honduras, Chase Manhattan owns 25 percent of the Banco Atlantida of Honduras and Citibank has 99 percent of the stock of Banco de Honduras, while Lloyds and Bank of America have wholly owned branches there. According to one source, the large American banks exercise almost total control over Honduran banking.[35]

In the early 1970s private development banks established by private business in each Central American country received funds from AID and in several cases from foreign banks and corporations. By the early 1970s, ADELA, an international corporation owned by 200 of the largest corporations and banks in the world, had equity in several of these banks. Shares in Financiera Industria y Agropecuaria, S.A. (FIASA) of Guatemala were also held by the Bank of London and Montreal, the Bank of America, and the Deutsch Sudamerikanische Bank, as well as by firms controlled by U.S. capital, Molinas Modernas, GINSA, and Industrial Horenera.[36] Private development banks have continued to be heavily dependent on loans from foreign institutions, enabling foreign corporate and financial stockholders to control the use of finance capital, and constituting one more mechanism for the integration of foreign capital and private domestic groups.

A further form of foreign financial influence became evident in the 1960s. When U.S. corporate subsidiaries began to proliferate, drawn by the Central American Common Market, U.S. banks also moved into the region through the establishment of branches in each country. The Bank of America led the way, setting up a branch in Guatemala in 1957 during the investment drive following the 1954 coup. Today the Bank of America is the major source of agricultural capital in Guatemala after the government. It is also the only corporation in the country belonging to Amigos del Pais, a right-wing business group with ties to the armed forces and allegedly to right-wing death squads. Amigos del Pais has spent millions of dollars in the United States in an effort to "clean up" the brutal image of Guatemala's dictators and to pressure for a resumption of U.S. military and economic aid, suspended due to the Guatemalan government's human rights violations. One recipient of these funds was the public relations firm Hannaford and Deaver, which received $11,000 monthly from Amigos del Pais and provided the organization with an important White House contact when its president Michael Deaver became policy adviser to President Reagan. The Bank of America has made frequent loans to Guatemalan military officers, including a loan of $750,000 to former president Gen. Lucas García, while he was defense minister, to finance his property in the oil-rich Franja Transversal del Norte.[37]

During the 1960s the Bank of America opened additional branches in Costa Rica, Honduras, and Nicaragua. The First National City Bank began operations in El Salvador in 1964, and several foreign banks formed financial companies in Costa Rica. Bank branches can draw upon local savings, in the form of deposits and savings accounts, for loans to private firms, including subsidiaries of multinationals. Often the amount of capital actually brought into a country by multinational corporations is quite small, since multinationals can depend on foreign and domestic loans. U.S. banks also provide other services for U.S. interests in Central America. The Bank of America was a founder and is one of about twenty banks and agribusiness corporations with interests in LAAD, the Latin American Agribusiness Development Corporation with extensive beef and agricultural interests in several Central American countries. The First National City Bank made the initial contact between the International Executive Service Corps (IESC) and Salvadoran businessmen, whose companies subsequently became major clients of IESC.

Foreign loans to government and private financial institutions, foreign equity in domestic banks, and the establishment of branches of U.S. and other banks have facilitated the penetration of foreign capital into Central America and strengthened the ties between foreign capital and local business groups. They have increased the financial resources available to multinational corporations with subsidiaries in Central America. In the short run they bailed out Central American governments whose resources were drying up as their expenditure needs were growing and who were unable or unwilling to increase taxes in the face of militant opposition by the dominant classes of their countries. In the case of Nicaragua, for example, foreign resources grew from 5 percent of the country's total financial resources in 1960 to 49 percent in 1969. In the three years prior to Somoza's downfall, 1976-79, Nicaragua's foreign debt doubled, from $642 million to $1.5 billion.[38]

In the long run, of course, foreign debts must be repaid, with interest, and financial dependence has meant a spiraling foreign debt and increasing balance-of-payments problems. This situation has been aggravated by government inefficiency in using funds and by corruption, the most spectacular instances of which were provided by the Somoza family in Nicaragua. Anastasio Somoza's appropriation of relief funds following the 1972 earthquake took such forms as the use of $3 million, provided by AID for housing construction, to buy a tract of land in Managua which he himself had previously purchased for $30,000, a net gain of $2,970,000, courtesy of U.S. taxpayers.[39]

Table 7.2
Foreign Debt ($ millions)

Country	1960	1970	1977	1980
Costa Rica	55	227	1,303	2,415
El Salvador	33	126	589	936.0
Guatemala	51	176	640	864.0
Honduras	23	144	787	1,608.6
Nicaragua	41	206	944	2,121.9

Source: Inter-American Development Bank, 1978, 1982

The cost of foreign loans has been aggravated in some cases by balance-of-trade deficits, with additional loans necessary to provide foreign exchange to offset negative trade balances. Despite the export drive of the 1970s, the structure of extra-regional exports has not changed markedly. The Central American economies continue to depend on exports of primary commodities, coffee, cotton, bananas, sugar, and beef, and export earnings are therefore determined largely by prices for these commodities on the world market. By the end of the 1970s export earnings began to decline sharply as a result of the world recession, while prices for imports have tended to increase over time, especially costs of fuel and other industrial and infrastructure inputs. Trade deficits, combined with loan costs, have resulted in a growing balance-of-payments deficit within the region as a whole, which increased from $320 million in 1970 to $845 million in 1981. During the same period government budgetary deficits increased from $692 million to $1.5 billion.[40] Loans from U.S. private banks for debt servicing provide a temporary solution but aggravate the problem in the long run, since these are usually short-term loans with high interest rates.

Nowhere have the combined effects of balance-of-trade deficits and dependence on foreign loans been more devastating than in Costa Rica, traditionally the most politically stable of the Central American countries. Costa Rica has for a long time suffered from a balance-of-payments deficit, in part the result of government expenditures on social welfare and economic infrastructure. During the 1970s, however, trade deficits increased precariously due to the higher costs of imports, especially oil, and the drop in prices for its export commodities, especially coffee. The negative trade balance, which tripled between 1976 and 1980, from $132.4 million to $443.7 million, was further aggravated by payments of interest and amortizaton of former loans. As early as the mid-1970s the Costa Rican government was borrowing heavily simply to pay off existing debts and to maintain a balance of foreign reserves. By 1980 it was no longer possible to obtain sufficient foreign credit and Costa Rica had a foreign reserve deficit of nearly $100,000, at which point foreign banks and lending agencies refused to lend additional funds. Costa Rica was declared in bankruptcy and suspended amortization and interest payments. The *colón*, its currency, was devalued by 465 percent and inflation skyrocketed, since the devaluation raised the costs of foreign inputs, affecting nearly all industrial products.

Today Costa Rica's foreign public debt is close to $3 billion with an aditional $1 billion in private debt, one of the highest per capita debts in the world. The situation has resulted in general production cutbacks and bankruptcy in the case of smaller and medium-sized firms unable to import raw materials and other inputs, cutbacks in real wages due to inflation, and rising unemployment, now about 20 percent.[41] Although Costa Rica's situation is extreme it is not unique. Both Nicaragua and Honduras face serious balance-of-payments problems and escalating debts resulting from dependence on foreign loans and reductions in export earnings.

The political implications of these economic conditions are obvious. The U.S. government attempted to manipulate aid to Nicaragua during the first year of the revolutionary government, and the Reagan administration has cut off this aid and reduced import quotas for Nicaragua's products. It has also used economic and military aid to Honduras, and even Costa Rica, as a means to secure support for its Central America policy.

The Common Market: An Assessment

There can be little doubt that in the two decades following the formation of the common market the impact of foreign capital on the Central American societies has been substantial. Prior to 1960 foreign capital had been confined largely to the various phases of banana production and export—the export enclave. While this gave the corporations enormous political influence in the affected countries, the visible effect on the rest of the economy was limited.

By 1980, however, foreign capital had permeated every facet of the Central American economies. Foreign corporations controlled the major manufacturing firms producing for internal and external markets and provided the needed imports of industrial machinery, parts, and supplies. Through loans, marketing arrangements, and the sale of fertilizers, farm machinery, and the like, foreign corporations and lending agencies were extensively involved in agricultural and livestock production, including not only production for export but also in some cases production for internal consumption. Foreign banks, especially those in the United States, government agencies, and multinational lending agencies had thoroughly penetrated the banking system through direct ownership or through loans to government and private banks. The major mining companies were foreign owned. Government infrastructure projects—hydroelectric plants, communications systems, airports—were financed through foreign loans (direct or through the BCIE), provisioned through imports of construction machinery, electronic equipment, and other supplies from foreign corporations, and often constructed under foreign contracts. Foreign capital was also increasingly involved in the construction of hotels and other services for the tourist industry.

The result of these trends was not, however, the self-generating, stabilizing, trickle-down growth that planners had envisioned at the beginning of the common market period. It was a growth based on a distorted industrial structure geared less to efficient production and exchange among the Central American economies than to the needs of foreign corporations for cheap labor and competitive advantages, and led to an aggravation of existing imbalances between the more and less industrially advanced Central American economies. It was a growth that resulted not in increasing self-sufficiency and the development of natural resources but in the depletion of forests and the displacement of local subsistence production by agro-export production, generating an increased dependence on the unstable and fluctuating prices on the world commodity market. It has been generated not through the mobilization of internal savings but through a dependence on external financial resources which was aggravated when world prices for traditional exports dropped, leading in turn to an ever-downward spiral of unfavorable balances of trade, dependence on foreign loans, and escalating debt.

A comment by two observers on the situation of El Salvador during this period is appropriate for the region as a whole:

> Modernization . . . was . . . like a skyscraper built on a crumbling foundation but no one dare call the structure unsteady. Not the oligarchies, who kept one foot in their agrarian past and one in the industrial present; not the military, who ruled only at the behest of the "Fourteen Families"; and not the United States, which was willing to settle for a semblance of change, so long as anti-communism remained the shared philosophy of both governments.[42]

Contradictions of Foreign-Generated Growth: Crisis and Mobilization

The impact of economic transformation resulting from foreign capital penetration as well as the economic crisis it helped to generate were experienced directly by the majority of Central Americans. There were changes in the amount and kind of employment, the products available for mass consumption, the cost of consumption in relation to earnings, and, most importantly, the extent to which ordinary people could provide for their own needs or were forced to depend on the market for the sale of their labor power and the purchase of basic commodities. The result of these changes was to diminish the traditional alternatives for coping with economic crisis, for example, more intense exploitation of the family's subsistence plots, and ultimately to both necessitate and facilitate new forms of organization and protest.

Changes in Employment and Work Conditions

Industrialization was expected by common market planners to generate new employment. It did, in fact, create a significant demand for labor, but this demand was highly uneven and disproportionate to the labor supply.

The general assumption by critics of foreign investment that it resulted in capital-intensive industrialization and therefore generated little employment is only partly true. While certain industries, particularly mining, petroleum, and food and beverage processing, were dependent on modern productive processes and generated relatively little employment, others, such as metal products, textiles, machinery, chemicals, foodstuffs, and accessory construction, were labor intensive. This was particularly true of the *maquilador* industries which were attracted to Central America, to El Salvador particularly, by the prospect of cheap labor. Employment was also generated indirectly by increased demand for raw materials, transportation, services, construction, and commerce. Jobs in the manufacturing sector increased in every Central American country between 1960 and 1978, and it is estimated that for each job created in industry, .82 jobs were created in other parts of the urban economy.[43]

The capital-intensive nature of industry is evident, however, in the fact that industrialization grew much more rapidly than employment in industry. Between 1961 and 1971 the manufacturing sector in El Salvador grew by 24 percent, but the number of people employed in industry increased by only 6 percent.[44] Furthermore, by the end of the 1970s, due to the economic crisis, many workers previously employed in industry were no longer employed. It was estimated that by this time 11 percent of the urban industrial workers had lost their jobs in Guatemala and Costa Rica, and 21 percent in El Salvador.[45]

While the ability of manufacturing industry to absorb labor was limited, structural changes in the countryside were creating rural unemployment and driving thousands of peasants into the cities. Access of small and medium farmers to land was shrinking due to the expansion of plantation agriculture for export. The transformation of subsistence farmers into cash crop producers (often as a consequence of foreign agribusiness intervention, as in the case of ALCOSA) linked them to dependence on the highly volatile world commodity market. Market production on family plots became difficult due to lack of access to credit, and supplemental income from artisan production suffered from competition with cheaper manufactured goods and imports such as nylon ropes and hammocks, plastic water jugs and dinnerware, and mass-produced clothing. Thus increasing sectors of the rural population became dependent on the market for income, either from the sale of crops or in the form of wages, with which to obtain the basic necessities they formerly produced themselves.

At the same time, agricultural employment was increasingly seasonal and declined during this period due to the introduction of labor-saving forms of cultivation, mechanization, or the shift of land from agriculture to livestock which required less labor. More and more plantations dispensed with the use of resident labor (*mozos, colonos*) and relied instead on a small permanent labor force with large quantities of temporary labor at planting and harvest times. The amount of land farmed in tenant relationships in El Salvador, for example, decreased by 77 percent between 1961 and 1971. Correspondingly, more and more peasants cultivated rented land or worked as wage laborers for large landowners. The proportion of Salvadoran agricultural workers who were completely landless increased from 12 percent in 1960 to 41 percent in 1975, and those who had two hectares of land or less increased from 72 percent to 90 percent.[46]

In Costa Rica, the shifting of large tracts of land from crop production to livestock has had a measurably negative effect on rural employment.[47] In Nicaragua, the dramatic increase in the land used for pasture during the 1960s and 1970s led to the displacement of small food producers from the central region of the country, where they had moved following their prior displacement from the coastal region due to the expansion of cotton production in the 1940s, to more remote areas of the country where they were reduced to slash-and-burn agriculture. By the 1970s roughly half of the economically active population in agriculture were seasonal cotton workers, which provided employment for two to three months of the year.[48] Unemployed and underemployed rural workers as well as children, young women, and widows, increasingly had no alternative but to migrate to the urban centers to seek the cash income that greater dependence on the consumer market and lack of access to land now required.

Income and the Cost of Living

Even the fully employed were able to reap few material benefits from industrialization. Wages remained virtually frozen during the 1960s and subsequently increased only slightly, partly as a result of temporary labor shortages and increased union activities after the earthquakes in Nicaragua (1972) and Guatemala (1976). The weakness of unions at the beginning of the common market period, together with government promises to private investors to maintain a docile labor force, accounts for the difficulty workers had in increasing their share of the wealth produced even in the most "privileged" sectors of employment.

Aggravating the situation of low wages was the steady rise in the cost of goods and services, particularly during the 1970s. Beginning in 1974, for the first time since World War II inflation affected the daily lives of the people of Central America. Inflation rates, which averaged 4 percent or less between 1960 and the early 1970s, began to reach two-digit figures by 1973. Between 1975 and 1980, prices increased 47 percent in Costa Rica, 53 percent in Honduras, 66 percent in Guatemala, 77 percent in Nicaragua, and 84 percent in El Salvador. Real wages for workers fell by 25 percent in Nicaragua, between 1967 and 1975, by 30 percent in Honduras, between 1972 and 1976, and in 1975 in El Salvador dropped back to 1965 levels after having risen briefly in 1970-71. The purchasing power of the *quetzal* in Guatemala, for those with access to cash income, declined by 55 percent between 1972 and 1978.[49]

While external conditions such as the rise in world oil prices accounted for some of the price increases, e.g., in fertilizers, gasoline, urban transportation, these increases were aggravated by conditions resulting from the internal social structure and the development model. In Guatemala small and medium peasants had been encouraged to depend on chemical fertilizers to achieve production increases in the 1960s rather than look toward the 57 percent of latifundia land estimated to be fallow.[50] The urban centers in turn depended on small and medium peasant food production to supply the local market since large landowners preferred the potentially higher profits of export-oriented crops.

Table 7.3
Price Index 1980
(1970 = 100)

Country	General Prices	Food Prices
Costa Rica[1]	279.4	309.9
El Salvador[1] (1978)	204.8	198.3
Guatemala[2]	166.1	156.1
Honduras[1]	210.3	230.1
Nicaragua[1,3]	258.2	315.6

Source: Compiled from tables in International Labour Office, *Yearbook of Labour Statistics 1981* (Geneva: ILO, 1981).

1. Metropolitan or urban areas
2. 1975 = 100
3. 1974 = 100

At the same time that the cost of fertilizers and other agricultural inputs increased sharply, government-subsidized agricultural credit was cut, making loans scarce and costly. Domestic food producers faced the choice of abandoning production altogether (as many did) or attempting to pass the increased costs on to the consumer. The consumer in turn not only had to pay higher prices for locally produced food but also confronted scarcities in those products, such as sugar and beef, which could bring higher prices on the export market, making producers reluctant to market them locally.

It is one of the ironies of the Central American development model that while increasing amounts of food were produced for the local market (as well as export) throughout the 1960s, food consumption did not improve and for some sectors actually declined. In the case of El Salvador, for example, the mechanization of agriculture on the large estates and the increased use of fertilizer, insecticide, and other inputs by small and medium farmers, meant that the production of export crops (coffee, sugar cane, and cotton) as well as basic food crops (corn, beans, and rice) increased during this period, reducing dependence on exports of these products. But because of the decline in the number of people producing for their own subsistence and the corresponding increase in those totally or partially dependent on the market for their basic food needs, reductions in real income (due to increased food costs) prevented these groups from improving or even maintaining their levels of food consumption.

In the region as a whole, scarcities, declining real incomes, and decreasing access to alternative means of subsistence resulted in high rates of hunger and malnutrition. An estimated 5 percent of the population in Guatemala consume 60 percent of the food and among the poorest 50 percent of Guatemalans over half of the children die before five years of age from hunger-related diseases. By the mid 1970s El Salvador was rated as the country lowest in the hemisphere in per capita caloric consumption.[52]

Unionization and Popular Organization

By the end of the 1960s the social landscape of Central America was changing. A greater number of industrial workers were concentrated into large, modern manufacturing plants such as those of Coca Cola, Del Monte, and Texas Instruments, resulting in interdependence in the production process and increased opportunities for communication among the workers regarding common grievances. Despite opposition by the government in most cases, independent unions and labor confederations were formed and strikes, work stoppages, and other collective actions by industrial workers took on an increasingly modern, proletarian character.

The social relations of many urban workers had changed, and with them their view of reality. So had those of the semiproletariat, landless rural workers dependent on permanent or seasonal work on coffee, cotton, or banana plantations and small peasants with whom they shared a growing dependence on the market. As Porras Castejon comments, with respect to Guatemala, market dependence decreased their isolation:

> From the social point of view, this incorporation of small producers into the market objectively links an important part of the peasant population to the mechanisms of international capitalism, the institutions of the State, etc. That is, it breaks the traditional isolation of the peasantry and permits a wider vision of the social mechanisms which determine, ultimately, the conditions of their production.[53]

Faced with the need for more cash income in the context of low wages, often with long hours and difficult working conditions, agricultural workers organized into rural unions and pressured for increases in the minimum wage and improvements in conditions of work. In Nicaragua it was on the coffee plantations of Masaya and Carazo, where seasonal workers shared with the permanent workers back-breaking work and inhuman living conditions, that agrarian commit-tees were first organized in 1976, later spreading to the coffee, sugar, and cotton plantations of Rivas and Chinandega. These committees constituted the nucleus of the Rural Workers' Association (ATC), formed in 1978 and today the major rural labor confederation in Nicaragua.[54]

The demands of rural workers were simple and basic—land, food, a living wage, potable water, electricity, less crowded and better equipped classrooms, less dangerous working conditions, better health services. In some cases organized workers succeeded in winning con-cessions. In Guatemala, in May 1980, 80,000 permanent and seasonal sugar cane workers, migrants and nonmigrants, Indian and ladino, staged an unprecedented strike to increase rural minimum wages from $1.20 to $3.20 a day, and marched along the South Coast Highway with machetes held high. When urban workers offered to go out in sym-pathy and raise increased wage demands of their own, the government ordered landowners to pay the increase.

But most strikes were met with serious repression, and the leaders even of those that achieved momentary gains were subjected to harass-ment and persecution. In El Salvador, two leaders of the independent labor federation FUSS (United Federation of Salvadoran Trade Un-ions) who supported a 1968 strike by ANDES (the teachers' union) were arrested and "disappeared"; their mutilated bodies were later found, having been washed ashore on the Pacific beaches of La Liber-tad.[55] Efforts to form a union in the cotton growing region of Chinandega in Nicaragua in the 1960s resulted in the assassination of 300 peasants and workers by the National Guard, one of many in-stances of brutal repression of organizing efforts by the rural population to improve their conditions.[56] In Guatemala, three leaders of the union of the Coca Cola franchise bottler, Embotelladora Guatemalteca, and three additional members of the union's executive committee were as-sassinated in the eighteen-month period between December 1978 and May 1980.[57]

In short, basic economic reforms were not on the agenda. The free market, status quo oriented model of growth called for a reconcen-tration of wealth, not its dispersion, and the political model accompan-ying it required a passive and above all cheap labor force, not one or-ganized to make demands. To the peasants and urban and rural work-ers seeking to achieve a decent standard of living, the ruling groups had nothing to offer but a virulent anticommunism and violent repression.

While the economic changes resulting from the U.S.-inspired and assisted model of growth established conditions for popular organization and revolt, the intransigence of U.S.-backed sectors and groups holding power within the Central American countries—the Somoza regime in Nicaragua, the dominant sectors of the bourgeoisie and their military allies in El Salvador and Guatemala—blocked all possibility of change within the system. Demands which were basically economic and reformist took on a political and revolutionary character in the context of Central America. Because reforms were not on the agenda of the ruling elites, revolution became a necessity for the newly mobilized masses. Repression fueled the fires of the revolutionary movements and deepened their commitment to total change.

Notes

1. See Ralph Lee Woodward, Jr., *Central America: A Nation Divided* (New York: Oxford University Press, 1976), pp. 177-83, on the early development of the banana companies in Central America.

2. On the reform movement and 1954 coup in Guatemala, see Suzanne Jonas and David Tobis, eds., *Guatemala* (New York: NACLA, 1974).

3. See Royce Q. Shaw, *Central America: Regional Integration and National Political Development* (Boulder, Col.: Westview Press, 1978).

4. Sources on the Central American Common Market and the shift in its direction with U.S. involvement may be found in Shaw, *Central America;* Suzanne Jonas, "Masterminding the Mini-Market: U.S. Aid to the Central American Common Market," in Jonas and Tobis, eds., *Guatemala;* and Karen Holbek and Peter L. Swan, *Trade and Industrialization in the Central American Common Market: The First Decade* (Austin: Bureau of Business Research, Graduate School of Business, University of Texas, 1972).

5. George Black, *Triumph of the People: The Sandinista Revolution in Nicaragua* (London: Zed Press, 1981), p. 39.

6. Tom Barry, Beth Woods, and Deb Preusch, *Dollars and Dictators: A Guide to Central America* (Albuquerque: The Resource Center, 1982), p. 17; Roger Burbach and Patricia Flynn, *Agribusiness in the Americas* (New York: Monthly Review Press, 1980), pp. 253-81; and *NACLA Report on the Americas*, November-December 1978, pp. 38-39.

7. SIECA, *El desarrollo integrado de Centroamérica en la presente decada: Bases y propuestas para el perfeccionamiento y la reestrucciación del Mercado*

Comun Centroamericano (Buenos Aires: INTAL/BID, 1973), Anexo 3, pp. 60-62.

8. SIECA, *El desarrollo integrado*, Anexo 9, p. 102; Marc Herold, "Direct U.S. Investment in El Salvador," unpub. ms., 1980.

9. CAMINO, *El Salvador: Background to the Crisis* (Cambridge, Mass.: Central America Information Office, 1982), p. 62.

10. Black, *Triumph of the People*, p. 38. For detailed information on the development of the major private sector groups in Nicaragua, see Jaime Wheelock Román, *Imperialismo y dictadura: Crisis de una formación social*, 3rd ed. (Mexico: Siglo XXI, 1979).

11. Herold, "Direct U.S. Investment," p. 22.

12. Vincent Cable, *Foreign Investment, Economic Integration, and Industrial Structure in Central America* (Glasgow: Institute of Latin American Studies, 1976), pp. 19-20.

13. Holbek and Swan, *Trade and Industrialization*, p. 24.

14. William E. Cline and Enrique Delgado, eds., *Economic Integration in Central America* (Washington, D.C.: Brookings Institution, 1978), p. 62.

15. Shaw, *Central America*, pp. 82-89, 94, 103-10.

16. This assessment seems to have been premature: intra-regional trade, which had increased 700 percent between 1960 and 1970, increased another 400 percent from 1969 to 1980, when it reached $1.16 billion (*Comercio Exterior*, August 1981, p. 919). Nor do fears of ECLA and SIECA to the effect that foreign investment would lead to massive profit repatriation seem to have been borne out, at least prior to the 1970s. U.S. Department of Commerce figures indicate a steady reinvestment of U.S. earnings in Central America, particularly in manufacturing. This can probably be explained by the virtual absence of local taxes as an incentive to foreign investment (Cable, *Foreign Investment*, 13).

17. Jaime Biderman, "The Development of Capitalism in Nicaragua: A Political Economic History," *Latin American Perspectives* 10, no. 1 (Winter 1983); *Multinational Monitor*, "El Salvador," May 1981.

18. Robert H. Holden, "Central America is Growing More Beef and Eating Less," *Multinational Monitor*, October 1981, pp. 17-18; J. Edward Taylor, "Peripheral Capitalism and Rural-Urban Migration: A Study of Population Movements in Costa Rica," *Latin American Perspectives* 7, nos. 2 and 3 (Spring/Summer 1980): 82-86.

19. See the case of Alcosa described by David Landes, Chapter 4, this volume. Donald Castillo Rivas, *Acumulación de Capital y Empresas Transnacionales en Centroamérica* (Mexico: Siglo XXI, 1980), pp. 131-33; Frances Moore Lappé and Nick Allen, "Central American Victims," *New York Times*, May 28, 1982.

20. On EXMIBAL see Fred Goff, "EXMIBAL: Take Another Nickel Out," in Jonas and Tobis, eds., *Guatemala*, pp. 160-61.

21. See Nancy Peckenham, "Guatemala: Peasants Lose Out in Scramble for Oil Wealth," *Multinational Monitor*, May 1981; and George Black, Norma Stoltz Chinchilla, and Milton Jamail, "Garrison Guatemala," *NACLA Report on the Americas*, March-April 1983.

22. NACLA, "Hit and Run: U.S. Runaway Shops on the Mexican Border," *NACLA's Latin American and Empire Report* 9, no. 5 (July-August 1975).

23. Steve Edinger, "What We are Fighting For: Proletarianization, Industrialization, and the Corporate State in El Salvador," unpub. ms., Berkeley, 1981, p. 30.

24. Castillo, *Acumulacion de capital*, pp. 143, 154-55, 167.

25. "The Big Splash in Little El Salvador," *Fortune*, September 1, 1967.

26. Asociación Latinoamericana de Instituciones Financieras de Desarrollo (ALIDE), *Financiamiento del Desarrollo en Centroamérica y en el Caribe* (Lima: ALIDE, May 1972), p. 353.

27. See U.S. Department of Commerce, *Overseas Business Report. World Trade: Outlook for 64 Countries*, OBR 81-24 (September 1981). Approximately 25-30 percent of the Central American imports are from within the region: the rest are divided among the EEC countries, especially Germany and Japan.

28. Clark W. Reynolds, "Fissures in the Volcano? Central American Economic Prospects," in Joseph Grunwald, ed., *Latin America and World Economy: A Changing International Order* (Beverly Hills: Sage Publications, 1978), p. 219.

29. Cable, *Foreign Investment*, p. 12.

30. Shaw, *Central America*, p. 91-92.

31. SIECA, *El desarrollo integrado*, Anexo 9, cuadro 1.

32. U.S. Agency for International Development (AID) *Congressional Presentation: Fiscal Year 1983*, App. 3: *Latin America and the Caribbean* (Washington, D.C.: AID, 1982), p. 42.

33. Bank of London and South America *Review*, "Central America: Patterns of Regional Economic Integration," June 1979, p. 339.

34. Barry et al., *Dollars and Dictators*, p. 53.

35. SIECA, *El desarrollo integrado*, Anexo 4; Gustavo Adolfo Aguilar B., "Honduras: situación actual y perspectivas políticas," in *Centroamérica en crisis* (Mexico: Centro de Estudios Internacionales, Colegio de México, 1980), p. 88.

36. Jonas and Tobis, eds., *Guatemala*, pp.147-48.

37. On Bank of America links with Guatemalan business interests and the military, see Alan Nairn, "Bank of America Asked to Explain Its Support for the Guatemala Death Squads," *Multinational Monitor*, March 1982.

38. René Herrera Zúñiga, "Nicaragua: El desarrollo capitalista dependente y la crisis de la dominación burguesa, 1950-1980," *Centroamérica en crisis*, p. 103; Barry et al, *Dollars and Dictators*, p. 219.

39. Stephen Kinzer, "Nicaragua: A Wholly Owned Subsidiary," *The New Republic*, April 9, 1977.

40. U.S. AID, *Congressional Presentation*, pp. 40-41.
41. Fco. Ramírez and G. Ramírez, "La crisis económica costarricense," paper presented at seminar "En busca de una alternativa propia," Managua, June 1982.
42. Robert Armstrong and Janet Shenk, *El Salvador: The Face of Revolution* (Boston: South End Press, 1982), p. 48.
43. Clark W. Reynolds and Gustavo Leiva, "Employment Problems of Export Economies in Central America," in Cline and Delgado, eds., *Economic Integration*.
44. Armstrong and Shenk, *El Salvador*, p. 47.
45. Edelberto Torres Rivas, *La crisis económica centroamericana: Cuál crisis?* (Managua: INIES, 1982), p. 7.
46. Carlos Samaniego, "Movimiento Campesino o Lucha Proletariada Rural en El Salvador," *Estudios Sociales Centroamericanos* 9, no. 25 (January 1980), pp. 125-44.
47. Taylor, "Peripheral Capitalism," pp. 83-86.
48. Biderman, "The Development of Capitalism in Nicaragua," p. 15.
49. *Latin American Economic Report* (May 4, 1979); *Latin America Regional Report: Mexico and Central America* (June 6, 1980); Harold Jung, "Class Struggles in El Salvador," *New Left Review* 122 (July-August 1980).
50. Gustavo Porras Castejón, "Guatemala: La profundización de las relaciones capitalistas," *Estudios Centroamericanos* 356/57 (El Salvador, July 1978), pp. 368-77.
51. Samaniego, "Movimiento Campesino," pp. 128-39.
52. Nick Allen, "Guatemala: Hungry for Change," *Food First Action Alert* (San Francisco: Institute for Food and Development Policy, March 1983), and Amnesty International, *El Salvador: General Background* (London: Amnesty, 1977).
53. Porras Castejón, "Guatemala."
54. Carmen Diana Deere and Peter Marchetti, "The Worker-Peasant Alliance in the First Year of the Nicaraguan Agrarian Reform," *Latin American Perspectives* 7, no. 2 (Summer 1981): 49-50.
55. Armstrong and Shenk, *El Salvador*, p. 52.
56. Deere and Marchetti, "The Worker-Peasant Alliance," p. 48.
57. Robert Morris, "Coke Adds Life?" in Jonathan L. Fried et al., eds., *Guatemala in Rebellion: Unfinished History* (New York: Grove Press, 1983), p. 177.

Notes on Contributors

Roger Burbach is director of the Center for the Study of the Americas (CENSA) in Berkeley, California, and coordinator of Policy Alternatives for the Caribbean and Central America (PACCA). He is co-author (with Patricia Flynn) of *Agribusiness in the Americas* (Monthly Review Press, 1980).

Norma Stoltz Chinchilla is an associate professor of women's studies and sociology at California State University, Long Beach.

Carmen Diana Deere is an associate professor of Economics at the University of Massachusetts, Amherst.

Patricia Flynn is a freelance journalist and an associate at the Center for the Study of the Americas (CENSA) in Berkeley, California. She is co-author (with Roger Burbach) of *Agribusiness in the Americas* (Monthly. Review Press, 1980).

Nora Hamilton is an associate professor of political science at the University of Southern California.

Marc Herold is an associate professor of economics at the University of New Hampshire.

David Landes is an economic consultant and associate at the Center for the Study of the Americas (CENSA) in Berkeley, California.

Index